As taught by David Ocheltree
Edited by Carol Quaintance

THE ART OF LEADERSHIP

Celebrating 250 Years of American Excellence

Join Yankee Doodle Dave as he leads you through a year-long program of leadership classes with history and Bible verses.

The Art of Leadership
Written by David Ocheltree
Edited by Carol Quaintance

Copyright © 2026
All rights reserved.
Published by Masthof Press

Library of Congress Control Number: 2025948132
International Standard Book Number: 979-8-89674-063-6

Masthof Press
219 Mill Road | Morgantown, PA 19543-9516
www.Masthof.com

Table of Contents

36. Yankee Doodle

The oldest of our National songs, whose origin has never been traced. Many sets of words have been associated with it, because during the Revolutionary War, it was used by both the British and Americans as a means of ridiculing the other. The text printed here is suggestive of a boy's point of view regarding the continental army.

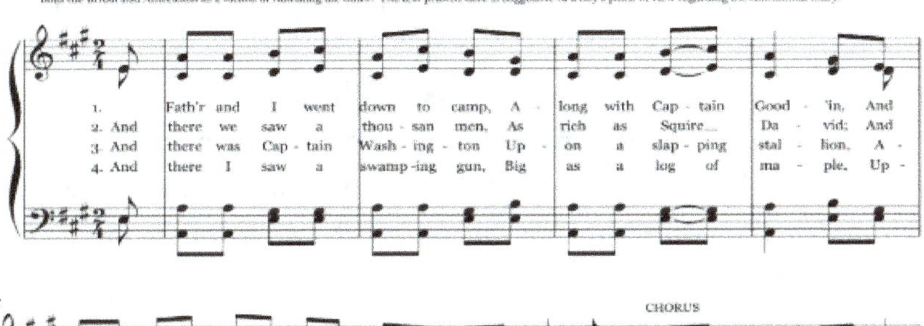

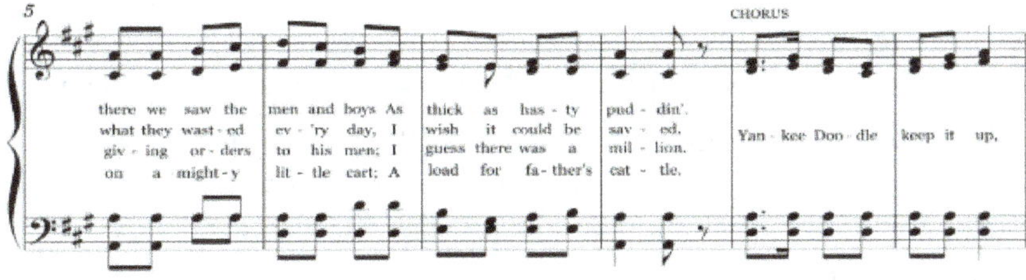

5. And every time they fired it off,
   It took a horn of powder;
   it made a noise like father's gun,
   Only a nation louder.

6. And there I saw a little keg,
   Its head all made of leather,
   they knocked upon't with little sticks,
   To call the folks together.

7. The troopers, too, would gallop up
   And fire right in our faces;
   It scared me almost half to death
   To see them run such races.

8. It scared me so I hooked it off,
   Nor stopped, as I remember,
   Nor turned about till I got home,
   Locked up in mother's chamber.

Dedication

To my Lord and Savior, Jesus Christ,
for without you none of this is possible.
I give all the praise and glory to you Lord.

To my beautiful bride Amanda. Thank you for all the support and dedication during the deployments, training exercises, and schools, which meant I missed out on a lot. Thank you for being that rock that kept this family together. The main reason I have been successful (both in and out of the military) is because of you and the support you give me each and every single day. You are truly amazing.

To my amazing daughter Isabella. Thank you for all your love and dedication. Being your Dad is possibly the best part of my day. Thank you for being such an amazing young lady. It has been a joy to watch you transform from the curious little girl to the beautiful young lady you are.

To the men and women of the United States Navy (especially the Chief's Mess, aka Goat Locker). Thank you for accepting me in the Mess and teaching me what it means to be a leader. Your teachings remain as relevant today as they were when I was first "pinned" with my fouled anchors and joined the Mess. Thank you for teaching me Servant Leadership.

To the brave men and women I served beside and deployed with the United States Marine Corps. You taught me what it was like to be part of a team and embraced me as one of your own; simply by calling me "Doc." Thank you for teaching me the meaning of honor, courage and commitment.

To the brave men of Military Training Team 6 (Team Forsaken) we are bonded in brotherhood forged in combat. Thank you for teaching me about courage, resilience and embracing discomfort.

To those fallen brothers in arms who did not return home from combat—thank you for teaching me about sacrifice and dedication to duty.

To all the Soldiers, Sailors, Airmen, Marines, Coast Guardsmen and civilians I have been privileged to lead in and out of the military. The lessons you have taught me daily are what have made me an effective leader. Thank you for teaching me humility and building teamwork.

For the leaders and owners at Kiepersol. Thank you for taking a chance on me and your continued support. Thank you for fostering a culture of continuous professional growth. Without your want for Leadership Development this would have never happened.

*Family photo of David with his wife Amanda
and their daughter Isabella.*

I had the privilege of serving alongside David during my time as Commanding Officer at Naval Air Station Key West, and I saw firsthand the integrity, creativity, and quiet leadership that define both the man and this work. With over 26 years in uniform, including command of both a Navy fighter squadron and a Naval Air Station, I've seen countless attempts to distill the essence of leadership—few succeed with the clarity and resonance that David has achieved here.

The Art of Leadership is more than a collection of illustrations; it's a visually compelling and philosophically grounded tribute to the values that guide real leaders: courage, humility, decisiveness, and service to others. David's ability to capture these principles with both simplicity and impact speaks volumes about his depth of experience and his talent as a communicator. This is the kind of work that belongs on the desks and shelves of those who lead—whether in uniform, in business, or in the community. It reminds us not just how to lead, but why we lead.

- BOBBY BAKER, *Captain, U.S. Navy (Ret.)*
Former Commanding Officer

As the Founder and CEO of Operation Second Chance, Inc., I am delighted to write this letter in support of David Ocheltree's book *The Art of Leadership*. Here at Operation Second Chance, we honor and serve our nation's veterans.

As a twenty-six-year career Naval Senior Chief Petty Officer and Hospital Corpsman, David knows what it means to put his life on the line and lead troops in combat and tend to his brothers in arms. His leadership training from our nation is exceptional. That coupled with his Master of Business Degree speaks greatly of his knowledge and experience in both the military and private sector.

David's guide for leadership training includes 250 years of American Excellence. Each chapter includes evidence of our founders' spirituality that birthed this nation. The pages march through history revealing leaders from George Washington, Abraham Lincoln and including great scientists and entrepreneurs.

In *The Art of Leadership*, David matches their stories to core qualities of bravery, morality, intuition and faith. It is my honor to help bring to the American public these cherished values so skillfully designed in the course work.

David has a strong passion for servant leadership, which has been demonstrated consistently in and out of the military. His actions consistently prioritize the needs and growth of others, fostering a collaborative and empowering environment. This is leading with humility and empathy. David's leadership style lies in serving others and helping them and the organization ultimately succeed. *The Art of Leadership* is a book that can help leaders today and the leaders of tomorrow learn what Servant Leadership is all about.

With a grateful heart,
Cindy McGrew

Foreword

This is a book that can help anyone who is a leader or may someday strive to become a leader. It tackles difficult concepts in an easy-to-follow manner for any age range.

- It is made up of 52 weekly lessons (approx.) 4-5 pages of easily digestible material
- Each weekly lesson is broken down into the following format:

(1) Pertinent topic to discuss on leadership

(2) Bible verse that discusses that specific topic

(3) Historical short story involving famous American leaders to further illustrate that point

(4) Different techniques that a leader can use in their work center today to address specific areas of concern in leadership development.

(5) Leadership Challenge – The reader will have a few tasks to work on to further shape and refine their leadership skills

(6) Each week there is an illustration of a character that I designed to further enhance the learning. His name is *"Yankee Doodle Dave."*

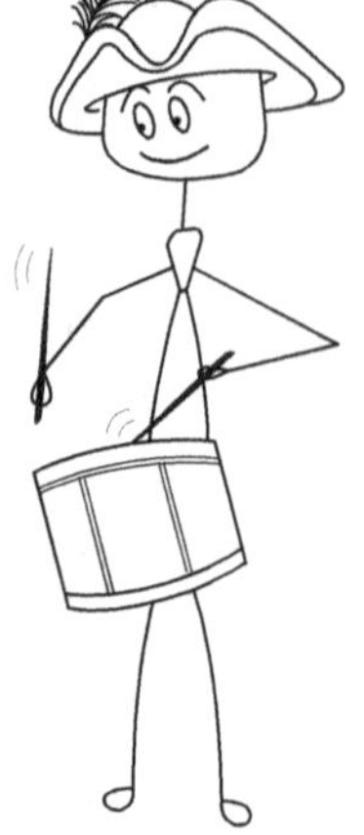

Introduction

Before I get started, I want to say Thank You! Of all the books you could have picked you chose this one to read. That means a lot. I am extremely grateful and appreciative to you and your precious time.

HISTORY

Please allow me to begin with a small amount of background and how the decision was made to create this book.

Immediately after I graduated high school, I enlisted in the United States Navy. During that time in the military, I saw more than one combat tour and multiple non-combat deployments. The one thing that the military takes very seriously is Leadership Development. Leadership Development is something that consumed well over half my time in the military. As I progressed up the chain of commands and advanced in rank I would receive different Leadership Development courses at each promotion. The following are some of the courses that I was privileged to attend:

- Foundational Leader Development Course
  (for E3 and E4 Sailors)
- Intermediate Leader Development Course
  (for E5 Sailors)
- Advanced Leader Development Course
  (for E6 Sailors)
- Chief Petty Officer Leader Development Course
  (for CPO/ E7 Sailors)
- Senior Enlisted Academy Leadership Course
  (for CPO – MCPO/ E7 through E9 Sailors)

I am sure there are courses that I attended that are not on this list. The point behind this was completely normal for me to believe that people in the private sector would receive the necessary training to perform as a leader. After all, leaders are leaders. All leaders should have the same experiences and education. This is what I thought. I have learned differently.

In 2018, I retired from the Navy after 26 years of service. Since then, I have taken the formal education and experience to start the next chapter in my life while working in the civilian job market. Since retirement, I have had the opportunity to work in various industries (manufacturing, agriculture, medicine and even hospitality). In every one of those organizations, they did not have a formalized leadership development program. When I talked with staff members brand new or seasoned, not one person told me they have ever received formalized leadership development training. Then when the leadership at every one of those facilities found out I had conducted leadership development training in the military the reaction was always the same.

"We would love it if you trained our staff." I was honored and privileged to be given the opportunity to do so.

This is when I realized I wanted to do something more. I wanted to come up with something to help all the leaders and potential leaders out there. I wanted to develop something that everyone could use as a training tool to help them in their journey in leadership.

In my current role as the Director of Human Resources at Kiepersol Enterprises I was asked that same question. I absolutely love helping others. The idea was for me to begin to create a Leadership Development Program for the staff. It started off by simply sending out weekly leadership development training messages to the company leadership. I realized after drafting numerous messages, I would put all those messages into one folder. Then I started to work on previous messages adding content, working on format and a lot of prayer.

This is how I decided to come up with this book.

HOW THIS BOOK WORKS

The typical book you pick up from the bookstore or online is read from cover to cover. To get the most out of this I am going to recommend something different. This book should be read at a different pace from other books. Here is my suggestion:

- When you first get it, I encourage you to read it from cover to cover—enjoy it.
- Once you have read it over, I encourage you to go back and re-visit it. This time around take your time.
- Try your best to only read one weekly assignment per week.

Complete the Leadership Challenge for that Week

- Share the weekly assignment with your staff during that week as well.
- At the beginning of the next week start with Week #2.
- Then repeat only completing one week at a time.
- However, if you have a specific issue you are dealing with, I suggest trying to locate that specific topic in the Table of Contents for specific guidance.

HOW TO LOOK AT THIS BOOK

The images listed on the previous page are anchors signifying the ranks of Chief Petty Officer, Senior Chief Petty Officer and Master Chief Petty Officer in the United States Navy. Allow me to share something with you specifically about those anchors. Notice the letters U.S.N. Those do not stand for United States Navy. They stand for something very different.

U – Unity:	Represents corporation, harmony and a unified purpose.
S – Service:	Signifies service to God, fellow man and the Navy.
N – Navigation:	Reminds Chiefs to stay on course, point the path for others to follow and lead with integrity. With a very small change you can look at leaders in your company with the same optic.

Use this book to develop this viewpoint. In my company we will have:

U – Unity:	Represents corporation, harmony and a unified purpose.
S – Service:	Signifies service to God, fellow man and our company.
N – Navigation:	Reminds leaders to stay on course, point the path for others to follow and lead with integrity.

GUIDE FOR THIS BOOK

Allow me to introduce you to "Yankee Doodle Dave." He will be your guide for this book as you journey on to becoming an inspirational leader.

Yankee Doodle Dave is a leadership development consultant with over 10+ years experience helping individuals and organizations reach their full potential. He specializes in coaching leaders at all levels and creating customized leadership development strategies that align with business goals. Yankee Doodle Dave has a talent for identifying and nurturing leadership potential, helping individuals develop the skills and confidence to lead with impact. He holds a Master of Business Administration (MBA) and is a certified facilitator of Leadership Development. He is known for his ability to create engaging and transforming learning experiences.

"What do you say we get this journey started?"

Why Leaders Need to Care About Their Employees on a Personal Level

"A new commandment I give to you, that you love one another; just as I have loved you, you also are to love one another. By this all people will know that you are my disciples, if you have love for one another."
- John 13: 34-35

HISTORICAL FIGURE:
Abraham Lincoln, 16th President of the United States

The first concept that this book will deal with is something some might even consider a little controversial. Some may say this viewpoint is not considered mainstream. This concept is:

Leaders need to care about
their employees on a personal level.

Allow that to settle in for a moment. That is correct. I stated that leaders do need to care about their employees on a personal level. I am not stating that you now need to befriend your employees and head to the nearest watering hole to share your deepest and darkest stories.

Several leaders in history are well known for their ability to show their care for their people. President Abraham Lincoln is famous for numerous reasons. Many people are not aware of the efforts he made to take care of his staff. President Lincoln was known for his ability to connect with people on a personal level, even with those whom he disagreed.

He understood the hardships faced by soldiers and civilians during the war and actively sought to alleviate their suffering. Lincoln was known for visiting soldiers in hospitals. He would often be found providing inspiring words of encouragement to the soldiers on the battlefield. His unwavering commitment to justice and equality helped unite the country and pave the way for a more inclusive future.

President Lincoln's legacy is one of compassionate and effective leadership. His actions and words continue to inspire leaders and individuals around the world to prioritize the well-being of those they serve. President Lincoln was a leader who utterly understood the importance of caring for this staff on a personal level. He deliberately chose cabinet members who had been his political rivals, including those who had opposed him for the presidential nomination. He personally believed in a concept of benefiting from a range of perspectives and expertise.

There are several stories that illustrate President Lincoln's caring nature towards his staff. He established an "open door policy" where anyone could come to him with problems or concerns, fostering trust and respect.

There is one specific story that I want to share that highlights President Lincoln's caring nature. It involves his long-time valet, barber, handyman and bodyguard by the name of William Johnson.

On November 18th, President Lincoln was travelling from Washington, D.C., to Gettysburg to deliver his famous address. President Lincoln was travelling with Mr. William Johnson.

It is important to remember America was in the middle of the Civil War and Mr. William Johnson was African American. Lincoln saw Johnson as a trusted and loyal aide, many people, including much of his own White House staff, harbored deep-seated prejudice. It is quite possible that President Lincoln spent much of his time reviewing his notes for the speech he planned on delivering.

On November 19th, Mr. Johnson more than likely helped President Lincoln get dressed in the morning as he would prepare to deliver his speech. After the event the party got back on the train. This is where things take a turn. President Lincoln fell ill and developed a blinding headache. William tended to President Lincoln as he would be lying in bed and placed a wet cloth on his brow.

When they returned to the White House doctors were summoned to care for the president. President Lincoln was diagnosed with smallpox. It is suggested that he most likely contracted it from his young son Tad. Just a few days earlier Tad had grown very sick from smallpox.

President Lincoln was bedridden for three weeks while he was ill with smallpox. Every day Johnson would wait on the President and nursed him back to health. Mr. Johnson continued his duties even when he himself became sick.

In January 1864, William Johnson was hospitalized with smallpox. The doctors were unable to save him. On January 28, 1864, he succumbed to the illness and died. Some theories speculate that he contracted smallpox from the President. That is only one theory.

Abraham Lincoln paid for William Johnson's burial, coffin and the remaining half of the two $150 loans that he co-signed for Johnson. Although a banker offered to forgive the second half of the loan, Lincoln insisted on paying the full amount because he endorsed the notes and felt bound to do so. Lincoln also paid for a headstone to be placed at the gravesite. The burial spot is located at Arlington National Cemetery, and it reads: "William H. Johnson/Citizen." This may not seem like a big deal in today's time. It was a massive deal in 1864.

For a headstone to identify a Black man as a "citizen" in 1864 was a highly significant and powerfully defiant act. At the time, the

U.S. Supreme Court's 1857 *Dred Scott* decision legally barred African Americans from citizenship, whether free or enslaved. The inscription was a forceful public contradiction of that ruling and an assertion of inherent rights.

President Lincoln was well-known for understanding and practicing care for his staff and subordinates. He earned the loyalty of his team by demonstrating empathy, respect and a willingness to shoulder blame for their mistakes. This approach helped him build a dedicated and effective administration, even among former political rivals.

Caring for your employees on a personal level means going above and beyond the professional sphere to show genuine concern for their well-being. This can involve activities like getting to know them on a personal level. Do you know if they are going through challenging times? When was the last time you showed appreciation for their contributions?

Our staff members are much more than a résumé and a collection of skills sets. They are a collection of personal, professional, spiritual and financial issues. At any point in time there could be potential issues in any of those areas of their lives. Those potential issues could prevent your staff from performing at their optimum level. This means that you as a leader need to get involved. You need to take time out and ask about their families, hobbies and interests and try to remember the details about their lives. It is important to get out there and be available to your staff. Just because you did it one time that is nowhere near enough. This is a constant pursuit where you should be constantly learning about your staff.

Think about the following scenario for a moment. You have two employees within your department. Look at the comparison between the different employees:

Employee A	**Employee B**
Never show up on time, always late	Always show up early
Cannot count on them	Extremely dependable
Uniform is never clean	Uniform is always immaculate
Never smile	Always smiling
Lackluster customer service	Outstanding Customer Service

Now imagine that your supervisor has asked your department to complete a project. This project will require more hours and adhering to a very tight deadline. Who would you pick to help with this project? This is an obvious choice.

Employee B should be picked 100 times out of 100. As a leader are you taking time out of your day to express your gratitude and appreciation for their contributions. It is great that you can count on them; but do they know you truly appreciate them? Simply extending some public recognition towards that staff member in a group setting can sometimes work. Sometimes something as small as a simple hand-written "Thank You" note goes a long way.

There is a program that I informally developed and put in place at a company to help with this concept. I called it the *"Spotlight of the Week."* During my weekly staff meetings, I would share specific highlights of one specific staff member. This *"Spotlight of the Week"* notice turned out to be a very fun thing that the staff really looked forward to every week.

HOW DO YOU DO THIS?

To show your staff you care for them on a personal level build genuine relationships through actively listening, recognizing their accomplishments, offering support and respecting their work/life balance. Here are some specifics on this:

1. Build Genuine Relationships:

- **Active Listening:** Make time to listen to your staff's concerns, ideas, and personal stories, showing genuine interest in their lives outside of work.
- **Personalized Recognition:** Acknowledge individual achievements, both work-related and personal, to show you care about their well-being as individuals.
- **Open Communication:** Foster an environment where staff feel comfortable sharing their thoughts, concerns, and ideas.
- **Show Gratitude:** Express appreciation for their contributions and hard work regularly.

2. Support and Development:

- **Provide Resources:** Offer access to mental health resources, training programs, and mentorship opportunities.
- **Emphasize Work/Life Balance:** Encourage flexible work arrangements and be mindful of employees' personal commitments.
- **Offer Opportunities for Advancement:** Support career growth and provide opportunities for taking on new responsibilities.

By implementing these strategies, you create a workplace where staff feel valued, supported, and cared for, leading to increased job satisfaction, engagement, and retention.

LEADERSHIP CHALLENGE

Here is my challenge to you. How are you trying to get to know your staff on a personal level? How are you displaying that you care for your staff on a personal level?

In this week's lesson was a story involving President Abraham Lincoln and his desire to care for his staff on a personal level.

To demonstrate care for staff on a personal level in the workplace, managers should focus on building trust, fostering open communication, and showing genuine appreciation for their contributions. This includes active listening, offering support, and recognizing their individual needs and strengths. By prioritizing employee well-being and development, organizations can create a positive and supportive environment where individuals feel valued and motivated.

This week different concepts were discussed to help leaders further understand the concept of caring for staff on a personal level. To demonstrate this within a professional context, you should focus on demonstrating respect, empathy, and support for their well-being and growth, both at work and in their personal lives.

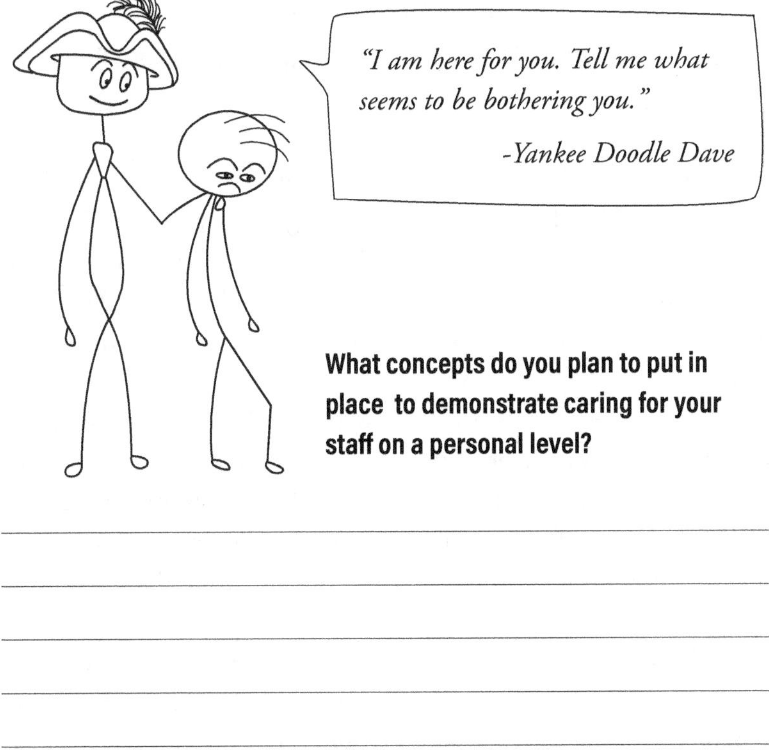

What concepts do you plan to put in place to demonstrate caring for your staff on a personal level?

____

____

____

____

____

"Leadership is not about being in charge. It is about taking care of those in your charge." - Simon Sinek

Be Proactive

"With God there is no limit to what you can do. There is no obstacle you can't overcome through Him, all things are possible."

- Matthew 19:26

HISTORICAL FIGURE:
General George Washington - Crossing the Delaware River

Today's Leadership Development topic has to do with a mindset. "Being Proactive" versus "Being Reactive."

One of the best examples to illustrate this is General George Washington's famous crossing of the Delaware River in 1776. This outlines proactive leadership during a critical point within the American Revolution.

After a series of defeats in New York and New Jersey, the Continental Army was demoralized, facing dwindling enlistments and the prospect of losing the war entirely. The British, under General William Howe, were preparing to settle into winter quarters, assuming Washington's army would remain inactive during the harsh winter months.

Instead of retreating to safe winter quarters, Washington conceived a daring plan to launch a surprise attack on the Hessian mercenaries garrisoned at Trenton, New Jersey. He meticulously planned a difficult Christmas night 1776 crossing of the icy Delaware River with 2,400 men and artillery, aiming to attack the Hessians by dawn. Despite the severe winter weather—a violent storm, including sleeting rain, snow, strong winds and below-freezing temperatures of 29- and 33-degree Fahrenheit—the Continental Army successfully crossed the river and marched toward Trenton.

When studying this event, it is important, if possible, to try to understand what was driving their thought process. It is very difficult to determine exactly what General Washington was specifically thinking at that moment. However, understanding the military situation, the climate and examining Washington's letters will reveal something very interesting. He was intensely focused on the elements of the risky plan while fully aware that he was gambling on this single, audacious move.

With military enlistments set to expire at the end of 1776, Washington knew his army was on the verge of total collapse. There was a sense of urgency concerning this situation. He had retreated across New Jersey after a series of defeats and felt the "game is pretty much up" if he could not act decisively. In a letter, he justified his actions by writing, *"Necessity, dire necessity, will justify my attack."*

He was also very aware that spies and deserters had likely informed the British and Hessian forces of a potential attack. As a result, he knew that the element of surprise was far from guaranteed, making the attack an even greater risk.

Despite the terrible weather conditions, dangerous delays and multitudes of reasons not to push forward, Washington resolved to continue moving forward. He concluded that there was no safe way to retreat across the river without being detected and harassed. The only viable path was forward, toward Trenton, no matter what.

This resulted in a decisive American victory! They captured nearly two-thirds of the Hessian force with minimal American casualties. This victory, followed by another at Princeton a week later, significantly boosted American morale and reignited support for the revolutionary cause. Washington's proactive and bold leadership demonstrated his strategic thinking, his commitment to the war effort, and his ability to inspire his troops despite overwhelming odds.

Thus, this victory significantly raised the morale of the Continental Army, which had suffered numerous defeats and was on the brink of collapse. The success at Trenton reignited patriotic support for the revolution among the colonists and encouraged re-enlistments and new recruits for the army. The capture of nearly 1,000 Hessian prisoners along with vital supplies like muskets, ammunition, and artillery provided much-needed resources for Washington's army.

The Battle of Trenton, followed by the Princeton victory was the turning point of the war, signaling the Continental Army's ability to challenge and defeat the British and Hessian forces.

This solidified Washington's leadership and strategic capabilities, reinforcing confidence in him as commander-in-chief. This famous account highlights Washington's proactive decision. By seizing the initiative and launching a surprise offensive he transformed the course of the American Revolution, breathing new life into the struggling Continental Army and the fight for independence.

The definition of initiative-taking is creating or controlling a situation by causing something to happen rather than responding to it after it has happened.

Stephen Covey's *The 7 Habits of Highly Effective People* outlines seven principles for personal and interpersonal effectiveness. The first principle is *"Be Proactive."* According to Dr. Covey, being proactive means taking responsibility for your life and choices, focusing on what you can influence rather than what you cannot. This involves making choices rather than reacting to situations.

In the workplace, a proactive approach leads to greater control, reduced stress, and improved outcomes compared to reactive ones. Proactive individuals anticipate potential problems, plan for them, and take steps to prevent them from occurring, while reactive individuals only respond after an issue arises.

Here's a more detailed breakdown of how to be proactive at work.

Anticipate and Solve Problems:

- **Identify Potential Issues:** Before they arise, try to foresee potential roadblocks or challenges in your projects or work processes.
- **Develop Solutions:** Brainstorm to prevent these problems or address them proactively.
- **Act:** Don't wait for problems to escalate. Act early to mitigate their impact.

Take Initiative and Responsibility:

- **Don't Wait to Be Told:** Identify opportunities to contribute—act without being explicitly asked.
- **Be a Self-Starter:** Proactively seek new projects or tasks—owning your work.
- **Own Your Mistakes:** Learn from errors, take responsibility—do not blame others.
- **Communicate Effectively:** Keep colleagues informed by sharing updates on your progress and any potential issues you've identified.
- **Ask Questions:** Clarify any uncertainties and seek input from others to ensure you're on the right track.
- **Provide Timely Feedback:** Share your thoughts and suggestions constructively to help improve team performance.

HOW DO YOU DO THIS?

To become more proactive in a professional setting focus on anticipating needs; planning and taking the initiative to improve processes; communicate effectively and participate in team efforts.

Here are some specifics on this:

1. Develop a Proactive Mindset:

- **Self-Awareness:** Understand your strengths and weaknesses to anticipate potential challenges and opportunities.
- **Growth Mindset:** Embrace challenges as learning opportunities and see setbacks as chances to improve.
- **Clear Goals:** Set specific, measurable, achievable, relevant, and timebound (SMART) goals to provide direction and purpose.

2. Anticipate and Plan:

- **Anticipate Needs:** Consider what's needed before it's requested. For example, if you know a client will need an updated report, prepare it in advance.
- **Plan:** Develop contingency plans for potential issues and problems.
- **Organize Your Work:** Create a system for managing your tasks, time, and resources to avoid being overwhelmed.

3. Take the Initiative and Participate:

- **Help:** Help colleagues with their tasks; seek opportunities to contribute to team goals.
- **Participate Actively:** Engage in meetings, offer suggestions, and share your ideas.
- **Embrace Challenges:** Seek out opportunities to learn and grow by taking on new responsibilities.

4. Continuous Improvement:

- **Seek Feedback:** Regularly solicit feedback from your colleagues and manager to identify areas for improvement.
- **Analyze Processes:** Observe workplace trends and identify ways to streamline processes and improve efficiency.

- **Strive for Excellence:** Continuously seek to improve your skills and knowledge to perform your job more effectively.

By implementing these strategies, you develop a proactive mindset and become a more effective and valued member of your team.

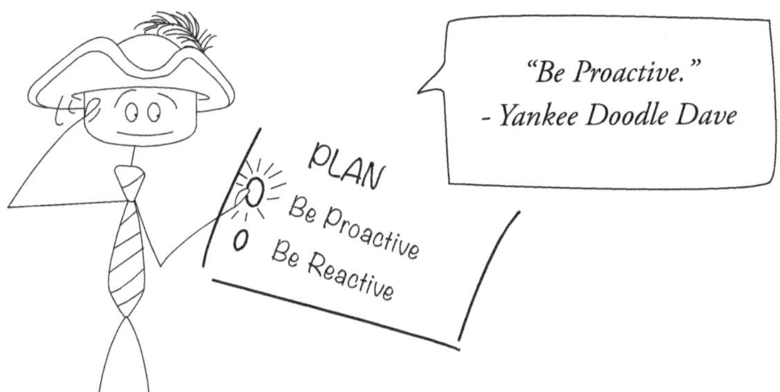

LEADERSHIP CHALLENGE

In this week's lesson we discussed the concept of "Being Proactive." This was highlighted very clearly by examples from General George Washington.

Being proactive in the workplace means taking the initiative and anticipating future needs or potential problems, rather than just reacting as situations arise. It involves identifying opportunities for improvement, suggesting new ideas, and taking ownership of tasks without being explicitly directed. A proactive employee anticipates, plans, and acts to achieve the desired outcome, contributing to a more efficient and productive work environment.

In this week different concepts were discussed to help leaders further understand the concept of being proactive. What concepts do you plan to put in place to demonstrate your ability to be proactive in the workplace?

In this setting you may not be looking to invent the form of transportation like Washington did. Look around your work center. Honestly, take a deep look around.

Being proactive could be something much more subtle. Is there something you are doing because you are in a "Reactionary State?" If so, what techniques listed above could help you and your department to shift into a "Proactive Mindset?"

____

____

____

____

____

____

____

"Happiness, like unhappiness is a proactive choice."
- Stephen Covey

Sales Through Hospitality

"Don't forget to show hospitality to strangers, for some who have done this have entertained angels without realizing it."

- Hebrews 13:2

HISTORICAL FIGURE:
Conrad Hilton, Founder of Hilton Hotels

In hospitality, leaders can drive sales by implementing strategies like up-selling, offering special deals, building relationships, and actively participating in sales efforts. They can also lead, for example, demonstrating professionalism and support for their team. Key hospitality sales skills include research, communication, and building relationships with clients.

Up-selling in restaurants involves suggesting more expensive or higher-margin items to customers, potentially increasing their order value without making them feel pressured. Effective up-selling strategies include training staff to be knowledgeable about the menu and making personalized recommendations based on customer preferences, using descriptive language to highlight the benefits of certain items, and offering pairings or additions.

Hilton understood that a positive guest experience was crucial for success. He prioritized cleanliness, comfort, and convenience, making his hotels stand out from the competition.

Conrad implemented strict standards for cleanliness, service, and accounting, ensuring consistency and efficiency across his hotels.

When Conrad Hilton built the first Hilton named hotel in Dallas in 1925, he envisioned a chain of first-class, modern hotels. His vision had what he called the "*Minimax Concept*." This concept was something where his hotels would offer the maximum amount of service and satisfaction for the minimum amount of cost.

One of the things that separated him from his competitors is that Hilton was not afraid of trying new things. He was an early adopter of amenities like air conditioning and in-room TVs, which became standard features in his hotels.

His goal was to operate the best hotel in Texas, providing reliable, comfortable, and reputable experience. He also focused on practical innovations, like designing the first Hilton to ensure no guest rooms faced the hot western sun. This is just one reason how he was committed to guest comfort.

Hilton's approach towards customers emphasized creating an experience that appealed to consumer desires, from design to amenities, aiming to make the hotel a destination. Conrad's sales strategy wasn't about just selling rooms. If you wanted to get a room, you could go anywhere to get that. For him, it was about selling an experience, a lifestyle, and a sense of luxury that attracted repeat customers and new guests.

Conrad Hilton conducted sales through hospitality by pioneering new, unique services that solved guest problems, like helping stranded travelers find rooms during wartime and anticipating needs with in-room amenities and an integrated reservations system. He also employed savvy marketing, leveraging celebrity culture and public relations for openings and using mass purchasing to improve efficiency and profitability. His vision focused on creating a unified, global hospitality experience where guests felt welcome, fostering a pioneering spirit to innovate and expand the hotel chain.

Like any person in life, he faced his set of obstacles. Hilton faced challenges like the Great Depression and the stock market crash. Conrad demonstrated resilience and adaptability, eventually regaining control of his hotels after facing setbacks.

Conrad Hilton's impact on the hospitality industry through sales was significant, transforming the business from a collection of independent hotels into a global, standardized brand. He pioneered the concept of the modern hotel chain, introducing features like room service and a focus on customer service, ultimately shaping the expectations of travelers worldwide.

Here's a more detailed look at restaurant up-selling techniques:

1. Train Your Staff:

- **Menu Knowledge:** Ensure staff is well versed in the menu, including ingredients, preparation methods, and any special offerings.
- **Descriptive Language:** Encourage staff to use descriptive language that makes the food sound appealing and highlights its unique qualities.
- **Personalized Recommendations:** Train staff to listen to customer preferences and suggest items that align with their tastes.
- **Role-Playing and Practice:** Conduct role-playing exercises to help staff practice up-selling in different scenarios.

2. Menu Engineering and Positioning:

- **Menu Design:** Strategically position high-profit margin items in prominent places on the menu, like the middle or top right corner.
- **Highlighting Specials:** Use clear language and attractive imagery to highlight daily specials and limited-time offers.
- **Creating Bundles:** Offer combo deals or meal bundles that include a main course, appetizer, and dessert, which can be more profitable than individual orders.

3. SUGGESTIVE SELLING:

- **Offer Pairings:** Suggest complementary wines or drinks to go with specific dishes.
- **Suggest Extras:** Recommend side dishes, additions, or appetizers that complement the main course.
- **Ask about Preferences:** Inquire about customer preferences to offer more tailored suggestions.
- **Highlight High-Profit Items:** Suggest items with higher profit margins, like specialty cocktails or premium entrées.

4. Create a Positive Dining Experience:

- **Emphasize Benefits:** Focus on benefits of the suggested item, not just the features.
- **Be Sincere and Enthusiastic:** Recommend with genuine enthusiasm and a focus on customer satisfaction.
- **Read Customer Cues:** Pay attention to customer behavior and nonverbal cues to determine the right time to up-sell.
- **Offer a Dessert to Go:** If a customer is full, but seems interested in a dessert, suggest "take it to go."
- **Build Loyalty:** Offer loyalty programs or incentives for repeat customers to encourage them to accept up-sell offers.

HOW DO YOU DO THIS?

1. Develop a Broader Set of Business Skills
2. Focus on the Value Proposition
3. Get Back to Sales Fundamentals
4. Prospect with Purpose
5. Leverage Social Selling
6. Prepare for Each Business Conversation

"Great service doesn't cost anything. Poor service can cost everything."

- Yankee Doodle Dave

LEADERSHIP CHALLENGE

Think about the story of Conrad Hilton and Hilton Hotels. He faced enormous setbacks (stock market crash and the Great Depression). His customer service and sales through hospitality tactics are what initially brought him success.

Have there been times when we have lost focus on what may have initially brought us success?

The concept of *"Sales Through Hospitality"* in the workplace involves leveraging customer service and relationship building skills to drive revenue and achieve business goals. This approach focuses on creating positive experiences that encourage repeat business, referrals, and ultimately, increased sales. It is not just about selling a product or a service but about creating value and fostering loyalty through exceptional hospitality.

In this week's lesson different concepts were discussed that can help leaders further understand the concept of *"Sales Through Hospitality"* and leveraging customer service and relationship building skills.

What concepts do you plan to put in place to demonstrate how you will be able to be that focus on *"Sales Through Hospitality?"* What techniques will you apply over the next week to ensure you as a leader, and your staff is focused on *"Sales Through Hospitality?"*

"The secret of success is to do the common thing uncommonly well."
- John D. Rockefeller

A Leader's Role in Customer Service

"A faithful, sensible servant is one to whom the master can give the responsibility of managing his other household servants and feeding them. If the master returns and finds that the servant has done a good job, there will be a reward. I tell you the truth, the master will put that servant in charge of all he owns."
- Matthew 24: 45-47

HISTORICAL FIGURE:
James Madison, 4th President of the United States

The topic for this week's Leadership Development is "A Leader's Role in Customer Service."

One of the best stories I could think of that exemplifies servant leadership is the story of James Madison.

James Madison was a founding father of our nation and the 4th President of the United States. He was a prolific writer. In fact, he is known by many as being the *"Father of the Constitution"* because he authored the first drafts of the *U.S. Constitution and the Bill of Rights.*

Most people may not know this, but James Madison is known as the "smallest president." He had a frail build and stood at the height of 5 feet 4 inches and tipped the scales at just over 100 pounds. His voice was so weak that people often had difficulty hearing his speeches.

James Madison had a long history of understanding others' needs and taking care of others (customer service). However, he was one that did not budge on his personal principles. Allow me to provide a small story to explain this. In colonial and early American elections, it was customary for candidates to provide voters with "spirituous liquors and other treats" to "*swill the planters*" and win support. This is a historical phrase used when voters were bribed during elections. The full phrase was actually "*swill the planters with bumbo.*" "*Bumbo*" was a popular rum drink for pirates and sailors during the 17th and 18th centuries, especially in the Caribbean.

In 1777, a young James Madison was very young (27 years old) and ran for the House of Delegates. He was very devout in his Christian faith and believed the "*swill the planters*" practice to be a form of bribery and corruption. He refused to follow this tradition and refused to offer alcohol to voters during that election cycle.

The result was that his opponent won. Despite the setback, James Madison was soon chosen for an open seat of Virginia's Council of State. By 1780, the 29-year-old was serving as the youngest delegate to the Continental Congress.

There are only three (3) individuals who contributed to all the following: they were present at the Constitutional Convention, were influential in the creation of the U.S. Constitution, creation of the Federalist Papers and the drafting of the Bill of Rights. Those men were: Alexander Hamilton, John Jay and James Madison. Think about that for a moment. That is quite remarkable.

Fifty-five delegates met in Philadelphia, Pennsylvania, between May 25, 1787, and September 1787. These men would not only reject the Articles of Confederation, but they would produce the first written constitution for any nation in the history of the world. James Madison was one of those fifty-five delegates. James Madison's major contributions to the U.S. Constitution include authoring the Virginia Plan as a blueprint for the new government. This served as the foundation for the Constitution, establishing a bicameral and a system of separation of powers. As evidenced by his role in the Constitutional Convention and the compromises reached, Madison excelled at finding common ground and negotiating solutions that addressed various interests. This aptitude for compromise is invaluable in resolving complex customer issues and finding solutions that work for everyone involved.

The Federalist Papers were written between October 1787 and May 1788. *The Federalist Papers* consists of 85 essays. The main purpose behind the *Federalist Papers* was to persuade the citizens of New York to ratify the proposed United States Constitution by explaining the benefits of a stronger federal government and detailing how the Constitution would function, including its checks and balances. James Madison wrote roughly one-third of those essays under the pseudonym "Publius." One of his key contributions includes Federalist No. 10, which explained how a large republic could prevent rule by majority faction and Federalist No. 51 argued for a checks and balance system. However, many of his other writings were published in newspapers and were meant to educate and persuade citizens to ratify the constitution. These series of articles (along with others written by Alexander Hamilton and John Jay) are known as *The Federalist Papers*. James Madison displayed strong communication skills translated to effective explanation of policies, procedures, and solutions, fostering understanding and building trust.

James Madison then served as a leader in the First Federal Congress. There he sponsored the first ten (10) amendments (The Bill of Rights). The Bill of Rights was added to the Constitution in 1791 to address widespread fears that the new federal government would become too powerful and infringe on individual liberties, like the British monarchy they had just overthrown. Madison's dedication to ensuring that different voices were heard and that fundamental rights were protected, as demonstrated by his championship of the *Bill of Rights*, speaks to a fundamental principle of effective customer service—ensuring that all customers feel heard, valued, and that their needs are properly represented.

Madison recognized the importance of acknowledging the opinions and beliefs of differing viewpoints, even when disagreements existed. This ability to understand diverse perspectives is crucial in effectively addressing customer concerns and providing solutions that satisfy a broad range of individuals. James Madison's historical actions and documented traits suggest he would be well-suited as a customer service leader. President Madison has numerous contributions to life as we know it today.

In essence, Madison's focus on listening; understanding diverse perspectives; negotiating and compromising; advocating for rights, and effective communication aligns well with the attributes of a strong customer service leader.

WHAT IS A CUSTOMER SERVICE LEADER?

It is important to understand what a customer service leader is. A customer service leader is someone who consistently shows a customer-focused approach to service within an organization. Leaders in customer service guide others with the mindset that excellence in serving customers starts with how company leaders act.

Leaders who are focused on customer service create an environment where team members are immersed in a strategic vision for meeting client needs. These leaders support employees by giving them the tools to successfully manage customer interactions, such as high-quality training, clear objectives and templates for addressing customer feedback.

WHY IS IT IMPORTANT TO BE A LEADER IN CUSTOMER SERVICE?

Customer-focused strategies affect nearly every aspect of a business. Opportunities to interact with consumers online, through mobile devices, and website platforms continue to increase. This makes customer service an important feature to manage sales growth and brand image. When leaders show their commitment to putting the customer first, they create a service-forward culture for the other employees. Excellence in customer service provides a versatile skill you can use across industries. Improving this ability may also help you rise as a top candidate for leadership positions.

FIVE STEPS TO GROW YOUR SKILLS AS A LEADER IN CUSTOMER SERVICE:

Improving your customer service abilities will help you become a better leader in any organization. Follow these steps to grow your skills as a leader in customer service:

Step #1: Demonstrate Your Customer Service Values

Show employees how you want them to treat customers by modeling the same behaviors as you interact with other team members. For example, if you expect staff to speak politely to customers, use the same polite language when you talk with employees. Ensure that you always display professionalism and do not lose your temper. A customer service strategy shown by the top leadership encourages the entire organization to repeat these values.

Remember this: Would you lose your temper or speak to a guest in a demeaning manner? Of course not. Then why is it acceptable to speak to staff in anything less than a respectable manner? The professionalism displayed to guests should be afforded to each and all employees.

Step #2: Give Employees Tools for Customer Service Success

Allow employees' autonomy to manage customer needs by providing them with the necessary training and development to guide their interactions. Provide guides such as scripts for speaking with customers, or templates for email and phone messaging. Grant employees the ability to make decisions that will quickly solve customer problems and address their concerns.

Remember this: Every role within your organization requires specific tools and training to ensure that they are successful. As leaders it is our responsibility that our employees are properly equipped to complete their tasks and administer the best customer service possible.

Step #3: Show Staff Members You Value Their Input

Showing that you value an employee more than data or statistics encourages others to trust your leadership and fosters stronger professional relationships. Give staff members the opportunity to provide input as you develop new customer service strategies. Allow team members the chance to grow; let them employ and manage customer service processes within their roles.

Remember this: If a guest came to you with a concern, you would stop what you are doing and give them your undivided attention. They would feel as if their voice was heard, and you cared for their well-being. Shouldn't we have the same approach if one of our staff members comes to us with concern? Don't they deserve the same attention and respect?

Remember this: One of the biggest reasons people are let go of a job is because of a bad culture fit. It is easy to rush to a quick decision during this process because of increased workloads and a decrease in manpower. My advice is to slow down and take your time here. Remember that this staff member is someone you want for the long haul. Sometimes rushing this decision ultimately results in what I call a revolving-door effect. People seem to be always coming and going.

When a guest comes into a facility, they clearly understand many things as we have demonstrated this to them: hours of operation; specific items they can order; cost of items, safety protocols, etc. Meticulous time and attention are spent ensuring that our guests have been properly educated with how our organization is supposed to operate. What would it look like if we took as much time educating our staff on the policies and procedures of your specific organization and how it should operate?

Yankee Doodle Dave is reminding you about the Leader's Role in Customer Service.

LEADERSHIP CHALLENGE

This week we learned about our 4th President of the United States, James Madison. The characteristics he displayed were those of a person who was a leader in customer service.

There are still several ways as a leader you can increase your *"Servant Mindset"* (Customer Service) within an organization. What are some ways over the next week that you can do that?

A servant mindset in the workplace is a leadership philosophy where the primary focus is on serving others, prioritizing their needs and well-being to foster a strong and effective team. It emphasizes putting the needs of employees, customers, and the community above the leader's own self-interest. This approach encourages empowerment, collaboration, and a focus on the growth and development of team members.

In this week's lesson different concepts were discussed that can help leaders further understand the concept of *"A Leader's Role in Customer Service"* and *"A Servant Mindset."*

What concepts do you plan to put in place to demonstrate how you will be able to focus on implementing a *"Servant Mindset"* in your workplace?

"There is only one boss—the CUSTOMER—and he can fire everybody in the company by spending his money somewhere else."
- Sam Walton

Why Leaders Need to Be Confident

"I can do all things through Christ who strengthens me."

- Philippians 4:1

HISTORICAL FIGURE:
President Theodore Roosevelt - "The Moose Speech"

The definition of the word confidence is the feeling or belief that one can rely on someone or something. The word "confidence" originates from the Latin word *confidential*, meaning "firm trust or reliance."

If you are looking for a story that depicts confidence, then allow me to share one with you. This is the story of an attempted assassination of former U.S. President Theodore Roosevelt.

President Theodore Roosevelt served as president from September 14, 1901–March 4, 1909.

One of the most famous stories illustrating Theodore Roosevelt's confidence occurred in 1912 when he was shot before giving a campaign speech in Milwaukee, Wisconsin.

The day was October 14th, 1912. Theodore Roosevelt had just completed two consecutive terms as a Republican president. Roosevelt lost the presidential nomination to incumbent Howard Taft. Theodore Roosevelt and his supporters split to form a new political party. Theodore Roosevelt was at the Gilpatrick Hotel in Milwaukee,

Wisconsin. He was scheduled to deliver a speech at the Milwaukee Auditorium. News had circulated that Roosevelt was in the hotel.

It was 8:10 p.m. Central Standard Time. A loud shot rang through the air! Theodore Roosevelt was shot at close range by John Schrank. Schrank was a saloonkeeper from New York. The bullet first passed through a folded 50-page copy of Roosevelt's speech (which he was about to deliver) and his steel eyeglass case, which were in his breast pocket. Roosevelt, who was an experienced hunter and anatomist, assessed that the bullet hadn't reached his lung because he wasn't coughing blood.

After assessing his own dime-sized wound and coughing into his hand to check for lung damage, he told an aide, "*He pinked me.*"

He rejected pleas from his concerned entourage to go to the hospital. He famously said, "*You get me to that speech. It may be the last one I shall ever deliver, but I am going to deliver this one.*"

Roosevelt had boasted about feeling "*strong as a bull moose*" after losing the Republican nomination earlier that year. This led him to form the Progressive Party, often called the "*Bull Moose Party.*"

Roosevelt declared that such violence would become commonplace if society ignored the rising economic inequality he was campaigning against. He used the event to warn against the division of "Haves" and the "Have Nots."

Theodore Roosevelt claimed that having led such a happy and fulfilling life, he had no concern about whether he was shot. This bold statement was a testament to his self-perception as a fearless and driven leader.

One of his famous quotes occurred during this speech by saying, "*I don't know whether you fully understand that I have just been shot; but it takes more than that to kill a Bull Moose.*"

Roosevelt gave a 90-minute speech, reportedly bleeding throughout. He held up the bullet-riddled speech manuscript, further showcasing his spirit. After the speech, doctors confirmed that the bullet was in his chest muscle but hadn't penetrated his lung.

They decided it was safer to leave it in than to remove it. Roosevelt carried that bullet for the remainder of his life!

This episode highlighted Roosevelt's personal courage and resilience. It also cemented his public image as a figure of determination and confidence. This moment galvanized his supporters and helped solidify the Progressive Party's platform, which focused on issues like social reform, economic equality, and conservation.

Confidence is crucial in leadership because it allows leaders to inspire trust, make decisive decisions, communicate effectively, and motivate teams to achieve goals, ultimately fostering a positive and resilient organizational culture.

Here's a more detailed explanation of why confidence is so important in leadership:

- **Inspires Trust and Respect:** Project an image of competence and assurance, which builds trust and respect among team members and stakeholders.
- **Facilitates Decision-Making:** Make timely and decisive choices, even under pressure, rather than procrastinating or avoiding difficult decisions.
- **Enhances Communication:** Communicate your vision and strategies clearly and persuasively, ensuring that your message is understood and followed.
- **Motivates and Inspires Teams:** Inspire your team to believe in your abilities and to strive for excellence, leading to improved performance and job satisfaction.
- **Promotes Resilience and Adaptability:** Equipped to navigate challenges and setbacks, to view them as opportunities for learning and growth, rather than insurmountable obstacles.
- **Creating a Positive Work Environment:** Foster a sense of security and stability within the team, creating a more positive and productive work environment.
- **Take Calculated Risks:** Be willing to take calculated risks and explore new ideas, which lead to innovation and growth.

- **Builds Momentum and Focus:** Build momentum and focus, inspiring people to give their best and achieve ambitious goals.
- **Sets the Tone for the Organization:** A leader's confidence sets the tone for the entire organization, influencing the behavior and attitudes of team members.

HOW DO YOU DO THIS?

Leaders demonstrate confidence through clear communication, decisive actions, and by fostering a positive and supportive environment. They should also be open to feedback, celebrating successes (both big and small), and empower their teams.

Here's a more detailed look:

1. Communication Is Key:

- **Be Clear and Concise:** Avoid jargon and ambiguity when communicating goals, expectations, and decisions.
- **Active Listening:** Pay attention to what others say, acknowledge their perspectives, and ask clarifying questions.
- **Share Information Freely:** Transparency builds trust and confidence within the team.

2. Actions Speak Louder Than Words:

- **Take Ownership:** Acknowledge mistakes and take responsibility for outcomes.
- **Be Decisive:** Make timely and well-informed decisions, even when faced with uncertainty.
- **Lead by Example:** Demonstrate the behaviors you expect from your team.

3. Foster a Supportive Environment:

- **Celebrate Successes:** Recognize and acknowledge both individual and team achievements, no matter how small.

- **Empower Your Team:** Delegate tasks, provide support, and trust your team's abilities.
- **Encourage Growth:** Provide opportunities for learning and development and help team members build their skills and confidence.

4. Build Self-Awareness and Adaptability:
- **Seek Feedback:** Actively solicit feedback from team members and be open to constructive criticism.
- **Reflect on Your Actions:** Regularly assess your leadership style and identify areas for improvement.
- **Be Flexible and Adaptable:** Adjust your approach as needed to respond to changing circumstances.

By consistently demonstrating these behaviors, leaders can build a strong foundation of confidence, which in turn inspires trust, motivates their teams, and drives positive results.

LEADERSHIP CHALLENGE
You may not be standing in front of a group of people about to deliver the famous *"Moose Speech"* as Theodore Roosevelt did. It

*Yankee Doodle Dave
is reminding you—
believe in yourself!*

is hard to even fathom courage and confidence one would have to simply keep delivering a speech even after you were shot.

We all deal with obstacles and difficulties in our lives. A wise person once told me that there are only two things that you can really control in our lives.

One is your Words
Second is your Actions

You may have influence on others, but I argue that you do not control others. For this let me speak directly to the parents of toddlers. Do you honestly control the words that come out of your toddler's mouth? Or do they happen to say the most random things at the most inopportune times? I think we know the answer to that one!

Maybe you do not have children. Perhaps you are a supervisor at an organization, and you have a few staff members that report directly to you. You get a call after normal working hours from your supervisor. They tell you about a situation involving one of your direct reports.

Your direct report was caught consuming alcoholic beverages during working hours.

As a leader do you believe you control the actions of those that work directly for you?

Here is my challenge for you. What can you do over the next week to increase your confidence level with your team? Or maybe something on a personal level?

____

____

____

____

"Brave leaders are never silent around hard things."
- Brené Brown

How Leaders Can Improve
Teamwork in the Workplace

*"Iron sharpens iron; so, a man sharpeneth
the countenance of his friend."*
- Proverbs 27:17

HISTORICAL FIGURES:
Coach Herb Brooks & 1980 U.S. Olympic Hockey Team

Leaders have such an incredible impact on an organization. One of the greatest areas they can impact is the overall teamwork seen in the workplace. A famous example of this would be found in the 1980 U.S. Olympic Hockey Team.

To really understand how incredible this is you must remember what was happening in world events. Tensions were incredibly difficult between the United States and the Soviet Union. This escalation was largely triggered by the Soviet Union invasion of Afghanistan in 1979. President Carter responded with measures like boycotting the 1980 Moscow Olympics and imposing a grain embargo. The Soviet Union retaliated by boycotting the 1984 Los Angeles Olympics. Further strains arose from the Pershing missile crisis and President Reagan's characterization of the Soviet Union as an *evil empire.*

On the world stage the Soviet Union was being painted in such a negative light. The Soviet hockey team was the odd-on favorite to win the gold in 1980. The Soviet players were full-time athletes, many of whom were commissioned officers in the Soviet Army and part of the famous Red Army hockey team. They had won gold in five of the six previous Winter Olympics and were expected to win again in 1980.

In comparison, the U.S. team was made up of a very young and rather unknown team. The team was comprised of amateur and college players. The odds were not in the favor of the United States. Coach Herb Brooks did not care about any of those factors. He provided unbelievable leadership to his team.

Prior to the game between Team USA and the Soviet Hockey Team, Coach Brooks delivered what is now considered a famous speech. It is referred to by sports writers as the "*You were born to be here*" speech. Here is some of what he said to his players before they took the ice:

> "*You were born to be hockey players. Every one of you. And you were meant to be here tonight. This is your time. Their time is done. It's over,*" saying "*Great moments are born from great opportunity.*" He also emphasized the team's ability to "**skate with them**" and "*shut them down*" because "*you are the greatest hockey team in the world!*"

His leadership led to his team upsetting the heavily favored Soviet team in the semifinal round with a score of 4-3. Two days later, the U.S. secured the gold medal by defeating Finland 4-2 in their final game.

"*The Miracle on Ice,*" the 1980 U.S. Olympic Hockey Team's victory over the heavily favored Soviet Union, was significant because it provided a major morale boost for America during a time of national self-doubt and geopolitical tension. It was a moment of unexpected triumph that resonated deeply with Americans, regardless of whether they were hockey fans. This is a perfect example of how leadership was critical in enhancing overall teamwork.

Coach Herb Brooks' words to his players instilled belief and a sense of destiny. He motivated them by shifting the focus from the "invincible" Soviets to the American team's potential. Coach Brooks fueled their belief in themselves and their shared vision.

To improve teamwork in the workplace, leaders must foster clear communication, encourage collaboration, and build a supportive environment that values trust and respect They can also implement strategies like setting clear goals, celebrating achievements, and creating opportunities for team building activities.

Here's a more detailed look at how leaders can improve teamwork:

1. Communication:

- **Open and Honest Communication:** Leaders encourage open and honest communication channels, allowing team members to share ideas, concerns, and feedback without fear of judgment.
- **Active Listening:** Leaders actively listen to team members showing their input is valued.
- **Clear and Frequent Communication:** Ensure that team members have clear and frequent communication about goals, expectations, and progress.
- **Two-Way Communication:** Make communication a two-way street, encouraging team members to share their perspectives and ideas.

2. Collaboration:

- **Create Collaborative Goals:** Establish shared goals and objectives to encourage team members to work together towards a common purpose.
- **Team Building Activities:** Organize team building activities to foster camaraderie and trust among team members.
- **Problem-Solving:** Allow team members to participate in problem solving activities and encourage them to collaborate on solutions

3. Supportive Environment:

- **Trust and Respect:** Create a workplace culture where trust and respect are valued and where team members feel comfortable sharing their ideas and concerns.
- **Conflict Resolution:** Be adept at resolving conflicts and finding solutions that promote teamwork and collaboration.
- **Celebrate Successes:** Recognize and celebrate team achievements and individual contributions to reinforce positive behaviors and foster a sense of camaraderie.
- **Empathy and Understanding:** Show empathy and understanding towards team members and their challenges, fostering a supportive and inclusive environment.

4. Other Important Factors:

- **Define Roles and Responsibilities:** Clearly define roles and responsibilities to ensure that each team member knows their individual contributions and how they fit into the overall team effort.
- **Lead by Example:** Model the behavior they expect from their team—demonstrating teamwork, communication, and collaboration in their own actions.

LEADERSHIP CHALLENGE

It may not be the 1980s and the relationship between the U.S. and Soviet Union has changed. Coach Brooks stepped up and provided the necessary leadership needed for the U.S. Hockey Team to come out on top.

You are a member of a different team. Your team happens to be in a different work setting.

One of the ways leaders improve teamwork in their workplace is by open and honest communication. Here is my challenge to every leader reading this:

"Teamwork Makes the Dream Work."

- Yankee Doodle Dave

Instead of reading an email or previous leadership development session, and going about your day, try this—organize a meeting with your staff to share this information with your team.

"Alone we can do so little; together we can do so much."
- Helen Keller

A List of Things I Have Done to Find True Happiness

"So, Jesus told them this story: If a man has a hundred sheep and one of them gets lost, what will he do? Won't he leave the ninety-nine others in the wilderness and go to search for the one that is lost until he finds it? And when he has found it, he will joyfully carry it home on his shoulders. When he arrives, he will call together his friends and neighbors, saying, 'Rejoice with me because I have found my lost sheep.' In the same way, there is more joy in heaven over one lost sinner who repents and returns to God than over ninety-nine others who are righteous and haven't strayed away!"

- Luke 15: 3-7

HISTORICAL FIGURE:
President George W. Bush – His Journey of Faith

This week's topic deals with Happiness. I would like to discuss the scripture listed above and how this pertains to happiness. This is a parable of the lost sheep found in the Book of Luke. This passage illustrates God's love and pursuit of those who are lost or have strayed from Him.

I would like to share a small story of someone with their own journey in faith. Their journey ended up being what he calls one of the best decisions he ever made. I happen to be taking about our 43rd President of the United States, George W. Bush. The story illustrates how President Bush strayed from the Lord but then returned.

George W. Bush grew up attending his parents' Episcopal church and later, as an adult, joined the United Methodist Church. While he was raised with religious influences, he himself describes a period where his faith lacked seriousness.

A pivotal moment for Bush's faith occurred during a conversation with the Reverend Billy Graham in 1985. Bush recounts in his autobiography that Graham's words *"planted a mustard seed in my soul"* leading him to re-evaluate his life and recommit himself to Jesus Christ. This meeting occurred when Billy Graham, a close friend of the Bush family, held a question-and-answer session on faith at the Bush family home in Kennebunkport, Maine.

The conversion helped George Bush leave behind what he referred to as "hard-partying, hell-raising life," including his struggles with alcohol. He described a turning point after his 40th birthday party when he woke up hungover and decided to quit drinking with his wife Laura's encouragement.

During his time as Texas governor and later as president, George Bush often spoke about the importance of his faith. He would cite Christ as his favorite philosopher, saying, "He changed my life." Bush consistently stated that he did not believe God told him what to do but instead prayed for wisdom, judgement and to remain calm. He adopted a daily routine of reading the Bible and devotional literature using prayer as a constant source of strength.

While some consider Bush a *"born-again"* Christian, particularly within evangelical circles, Bush himself has tended to emphasize a *"recommitment"* to Christ rather than a sudden born-again experience. He describes it as a "walk" of faith and a continuous process rather than a single dramatic moment.

President Bush's faith deeply influenced his presidency. He frequently invoked God and used religious language in speeches. His faith also played a role in his support for faith-based initiatives and in shaping his views on various policies, though the precise connection between his faith and specific policy decisions has been a subject of debate.

Bush said, *"My relationship with God through Christ has given me meaning and direction. My faith has made a big difference in my personal life, and public life as well."*

It's clear President George W. Bush's decision to deepen his faith and commit to following Jesus was a profoundly significant event in his personal life and subsequently impacted his public life.

It highlights that God rejoices more over one sinner who repents than over many righteous people who don't need repentance. The shepherd's actions of leaving the ninety-nine to find the one lost sheep, and his subsequent joy upon finding it, symbolize God's relentless pursuit of those who are lost.

If we are being honest with ourselves, no one wakes up in the morning and says, *"I do not want to be happy today."*

This is a ridiculous notion. However, the idea of being happy seems to affect so many people. In fact, Google reported that the term "how to be happy" is searched 45 million times every month. Happiness seems to be something that many people are searching for.

I would like to provide you with some very specific things that you can do in your life to increase your happiness level. This is by no means a comprehensive list of what someone needs to do to find happiness. This is a short list of things that I have personally done.

Before we get to those specific things there are a few things you need to truly understand about true happiness. It is not based on any material possession. Having more money, more clothes or even power will not help deliver true happiness. It is true that those things can solve some problems and relieve some stress. Material possessions will never deliver true happiness.

The idea that something will "not guarantee happiness" reflects a common sentiment in philosophy, and popular culture. It serves as a reminder that external achievements, material possessions, or life circumstances are not reliable paths to lasting contentment.

Here is a list of things I did to find true happiness:

1. Accept Jesus Christ as My Lord and Savior

For much of my life I had this concept that I felt this constant need to be in control. I felt like my plans or my way of doing things were going to make things happen. It was not until I realized my way is not the best way at all. In fact, my way was possibly the worst way.

I stopped everything and dropped to my knees and asked God to take control of everything. It did not matter what it was—personal, professional, spiritual, financial—everything. My life was a train wreck and what I was doing was not working.

Once I gave up control and accepted Jesus as my Lord and Savior; I felt an amazing feeling. I felt amazing warmth, peace, and an overwhelming sense of joy. At that moment, I began creating this connection along with a sense of faith, love and happiness.

2. Don't Take Things Personal

Your day is constantly bombarded with things that people do or what people say. Perhaps it is what they do not do, or what they do not say. You need to remember this has "Nothing to Do with You!" It has everything to do with them.

All their actions, words, lack of actions and lack of words is all about them and their internal struggles. It may even have to do with a possible childhood trauma (who knows). What is happening has absolutely nothing to do with you.

Example: You are driving to work, and someone cuts you off in traffic. Then they decide to drive ten miles under the speed limit for the next mile. The longer you drive right behind them the more frustrated you get. Next thing you know the both of you are turning into the employee parking lot. The person in front of you is one of your co-workers. Would you want to talk to this co-worker about their driving skills? Maybe you could take a different tactic.

If you stopped and took the mindset that this is not about you; things change drastically. Maybe they just received devastating news about a family member, maybe they are going through severe financial issues or perhaps they are physically ill? The list can be quite extensive. What if you approached this situation, where their actions and words had nothing to do with you and everything to do with them?

3. Have Connections & a Strong Support System

You should surround yourself with positive people that have your best interest at heart. When you have good people around you, they will act as a support system.

- If you have personal issues, you should have someone you can call.
- If you are going through financial difficulties, have someone you can borrow money from or simply talk about it with.
- If you are having housing problems, have someone that has a couch you can crash on.

Having this support system means you will always be surrounded by people that have your back. These people can be found in virtually any area of your life (work, family, school, church, etc.). This does not have to be a large group at all. It could simply be one friend. The power of one good friend makes a huge difference.

4. Stay Curious & Open Minded

Think about this for a moment. Try to imagine some of the most miserable people that you know. Think about what makes them so upset and miserable. For many of them there is a common thread.

Many of them are closed off and not open to new ideas. These are people that know everything and are not willing to try anything else. Those who never do anything new are usually some of the most unhappy people.

We should embrace new ideas and listen to different perspectives. Having a sense of wonder and wanting to grow fuels happiness. Learning and growing is something you should be passionate about.

Example: Imagine you are in a room with a 5-year-old child. This child is telling you in detail all about their toys and their coloring books. They also ask you to play a game with them using their imagination. To them their imagination is a huge part of their life.

Would you allow yourself to look at things from this 5-year-old's viewpoint? Would you be willing to be open minded to use your imagination or would you stay closed off?

5. Stop Regarding the Past

It is called the past for a reason. The Latin word for past is *preatrium*. This means olden times or the past. It cannot be changed. Spending time worrying about the past is a waste of time.

Do not forget the past. You can cherish good memories, but you should learn from your mistakes, so they never happen again. Stop regretting the past!

6. Stop Worrying about the Future!

There are actual studies that state that over 85% of the stuff we worry about never actually happens. Think about how much time we waste worrying about things that never happen. This is a complete waste of time and energy.

7. Stop Looking for Happiness in Other People

It is not the job of other people to make you happy. In fact, it is virtually impossible for them to completely fulfill all your happiness. Happiness is something that is inside every one of us. When you think about it like that it takes on a whole new meaning.

Happiness is not something that I get to keep and hold for myself. True happiness is something that I get to share with others.

LEADERSHIP CHALLENGE

I want you to stop and truly think about this for a moment. Think about the people you know in your life who are truly happy. What do you believe about those people allows them to be happy?

If I had to guess, they would fit in one or more of the categories listed above. There are only seven (7) things that I have put down on my list for striving towards true happiness.

"Accepting Jesus Christ as my Lord and Savior was the best decision of my life."

- Yankee Doodle Dave

- Accept Jesus Christ as My Lord and Savior
- Don't Take Things Personal!
- Have Connections and a Strong Support System
- Stay Curious and Open Minded
- Stop Regarding the Past
- Stop Worrying About the Future
- Stop Looking for Happiness in Other People

Pick at least one (1) of the categories listed above. I invite you to select any one of those techniques to begin your journey. If you would like a selection, I would start with the first choice.

NOTE: Take it from me, if you have not accepted Jesus Christ as your savior this is where you need to start. Here is a sample prayer to do so:

"Lord Jesus, I know that I am a sinner, and I ask You for Your forgiveness. I believe that You died on the cross for my sins and rose again. I turn from my sins and invite You to come into my heart and life. I want to trust and follow You as my Lord and Savior. Thank You for Your grace and love. Amen."

Taking a Leading Role in Communication

"But now you must put aside all such things as these: anger, rage, malice, slander and filthy language from your lips."
- Colossians 3:8

HISTORICAL FIGURE:
President John F. Kennedy - "The Moon-Shot Speech"

Today's leadership development topic must deal with taking a lead role in communication. Why is this important?

The year was 1962 and the President of the United States was John F. Kennedy. At the time tensions were unbelievably high with the Soviet Union. President Kennedy was at Rice University in Houston, Texas. September 12, 1962, Kennedy changed the course of our nation with the speech he gave.

On September 12, 1962, the weather was warm and humid. It was likely that many of the people in Houston were still feeling the effects from Hurricane Carla, which made landfall in Texas a year earlier, in September 1961. Over half a million residents were evacuated, and property damage was extensive, with over 1,900 homes and 980 businesses being destroyed along the coast. It was a dark time in American history, and the people were looking for some hope.

The hope came from the President when he gave his speech. The speech he gave at Rice University was called the *"Moon-Shot."* It significantly impacted the nation's space program and its role in the Cold War. Its significance lies in its ability to inspire a nation, galvanize public support for a massive undertaking and ultimately lead to the first human landing on the moon.

There are estimates that between 35,000 to 40,000 people attended John F. Kennedy's "Moon-Shot" speech at Rice University. Those people in attendance became witness to President Kennedy's gift of public speaking. He had a masterful use of rhetoric, inspiring themes, and charismatic delivery that was perfect for his audience. Unlike earlier politicians with more formal oratory styles, Kennedy's speeches felt fresh, modern and very personal.

President Kennedy was thinking about a technologically challenging, but achievable, national goal that would demonstrate American leadership in the Cold War. The idea was to expand human knowledge and inspire public support and investment in space exploration. The ultimate aim was to land a man on the moon and return him safely before the decade was out. This was an effort that ultimately became Project Apollo.

President Kennedy's speech rallied the nation behind the ambitious goal of landing a man on the moon before the end of the decade. This led to a massive mobilization of resources, both financial and human, to support NASA's Apollo program.

The speech positioned the Moon landing as a symbol of American ingenuity, technological prowess, and national pride.

This was especially important due to the continued Space Race with the Soviet Union. These efforts aimed to demonstrate that the United States could achieve great things and lead the world in scientific and technological advancements.

During the speech President Kennedy shared a small story while he was at NASA. While on his tour, President Kennedy noticed a janitor sweeping the floor. He approached the janitor and asked him, *Excuse me, what are you doing?*

The janitor's profound response was, "*Mr. President, I'm helping to put a man on the moon.*"

The janitor's answer highlighted how his work supported the overall mission. He understood that keeping the facility clean and orderly was essential for the engineers and scientists to focus on their complex work.

The story emphasizes that meaningful work comes from connecting one's daily tasks to a larger purpose.

Beyond its immediate impact, the speech has inspired generations to pursue careers in science, technology, engineering and mathematics (STEM). The "*Moon-Shot*" became a metaphor for ambitious goals and the power of human endeavor.

It became a defining moment in American history and a source of national pride; fostering a sense of accomplishment that resonated across the nation. Kennedy's famous line "*We choose to go to the Moon…not because they are easy, but because they are hard,*" became a powerful message about the importance of tackling difficult challenges and pushing the boundaries of human potential.

When it comes to communication, leaders make an incredible impact on an organization. Our actions have such an incredible impact on those around us. We are all leaders, and it is up to every single one of us to make that difference. Leaders must take the lead in communication to inspire, motivate, and guide their teams, foster trust, collaboration, and a shared understanding of goals, ultimately driving better results and a more positive work environment.

Here's why effective communication is crucial for leaders:

- **Inspires and Motivates:** Leaders who communicate clearly and effectively inspire teams to achieve common goals and motivate them to work towards a shared vision.

- **Builds Trust and Rapport:** Open and honest communication fosters trust and strengthens relationships between leaders and their teams, creating a more positive and productive work environment.

- **Enhance Collaboration:** Effective communication facilitates collaboration by ensuring everyone is on the same page and understands their roles and responsibilities.

- **Improvements in Decision-Making:** Clear communication allows leaders to gather information, assess situations, and make informed decisions that benefit the team and the organization.

- **Resolves Conflict:** Effective communication skills, including active listening and empathy, are essential for resolving conflicts and building consensus.

- **Fosters Employee Engagement:** When leaders communicate regularly and openly, employees feel valued and heard, leading to increased engagement and job satisfaction.

- **Productivity:** By ensuring everyone understands their roles and responsibilities, and by fostering a collaborative environment, effective communication can lead to increased productivity and efficiency.

- **Effective Communication:** Leaders must lead by example and model effective communication skills to inspire their teams to communicate effectively as well.

- **Adapts to Varied Audiences:** Leaders must be able to communicate effectively with different audiences, tailoring their messages to meet the needs of each group.

- **Provides Clear and Concise Instructions:** Leaders must be able to give clear and concise instructions, ensuring that everyone understands what is expected of them.

- **Demonstrates Empathy:** Leaders should demonstrate empathy and understanding, listen actively to their team members and show genuine interest in their concerns.

HOW DO YOU DO THIS?

Leaders can take a lead role in communication by actively listening, setting clear expectations, encouraging open dialogue, and demonstrating transparency. They should also be mindful of their body language, choose words carefully, and foster a culture where feedback is valued.

Here's a more detailed look at how leaders can enhance their communication:

1. Active Listening:

Leaders should prioritize attentive listening, giving their full attention to the speaker, and responding thoughtfully to ensure mutual understanding. This involves limiting distractions, focusing on the speaker's perspective, and asking clarifying questions.

2. Setting Clear Expectations:

Clearly defined goals and standards ensure everyone is on the same page, reducing confusion and increasing productivity. Regularly revisiting expectations helps keep the team aligned and focused.

3. Encouraging Open Dialogue:

Leaders should create a safe space where team members feel comfortable sharing their thoughts and ideas. This can be achieved by actively soliciting input, asking good questions, and being open to feedback.

4. Demonstrating Transparency:

Being transparent and open builds trust and makes communication more effective.

Leaders should be honest and sincere in their communication, allowing their personality and values to shine through. This includes being open about decisions, acknowledging mistakes, and explaining the rationale behind actions.

5. Body Language and Non-Verbal Cues:

Leaders should be mindful of their body language, as it can significantly impact how their message is received. Maintaining eye contact, using open and inviting postures, and conveying warmth through facial expressions can enhance communication.

6. Choosing the Right Medium and Tone:

Leaders should select the appropriate communication channel for the message, considering factors like audience, urgency, and complexity. They should also be consistent in their tone of voice and ensure their language is inclusive and accessible.

7. Providing Constructive Feedback:

Leaders should offer specific and actionable feedback, focusing on how team members can improve their performance. Feedback should be delivered in a constructive and supportive manner, helping team members feel valued and motivated.

8. Building Trust:

Effective communication is crucial for building trust between leaders and their teams.

By being transparent, responsive, and empathetic, leaders can foster a culture of trust and psychological safety.

LEADERSHIP CHALLENGE

The chances are that the next time you are asked to deliver a speech it will not be one that changes the course of the nation. That is okay. It is not the 1960s and you are not President Kennedy delivering a speech concerning our Space Program.

As a leader you do have the ability to assume a leading role in communication in your organization. Several tactics were discussed in this week's lesson that can help you in your leadership role in communication.

What are some things you plan on doing to increase communication with your staff this week?

Yankee Doodle Dave is helping people understand the concept of: "Taking a Leading Role in Communication."

The Importance of Explaining "the Why" to Your Staff

"Whatever you do, work heartily, as for the Lord, and not for men, knowing that from the Lord you will receive the inheritance as your reward. You are serving the Lord Christ."

- Colossians 3: 23-24

HISTORICAL FIGURES:
The Wright Brothers, Fathers of Modern Aviation

The topic on today's leadership development deals with the concept of "The Importance of Explaining '*the Why*' to Your Staff." Understanding "*the why*" is very important. To illustrate this, I would like to share a short story about two very famous brothers—"The Wright Brothers."

Some people may not know where Orville and Wilbur Wright found their love for aviation. To understand you need to learn a little about their father Milton Wright. He was a bishop in the Church of the United Brethren of Christ. For many years he served as a leader and influential clergyman of a conservative faction within the denomination.

In 1878, Milton Wright came home from a church business trip. While he was away on business, he purchased his boys a gift. It was a rubber band-powered toy helicopter. It was a miniature version of a design by French inventor Alphonse Penaud. The boys were fascinated by the toy. The toy hovered when they twirled the rubber band motor. This was a toy rarely seen at this point in America. The gift of the paper, bamboo, and cork helicopter is credited by Orville as the spark that ignited the brothers' lifelong passion for flight, leading them to build their own models and eventually develop the first successful aircraft.

That wooden toy fueled their dreams. It was 1903, and the brothers were in Kitty Hawk, North Carolina. Orville and Wilbur, achieved the first successful, sustained, and controlled powered flight of an airplane on December 17, 1903, at Kitty Hawk, North Carolina, near Kill Devil Hills. Orville piloted the first flight, which lasted 12 seconds and covered 120 feet. This is what record books have documented. The real question is *Why*? Why were they building a flying machine? What fueled their perseverance in the face of numerous challenges?

The Wright brothers invented the airplane to solve the challenge of controlled, powered flight, driven by their fascination with the possibility of human flight and their belief that they could build a machine that could fly like a bird. They aimed to create a flying machine that could be controlled by a pilot, unlike previous attempts that often ended in uncontrolled crashes.

They were successful in doing that by employing several factors. They used a methodical approach, innovative problem solving and practical skills. They focused on solving the crucial problem of flight control, using wind tunnel test designs and continuously refining their designs through trial and error.

In the beginning, the brothers self-funded their work, relying on their earnings from their bicycle shop. This was fine to get things started. They wanted to change history. To change history, they needed to do something different. They later attracted investors by highlighting their systemic approach to de-risking their technology. Their focus was incremental progress from gliders to powered flight, emphasizing their passion for solving the problem of human flight. Explaining their "*Why*" enabled the Wright brothers to secure external investors. This action ultimately led to their ability to have the necessary tools for a successful flight.

Change is an inevitable part of life. It can be seen in our personal and professional lives. Even though change occurs on such a frequent basis many people are hesitant in embracing it. Simply stating a change in policy or procedures will not be enough. As a leader you will need to have their buy-in. Employees' buy-in is critical because it leads to increased motivation, productivity and engagement. When employees feel invested in the company's success, they understand the value they bring, and actively participate in achieving organizational goals, resulting in better overall performance and outcomes for the business; essentially, when employees "buy into" a decision or change, they are more likely to support and actively work towards its implementation, leading to smoother transitions and higher success rates. As a leader one of the best ways to get buy-in is simply explain the *"Why."*

Explaining the *"Why"* to employees means clearly communicating the larger purpose of why things are happening. This new policy or procedure is important to you. How does it affect them? As a leader, explain how their work impacts the company's mission and overall success.

How to Effectively Explain the "Why":

- **Clearly Articulate the Company Mission:** Communicate the company's core purpose and values to all employees.

- **Connect Tasks to Goals:** Explain how individual tasks contribute to larger departmental & organizational goals.

- **Share Strategic Plans:** Provide insights into the company's future direction and how employee contributions fit into the bigger picture.

- **Use Storytelling:** Share real-life examples of how employee efforts have positively impacted customers or the company.

HOW DO YOU DO THIS?

Leaders can effectively explain the "*Why*" by connecting their decisions and actions to a larger purpose, vision, or mission, and by clearly communicating the benefits and impact of those decisions on individuals and the organization. This approach fosters understanding, engagement, and commitment from their teams.

Here's a more detailed breakdown:

1. Start with the "Why":

- **Connect to a Higher Purpose:** Articulate the deeper meaning behind their decisions, linking them to the organization's core values, mission, or a broader societal impact.
- **Highlight the Impact:** Explain how the decision will affect individuals, teams, and the organization, emphasizing the positive outcomes and benefits.
- **Share Personal Reasons:** Share your own motivations and passion for the work, make it more relatable and inspiring for the team.

2. Communicate Clearly and Consistently:

- **Use Simple and Accessible Language:** Avoid jargon and technical terms, ensuring that everyone understands the message.
- **Provide Context and Examples:** Illustrate with real-world examples and stories that resonate with the team.
- **Reinforce the Message:** Repeat the "why" regularly, in different ways, to ensure it's understood and internalized by the team.

3. Encourage Two-Way Communication:

- **Invite Questions and Feedback:** Create a safe space for team members to ask questions and express their perspectives on the "why."
- **Facilitate Open Dialogue:** Encourage team members to share their own interpretations of the "why" and how it relates to their work.

By consistently explaining the "*Why,*" leaders can create a more engaged, motivated, and high-performing team that is aligned with the organization's goals and values.

LEADERSHIP CHALLENGE

In this week's lesson we learned about the Wright brothers and for them the "Importance of explaining why to those around them." Who knows where we would be today within the field of aviation if they had not stopped and simply explained "*Why.*" Here is a scenario where explaining the "*Why*" would be important:

Scenario: You are at your work center at your organization. A new policy is being introduced affecting the Tip Share policy. This will ultimately affect many of your staff members' take-home pay. You know that many of them will be unhappy with the change.

"*Sometimes your staff simply want to know why things are happening the way they are. If you can, slow down and tell them why*"

- Yankee Doodle Dave

You have shared your concerns with the leadership team at your organization. They have informed you that policy changes are critical for strategic growth for the company.

It would be easy to simply state this is a policy change coming from the top. You are a leader that wants to take ownership of your actions. How would you communicate the *"why"* about this change in policy to your staff? How would you get their buy-in?

Here is my challenge. How do you handle this situation? Do you simply blame the Senior Leadership for the change? Or do you own the situation and attempt to get their buy-in?

How to Have a Difficult Conversation

"Be wise in the way you act toward outsiders; make the most of every opportunity. Let your conversation be always full of grace, seasoned with salt, so that you may know how to answer everyone."
- Colossians 4:5-6

HISTORICAL FIGURES:
Steve Jobs, Apple Co-Founder & Board of Directors

This can be personally, professionally or even spiritually; no one enjoys being put in a place where you must have a difficult conversation.

The year was 1985. It is hard to believe big hair and neon colors were all the rage. "Back to the Future" was in the theaters at that time. Madonna's album "Like a Virgin" was in the Billboard Top 100. Microsoft released Windows 1.0 in November 1985.

In 1985, in Cupertino, California, at Apple's headquarters a very difficult conversation was about to take place. The difficult conversation was between Apple's Co-Founder, Steve Jobs, and the Apple Board of Directors.

In 1985, an Apple Macintosh 512K computer had an introductory price of $2,795 before a price cut later that year made it available for $2,499. The original 1984 Macintosh 128K was priced at $2,495. If you had an average inflation rate of 2.79% per year between 1985 and today this would mean the cost would be: $7,502.76.

There was a very interesting and kind of unknown story about Steve Jobs that occurred just a few years earlier in 1981. Steve Jobs implemented a policy at Apple to eliminate typewriters from the office, viewing them as obsolete tools and believing personal computers would create more engaging and creative work for employees. Jobs' vision was that computers would not only automate tasks but also open the company's culture by allowing employees to focus on more rewarding and impactful work. The goal was to prove typewriters were outdated within Apple before trying to convince customers, demonstrating the value of a computer-centric workplace.

To understand how visionary this was, public schools in the United States continued teaching typing classes with typewriters well into the 1990s. Steve Jobs was a true visionary.

John Scully was brought in at Apple as their CEO in 1983. Scully was brought in to oversee the strategic direction of Apple. One of the pet projects he was overseeing was regarding the *Macintosh Project*. The *Macintosh Project* was a key focus for Apple, transitioning from the initial development phase to a commercially available product. The Macintosh, conceived by Jeff Raskin, was designed to be user-friendly with a graphical user interface (GUI) and a mouse, a departure from the text-based interfaces of the time. While the *Macintosh Project* was underway, Apple also released the Lisa 2/10, which was later rebranded as the Macintosh XL and ran Macintosh software via an emulator. Ultimately, the Lisa project was discontinued in April 1985 to prioritize Macintosh.

The *Macintosh Project* came with its potential learning lessons. The high price of this system was a potential barrier for many potential buyers. The initial cost was $2,495.

There was limited memory and processing power. The Macintosh only had 128K of RAM and a single floppy disk drive. This limited its capabilities and required frequent disk swapping.

The initial software was also limited. This made it difficult for users to find useful applications.

There was a period of internal conflict over the direction of the company and the performance of the Macintosh. The Board of Directors were feeling very frustrated and wanted to pull the company in a different direction from what Steve Jobs wanted. This ultimately led to Steve Jobs effectively being forced out of the company and resigning his position.

Perhaps you are not the Co-Founder of Apple. That is understandable. Maybe it is easier to imagine having difficult conversations with some examples that may be a little easier to relate to.

Imagine these situations:

Example #1: You are at home, and it is now 1:00 a.m. and your teenage daughter has missed curfew by an hour. She enters the door and sees you in the front room waiting for her. How do you handle the situation?

Example #2: You are at work and need to complete a financial report. During your audit there are numerous discrepancies. The more you dig you realize that these undocumented deposits were all completed by your supervisor. Just then that person (your supervisor) walks into your office. How do you handle the situation?

Example #3: It has been brought to your attention that one of your staff members is lacking personal hygiene. It is causing a problem within the work center. People are taking notice of this and not wanting to spend time around this person. They bring this to your attention so you can handle it. How do you handle it?

HOW DO YOU DO THIS?

To navigate difficult conversations at work effectively, prepare by understanding the situation and your goals, choose the right time and place, and focus on facts and solutions rather than emotions. Emphasize active listening, use "I" statements, and acknowledge the other person's perspective to foster a productive dialogue.

Here's a more detailed breakdown:

1. Preparation Is Key:

- **Understand the Situation:** Before the conversation, gather all relevant facts and identify the core issue.
- **Define Your Goals:** What do you hope to achieve with this conversation? Having a clear objective will help guide the discussion.
- **Consider the Other Person's Perspective:** Try to understand their point of view, which can help deescalate the situation and promote empathy.

2. Choose the Right Time and Place:

- **Private and Neutral Location:** Choose a location where you can speak freely without interruptions or eavesdropping.
- **Schedule Sufficient Time:** Ensure you have enough time to have a thorough and productive conversation.

3. Manage Your Emotions:

- **Stay Calm and Composed:** Difficult conversations can be emotionally charged, so it's important to maintain composure.
- **Practice Active Listening:** Pay close attention to what the other person is saying, both verbally and nonverbally.
- **Use "I" Statements:** Frame your concerns using "I" statements to avoid sounding accusatory or judgmental.

4. Focus on Facts and Solutions:

- **Stick to the Facts:** Avoid personal attacks or generalizations and focus on the specific issue at hand.
- **Frame the Conversation as a Problem-Solving Exercise:** Work together to find solutions that address the problem.

5. Document Conversation:

- **Take Notes:** Document the key points of the conversation and any agreements reached.
- **Follow Up:** If necessary, send a follow-up email summarizing the conversation and the next steps.

To effectively handle a difficult conversation, prepare beforehand, stay focused on the issue, listen actively, and be solutions oriented. Express your feelings and needs clearly using "I" statements and be prepared to hear different perspectives. If emotions run high, take a break and revisit the conversation later.

"Difficult conversations are not fun for anyone involved. Before you start, review some of the techniques in this week's lesson. Take a breath and you will be just fine."

- Yankee Doodle Dave

LEADERSHIP CHALLENGE

In this week's lesson, we learned about how the Board of Directors at Apple had a very difficult conversation with Steve Jobs.

Here is my challenge to you. As leaders, how do you handle either of these situations? Can you use courage to deal with these scenarios? Do you stand back and accept the behavior? Or do you have the courage to have a difficult conversation?

____

____

____

____

____

____

____

"When we avoid difficult conversations, we trade short-term discomfort for long-term dysfunction." - Peter Bromberg

Ego and Why We Need to Continue to Grow

"Let nothing be done through selfish ambition or conceit, but in lowliness of mind let each esteem better than himself."

- Philippians 2:3

HISTORICAL FIGURE:
Thomas Jefferson, 3rd President of United States

Today's Leadership Development session is on our Ego. More importantly, why do we need to continue to grow?

In leadership I am referring to an "ego" as an individual's sense of self-importance, often manifesting as a strong need for recognition, power, and validation, which can be detrimental if inflated. This leads to arrogance, defensiveness, and a disconnect from the needs of the team when not kept in check. This is essentially the tendency to prioritize one's own perspective over others' when leading.

Let me share a story of someone who understood the concept of needing to continuously grow and develop. This would be the third President of the United States, Thomas Jefferson. He served as president from 1801-1809.

Thomas Jefferson developed what is known as his "Garden Kalendar." You read this correctly. It is Kalendar with a "K." This was because of a then-common spelling convention of the word. During the 18th century and earlier, the spelling of English words was not as standardized as it is today. You can view this today through the Massachusetts Historical Society in their Thomas Jefferson Papers collection and in a physical, annotated print edition available from the Monticello Shop. The original manuscript is held within the Massachusetts Historical Society.

This was a comprehensive garden book, which chronicled his extensive agricultural experiments and observations of plant life at Monticello. Over several decades, Jefferson meticulously recorded planting dates, germination, harvests, weather, and even experiments with 330 varieties of 70 species of plants from around the world. Some of those included vegetables from Italy, France and Mexico. The Garden Kalendar served as a personal diary and a practical guide, demonstrating Jefferson's scientific approach to gardening and his goals of selecting the best plant varieties for his estate.

The main vegetable garden at Monticello is 1,000 feet long and 80 feet wide. This covered over a two-acre terrace. The garden is divided into sections including plots for vegetables, berries, and other edibles.

Thomas Jefferson embodied a commitment to continuous learning and intellectual curiosity, believing that knowledge was essential for human, political, and scientific progress. He was a self-taught architect, a statesman, a scholar, and a passionate gardener who meticulously documented his botanical experiments at Monticello. This dedication to lifelong learning informed his innovative and forward-thinking approach to leadership.

Jefferson possessed an insatiable curiosity and pursued knowledge across various disciplines throughout his life, including mathematics, science, classical history, languages, philosophy, and Native American culture. His formal education laid the groundwork, but his drive for knowledge extended far beyond it. He amassed three substantial personal libraries in his lifetime, demonstrating his dependence on books as a source of information and inspiration.

He was deeply influenced by enlightenment thinkers like John

Locke, Francis Bacon, and Isaac Newton, shaping his philosophy and political career. These ideas fueled his belief in human, political, and scientific progress, which he considered infinite.

Jefferson displayed a capacity for adapting his views and acknowledging when he was wrong, particularly when faced with new evidence or the judgment of others he trusted. This was evident in his initial concerns about the Constitution and his eventual acceptance of the document, as well as his willingness to expand his interpretation of the Constitution to facilitate the Louisiana Purchase, a move that went against his strict constructionist leanings.

Despite facing personal tragedies like the death of his wife and a period of depression, Jefferson found strength in purpose and continued his dedication to learning and public service. He viewed life as an opportunity for exploration and gaining knowledge, embracing challenges as opportunities to learn and improve.

Thomas Jefferson strongly believed that an educated populace was crucial for the success of the American experiment in self-government. This conviction led him to found the University of Virginia, designing its campus to reflect his educational philosophy. He aimed to empower every citizen with the knowledge needed to understand their duties and rights, believing that "free inquiry must be indulged."

Jefferson's continuous personal growth was fueled by his intellectual curiosity, his embrace of enlightenment ideals, his adaptability, and his unwavering commitment to education and the pursuit of knowledge. He served as a lifelong student, constantly striving to learn and refine his understanding of the world and his role within it. He was noted for having a "selflessness" in his approach, marked by a quiet demeanor. He would understand arguments and had an almost "excessive willingness to hear from everyone else and seek consensus." There was not a need to get credit for his ideas. Many times, Jefferson demonstrated qualities of selflessness and a focus on the common good in leadership.

We don't like to think that someone else is better than us or that we have a lot left to learn. Once you humble yourself you open yourself to true growth.

You must always keep a student mindset, which is willing to grow. You can't learn if you think you know everything. Remaining humble is vital. You cannot get better if you consider yourself the best.

HOW DO YOU DO THIS?

Leaders continue to grow by embracing lifelong learning, seeking feedback, and developing both hard and soft skills. They actively seek opportunities to learn from experience, mentors, and diverse sources of information like books, podcasts, and courses. Additionally, leaders must be self-aware, understand their strengths and weaknesses, and be willing to adapt and improve.

Here's a more detailed look at how leaders grow:

1. Lifelong Learning:

- **Stay Updated:** Leaders should consistently update their knowledge and skills by engaging in continuous learning, which can include formal courses, workshops, reading, and staying informed about market trends and technologies.
- **Embrace Change:** Leaders must be adaptable and willing to learn new things to stay relevant and effective in a constantly evolving world.

2. Seeking Feedback and Reflection:

- **Self-Reflection:** Regularly reflecting on experiences, identifying areas for improvement, and connecting with their purpose helps leaders understand their strengths and weaknesses.
- **Seeking Feedback:** Actively seeking feedback from team members, mentors, and peers provides valuable insights into leadership effectiveness.

- **Constructive Criticism:** Leaders should be open to receiving constructive criticism and using it to refine their approach.

3. Developing Key Skills:

- **Hard Skills:** This includes mastering specific knowledge and technical abilities related to their field and leadership role.

"If you are not growing you are dying."

-Yankee Doodle Dave

LEADERSHIP CHALLENGE

Thomas Jefferson clearly understood the concept of needing to grow continuously. He also understood the need to humble himself.

Imagine you were put in his situation. Maybe not as the 3rd President of the United States, but maybe you replaced someone in a work situation. You were put in place because you were told you were the rock star. You are the one that people come to—to make things happen. In your situation, another person was removed because they were not cutting the standard. It might seem very easy to sit back and think that you have finally made it.

Will you be comfortable with where you are and say, "I have finally made it?" Will you humble yourself to continue to learn? If so, how would you continue to grow?

Building Trust in the Workplace

"May the God of endurance and encouragement grant you to live in such harmony with one another, in accord with Christ Jesus, that together you may with one voice glorify the God and Father of our Lord Jesus Christ."

- Romans 15: 5-6

HISTORICAL EXAMPLE:
Apollo 13 Space Mission

This week's topic deals with "Trust in the Workplace." Trust in the workplace means that your employees enjoy a culture of honest, psychological safety, and mutual respect.

A powerful story illustrating trust in the workplace is the Apollo 13 mission. In 1970, during a lunar mission, an oxygen tank exploded, putting the crew in grave danger. The teams at NASA, both on-site and back at mission control, had to trust each other implicitly to solve the crisis and bring the astronauts home safely. This involved a high degree of vulnerability, open communication, and a shared commitment to a common goal, demonstrating how trust is essential for overcoming adversity and achieving success, even under immense pressure.

The mission set a Guiness World Record for the farthest distance from Earth, and mission control's innovative problem-solving, including jury-rigging a CO_2 scrubber that saved the astronauts.

There are some key aspects of the Apollo 13 story that highlight trust building. Engineers and astronauts had to openly admit their limitations and share concerns to find possible solutions. Being honest and transparent in their communication was critical. Everyone needed to be upfront about challenges and potential risks.

The crew of Apollo 13 consisted of three people. Those people were: Commander Jim Lovell, Lunar Module Pilot Fred Haise and Command Module Pilot Jack Swigert.

Jim Lovell was a veteran astronaut who had flown on three different missions including Apollo 8. In Jim Lovell's perspective, Apollo 13 was going to be a pivotal shift towards scientific exploration.

For Fred Haise, this was his first mission. He was completely focused on the demanding job of landing on the moon and conducting surface excursions.

Jack Swigert's preparation for Apollo 13 was unique as he was a last-minute replacement for Ken Mattingly. Mattingly was exposed to the measles just days before launch.

To move forward things had to be solved differently. They had to have a shared sense of responsibility. A collective sense of responsibility for the mission and the crew's safety fostered a strong sense of teamwork and trust.

To build trust, the crew of Apollo 13 relied on their extensive training, decisive leadership, and calm, precise communication. This trust was extended to Mission Control and was solidified through their shared focus on problem solving during the in-flight emergency.

The trust between the crew in space and the controllers on Earth was built on a few key principles. The first of which is decisive leadership. Both Lovell and Flight Director Gene Kranz demonstrated calm and steady resolve during the crisis. Kranz's clear call to "work the problem" immediately focused the entire team on one shared objective to get the crew home.

The second principle would be relinquishing control. Kranz trusted his team of experts to take ownership of their specialist areas and work tirelessly toward a solution. Similarly, the astronauts had to trust that Mission Control had their best interests in mind. Commander Jim Lovell later explained, *"You gotta trust each other to do the right thing, push the right buttons."*

The third principle would be their vast experience and preparation. The Mission Control teams and astronauts worked together for thousands of hours before the mission. This deep experience and prior relationship ensured that candid communication and loyalty paid off during the unpredictable emergency.

Historically, in the military and space community there is an inherent respect provided simply with one's rank. Solving this problem requires a different thought process. Regardless of rank, every member of the team was valued for their expertise.

There was a need to focus on the greater good. There was a primary focus on the overall mission—success in bringing home the astronauts. This superseded individual concerns or personal egos. You can reference last week's lesson (Week #11: Ego and Why We Need to Continue to Grow) for further information.

The mission success of Apollo 13 was the result of numerous factors but most importantly focusing on simply bringing the astronauts home. The team's actions, under extreme pressure, demonstrated their commitment to each other and the mission, building trust over time. This story serves as a compelling example of how trust is not simply given, but earned through consistent, honest, and collaborative behavior, particularly when facing significant challenges.

Trust in the workplace matters because it:

- Helps employees feel secure in their jobs, which reduces turnover.
- Builds employee engagement, which often leads to higher quality of work and better results for the company.
- Promotes an environment of psychological safety where people feel comfortable asking questions, sharing ideas, and expressing thoughts.

Here are a few strategies on how you can help build "Trust in the Workplace":

1. Listen More Than You Speak: Your employees are unique individuals who have their own ideas and viewpoints. Ask them to speak their mind, and when they do, genuinely listen. This is the foundation of building a positive workplace relationship built on trust.

2. Show Fellow Employees Appreciation Often: Everyday appreciation builds a sense of community and helps employees feel emotionally secure. When you recognize your team often, they will be more likely to trust you. You may show recognition by simply offering verbal praise or even complimenting them on their performance.

3. Empower Your Team by Trusting Them First: Empower your team by encouraging them with professional development and performing autonomously. Invite them to attend meetings or participate in projects they would not normally attend. They will remember the trust you showed them, and you will benefit from their unique perspective.

4. Be Honest and Transparent: Telling the truth can be tough. It can seem easier to tell your employees what they want to hear (especially during difficult times). But being honest, while being sensitive to their feelings, encourages trust in you. You should also be transparent when it comes to discussing changes in the workplace so that your employees are always in the know.

5. Ask for Help: Asking for help invites open communication. It shows you are comfortable with transparency and willing to work toward a solution. This creates an environment where others feel more comfortable seeking help when they need it. This creates a stronger and more trusting dynamic for your team.

HOW DO YOU DO THIS?

Building trust in the workplace is crucial for team cohesion and productivity. Key strategies include open communication, demonstrating reliability by following through on commitments, and fostering a culture of feedback and appreciation. Authenticity, vulnerability, and mutual respect also play vital roles in establishing trust.

Here's a more detailed breakdown:

1. Open Communication:

- **Transparency:** Share information openly and honestly, keeping employees informed about company news and decisions.
- **Two-Way Communication:** Encourage open dialogue and actively listen to employee feedback. This could involve regular check-ins, surveys, or creating space for employees to voice their opinions.
- **Clear Expectations:** Ensure everyone understands their roles, responsibilities, and performance expectations.

2. Reliability and Consistency:

- **Follow Through on Promises:** Be dependable and consistent in your actions. If you say you'll do something, do it.
- **Be Reliable:** Show up when you say you will and meet deadlines.
- **Be Consistent:** Align your words and actions, demonstrating that you practice what you preach.

3. Feedback and Appreciation:

- **Solicit Feedback:** Actively seek feedback from employees and be open to hearing both positive and constructive criticism.
- **Give Feedback Constructively:** Provide regular feedback, both positive and developmental, in a supportive and constructive manner.

- **Show Appreciation:** Recognize and reward employees for contributions and efforts.

4. Authenticity and Vulnerability:

- **Be Yourself:** Be genuine and authentic in your interactions with others.
- **Show Vulnerability:** Share your experiences, including successes and failures, to build rapport and demonstrate that you are human.
- **Be Empathetic:** Understand and acknowledge the emotions of others.

5. Building Relationships:

- **Get to Know Your Team:** Take the time to understand your colleagues' strengths, weaknesses, and what motivates them.
- **Foster a Sense of Belonging:** Create an inclusive environment where everyone feels valued and respected.
- **Encourage Mentorship:** Facilitate relationships where team members can learn from each other.

6. Accountability:

- **Take Responsibility:** Be accountable for your actions and mistakes.
- **Create a Culture of Accountability:** Encourage everyone to take ownership of their work and be responsible for their contributions.

LEADERSHIP CHALLENGE

This may not be as stressful as getting astronauts returned home from space. Building Trust in the Workplace does come with a certain number of stressors and complexities.

Several strategies were discussed in this week's lesson to help leaders build trust in the workplace. Try to implement at least one of these tactics into your workplace.

What tactics can you put in place to "Build Trust in Your Workplace"?

____

____

____

____

____

____

"Trust is the highest form of human motivation."
- Henry Ford

"This is not something that happens right away or overnight. Building trust in a workplace takes time."

-Yankee Doodle Dave

Why Good Leaders Must Be Good Followers

"But among you it will be different. Whoever wants to be a leader among you must be your servant."
- Matthew 20:26

HISTORICAL FIGURE: George Washington – Listening to His Military Council and Delaying the Attack on Boston

To be a good leader, one must be a good follower. I mean "follower" in the sense of gaining alignment with the leader, supporting the leader, and fulfilling your defined roles and responsibilities to the best of your ability. To be a good leader (especially in middle management), one must be a good follower.

This week's lesson deals with George Washington. Though he is known as a decisive leader, George Washington also demonstrated a capacity to listen to and follow the advice of others. Rather than leading as an unquestioned autocrat, he was consultative and collaborative, both as a general during the Revolutionary War and as the first president.

Allow me to share a small story about George Washington. This story illustrates his ability to follow in his decision to defer to his military council in 1776 rather than launching an immediate, high-risk attack on the British in Boston.

In the late summer of 1776, after the American army had forced the British out of Boston, the enemy forces returned, heavily reinforced. General William Howe now commanded a powerful British fleet and a large, disciplined army. In contrast, Washington's troops were a ragtag collection of poorly trained and ill-equipped soldiers.

After receiving intelligence that General Howe intended to attack New York City, Washington planned a swift, audacious counterstrike on the British in Boston. He was confident he could retake the city with a sudden assault.

On July 10, 1776, Washington gathered his senior officers for a council of war to present his plan. When conducting a meeting with his military council, George Washington would have been formal, deliberate and respectful of his officers' opinions. In the end he remained the decisive Commander. His approach blended with the gravity of his role in the American Revolution. During these meetings he would preside but often listened more than he spoke.

George Washington's military council was not just one single permanent body, but rather a varied group of officers he consulted for advice during Councils of War. Key members across these councils included Major Generals Artemis Ward, Charles Lee, Philip Schyler and Israel Putnam; Brigadier Generals Natahan Green, Horatio Gates and trusted aides like Alexander Hamilton and the Marquis de Lafayette.

In this specific meeting, MGEN Charles Lee, BGEN Nathanael Greene, and BGEN Israel Putnam, were strongly against the idea. They argued that the Continental Army was not ready for a frontal assault against a professional British army. There was also a belief that the risk of heavy casualties was too high. General Washington's senior officers knew they lacked the necessary siege equipment and heavy artillery to succeed. With a major confrontation expected soon in New York, they could not afford to lose experienced soldiers in a poorly conceived attack on Boston.

General Washington, described as having a fiery temper, was impatient and determined. He had a strong inclination to move forward with his plan. However, faced with the united and logical opposition of his team, he paused to listen. After an extended and thoughtful discussion, he decided to abandon his own instincts and follow their advice instead. He knew he had to follow!

By delaying the attack on Boston and consolidating his forces, Washington was able to turn his attention to a more pressing threat in New York. While the Continental Army suffered defeats in the battles for New York City, Washington was able to keep his army intact, which was a strategic victory. General Washington displayed a key leadership quality in listening to his advisors. This decision showed his capacity to consider other perspectives and did not let his impatience lead him to a costly mistake.

This event demonstrates Washington's wisdom in subordinating his personal ego and initial impulse to the collective intelligence of his team. It showed his leadership was not about always being first but about making the best decision for the larger cause—even if it meant following the counsel of others.

In the example listed above of George Washington, we learn why leaders need to be followers to learn. Further understanding the needs and perspectives of others is critical for effective leadership. Leaders who are willing to learn from their followers can adapt and improve their strategies. When leaders demonstrate humility and a willingness to learn, it encourages others to participate and contribute. A leader who values collaboration and learning ultimately creates a more thriving and sustainable environment.

HOW DO YOU DO THIS?

Leaders need to be good followers in the workplace because it allows them to better understand the perspective of their team members. It also allows them to gain valuable insights from others, build stronger relationships, and effectively delegate tasks by knowing when to step back and let others take the lead. These actions ultimately contribute to a more cohesive and productive team environment. In the end, being a good follower helps a leader develop the necessary skills to guide and motivate others effectively.

Key Points About Why Leaders Should Be Good Followers:

- **Empathy and Perspective:** By actively following, leaders can better understand the challenges and viewpoints of their team members, this fosters empathy and improves communication.
- **Learning and Development:** Observing other leaders and how they navigate situations can provide valuable learning opportunities for aspiring leaders.
- **Team Collaboration:** When leaders are willing to follow certain tasks, it encourages a collaborative environment where everyone feels valued and empowered to contribute.
- **Building Trust:** When a leader demonstrates the ability to follow, it builds trust with their team as they show respect for different roles and responsibilities.

"A good leader is also a good follower."

- Yankee Doodle Dave

LEADERSHIP CHALLENGE

There are reasons why you were selected for the leadership position you are in. No one is doubting that. In this week's lesson, we looked at a few examples involving George Washington. General Washington listened to his military council and went against his initial reaction to attack British troops in Boston. This process illustrated how he was a Good Follower.

During this next week (and the weeks to follow) how can you demonstrate being a good follower in your department? Please feel free to share any comments or best practices with your group. Learning from one another is how we will grow.

"A good leader encourages followers to tell him what he needs to know, not what he wants to hear."
- John C. Maxwell

Why a Leader's Actions Are Important

"Be shepherds of God's flock that is under your care, watching over them – not because you must, but because you are willing, as God wants you to be; not pursuing dishonest gain, but eager to serve."
- Peter 5:2

HISTORICAL FIGURE:
Frederick Douglass, American Abolitionist

A leader's actions are important because they directly influence the culture of an organization, impacting employee morale, engagement, and overall performance. Essentially, a leader's behavior sets the standard for others. This creates a ripple effect where their actions inspire, motivate, and guide their team towards achieving goals, making them a critical factor in an organization's success.

This week the focus is going to be on a leader who understood that their actions were important. That leader was Frederick Douglass. Frederick Douglass' life itself is a powerful testament to the importance of action in achieving freedom and progress.

Frederick Augustus Washington Bailey was born on February 14, 1818, into slavery on the Eastern shore of Maryland.

On January 1, 1834, he began to work for Edward Covey. The widely recounted story of Douglass' physical resistance to Edward Covey, a "slave breaker" known for his cruelty, marks a pivotal moment in his life where he consciously chose to fight back instead of submitting himself to abuse. In August 1834, Douglass fights back against Covey, resulting in Covey not attempting to whip him again. This act of defiance, though risky, reawakened his sense of self-worth and strengthened his resolve to be free.

According to the Bill of Rights Institute. It taught him that *"he who would be free must himself strike the blow."*

In 1836, Frederick Douglass is involved in a failed attempt to escape slavery. He was arrested and jailed in Easton, Maryland. He subsequently returned to his enslavement and was eventually sent to work in the Baltimore shipyards. This is where he learned skills that would later help him in his successful escape.

Frederick escaped from slavery on September 3, 1838. He fled to Baltimore by train, disguised as a sailor, using the documents of a free black sailor. He eventually settled in New Bedford, Massachusetts, where he married Anna Murray and began his life as a free man and abolitionist.

His persistent efforts to teach himself to read and write, despite laws and social constraints prohibiting enslaved people from doing such were amazing. This demonstrated the power of education as a tool for personal empowerment and ultimately, for challenging the system of slavery itself.

As Douglass himself stated, *"Knowledge unfits a child to be a slave."*

Douglass could have simply enjoyed his newfound freedom. Instead, he took the courageous step to become a leading voice in the abolitionist movement, travelling extensively to give powerful speeches and publishing his autobiography to expose the brutality of slavery to the world. This demonstrates the importance of using one's voice and experiences to advocate for change and fight for the rights of others.

During the Civil War, Douglass actively worked to convince African Americans to join the Union Army, including his own sons. He believed that acting and participating in the fight for freedom was essential for achieving lasting change and securing a future for his people.

There is an interesting story involving Frederick Douglass after the Civil War. Frederick Douglass was nominated as the vice-presidential candidate by the Equal Rights Party in 1872. Victoria Woodhull was the presidential nominee. An interesting part about this was that the nomination was made without Douglass' knowledge or consent. As a Republican, Frederick Douglass was already supporting President Ulysess S. Grant's reelection bid and never became a serious candidate for the vice presidency.

In essence, Frederick Douglass' life illustrates that freedom, equality, and social justice are not passively bestowed. They must be actively pursued and defended through courageous and persistent action, even in the face of immense adversity. His actions, both personal and public, had a profound and lasting impact on the fight against slavery and civil rights in the United States. His efforts inspired others to act and work toward a more just and equitable society.

Frederick Douglass was an influential figure whose actions had a significant impact on the abolitionist and civil rights movements in 19th-century America. His importance stems from his experiences as an enslaved person and his dedication to fighting for the rights of African Americans and women.

Key Aspects of Leading by Example:
- **Model Desired Behaviors:** Showcase the behaviors you want your team to emulate like punctuality, positive attitude, collaboration, and commitment to quality work.
- **Strong Work Ethic:** Be willing to put in the effort required to achieve goals, including taking on challenging tasks and going the extra mile when needed.
- **Open Communication:** Clearly communicate expectations, goals, and decision-making processes to your team, while also actively listening to their feedback.

- **Integrity and Ethics:** Adhere to high ethical standards in your actions and decision-making, demonstrating personal accountability for your choices.
- **Positive Attitude:** Maintain a positive outlook, even during challenging situations, to uplift your team's morale.

Example Scenarios:
- **Early Arrival:** If you expect your team to be on time, consistently arrive early at meetings or work yourself.
- **Taking Responsibility:** When a mistake occurs, openly acknowledge your role in it and take corrective action.
- **Giving Constructive Feedback:** Provide specific and timely feedback to team members, both positive and critical, to help them grow.
- **Supporting Colleagues:** Actively help team members who are struggling with tasks or facing challenges.

HOW DO YOU DO THIS?

Leaders have important actions centered around setting direction, motivating and inspiring others, and fostering a positive and productive environment. Key actions include decision-making, demonstrating integrity, and being adaptable. They also focus on personal development, building strong relationships, and encouraging growth within their teams.

Here's a more detailed look at some of those actions:

1. Setting the Vision and Direction:
- **Clearly Communicating:** Articulate a vision that inspires and unites the team, while also setting clear expectations for performance.
- **Focus on "How" and "Why":** Explain not just what needs to be done, but also the reasons behind the actions, to foster deeper understanding and commitment.

2. Inspiring and Motivating:

- **Lead by Example:** Demonstrate qualities you want to see in others, like integrity, hard work, and a positive attitude.
- **Foster a Positive Environment:** Create a workplace where people feel valued, respected, and motivated to perform their best.

3. Building and Maintaining Relationships:

- **Open Communication:** Encourage open dialogue and create a safe space for team members to share their ideas and concerns.
- **Provide Support and Guidance:** Coach, mentor, and offer support to help team members grow and develop their skills.

4. Decision-Making and Problem-Solving:

- **Make Timely Decisions:** Be decisive and take responsibility for making informed decisions, even in challenging situations.
- **Encourage Collaboration:** Foster teamwork and encourage team members to contribute their expertise to problem-solving.

5. Adaptability and Resilience:

- **Embrace Change:** Be flexible and adaptable in the face of changing circumstances and new challenges.
- **Maintain a Positive Attitude:** Stay positive and resilient during difficult times and encourage the same in their team.

LEADERSHIP CHALLENGE

By focusing on these key actions, leaders can create a positive and productive environment where individuals and teams thrive. In this week's lesson we learned about Frederick Douglass and how his actions as a leader were important.

Think about a relationship in your life (personal or professional). Remember how long it took to build trust and cultivate that relationship. Also remember how fast you can lose trust through one simple unethical action. This is why a leader's actions are so incredibly important.

There are countless stories of highly-respected and successful leaders who have been removed from their positions after finding some type of unethical behavior. In 2024, numerous leaders in business were removed from their positions because of unethical behavior. Martin Winterkorn (CEO for Volkswagen) was fired after the company was caught manipulating emissions tests on diesel vehicles. Steve Esterbrook (CEO from McDonald's) was fired for having an inappropriate relationship with a subordinate employee. These are just a small example of the countless examples of leaders who would be in their positions today if they did not display unethical behavior.

Here is my challenge to you. What actions do you plan to take this week to set a positive example within your team?

"A leader's actions set the tone and shape culture. They are also responsible for building trust and influence in the work center."

- Yankee Doodle Dave

What Is the Difference Between Leadership and Manipulation?

"For such people are not serving our Lord Christ, but their own appetite, by smooth talk and flattery they deceive the hearts of the naive."

- Romans 16:18

HISTORICAL FIGURES:
President Woodrow Wilson & President Theodore Roosevelt

What is the difference between leadership and manipulation? Leadership and manipulation are closely related, but one is deemed to be bad and the other is considered good. They are closely related because they are both trying to do the same thing. The aim of both leadership and manipulation is to get people to do what they want to do. The highest form of leadership and manipulation is to get people to do what you want them to do—because they want to do it.

To understand the difference between manipulation and leadership I would like to compare two presidents—President Woodrow Wilson and President Theodore Roosevelt.

President Woodrow Wilson was a former president of Princeton University before his presidency, earning him the nickname "The Professor." Wilson also earned a doctorate degree in history and political science from Johns Hopkins University.

In April 1917, one week after the United States entered *World War I*, President Woodrow Wilson established the Committee on Public Information (CPI) to rally public opinion behind the war effort. The CPI, headed by George Creel, became the modern U.S. government's first major propaganda machine.

Its tactics were far-reaching, establishing a national newspaper, publishing press releases, and engaging with the press around the clock.

It disseminated the Wilson administration's message via articles, cartoons, books, advertisements, feature films, posters, and pamphlets distributed by the millions. It enlisted leading journalists, advertising executives, artists, and even university professors to create and lend legitimacy to its propaganda.

While Creel insisted the CPI was a conduit for reliable information, it regularly sanitized news, distorted facts, and played on emotions. The organization also established front organizations and secretly subsidized news outlets and bribed journalists overseas. At home, the CPI challenged the loyalty of those who questioned its methods and collaborated with federal intelligence agencies to stifle dissent, trampling on civil liberties in the process.

Historian John Maxwell Hamilton notes that the CPI, *"shot propaganda through every capillary in the American bloodstream, proliferating pro-Allied and xenophobic anti-German messaging."*

The CPI pressured American media to censor news and coordinated with other government agencies, including the Postal Service, to restrict dissenting content.

Hamilton's book, *Manipulating the Masses: Woodrow Wilson and the Birth of American Propaganda,* draws on over 150 archival collections to tell the full story of the CPI's use of mass communication to advance U.S. foreign policy during *WWI.* He argues that the CPI represents the "original sin" in the U.S. government's relationship with the media, a foundational mix of spin and distortion that continues to echo in the contemporary era of presidential tweets and weaponized media.

Hamilton contends that *"every element of today's 'information state' had antecedents in the CPI, highlighting the enduring threat posed by government propaganda and the shortcuts that even well-intentioned propagandists take to sway opinions."*

To understand the concept of manipulation versus leadership, you need to examine a leader who influenced others without manipulation. A prime example is Theodore "Teddy" Roosevelt.

President Roosevelt graduated from Harvard but left law school at Columbia without receiving a degree. He had become focused on politics and lost interest in a legal career. Roosevelt was legally blind in one eye after a boxing injury at the White House. The President continued with his boxing hobby well into his presidency. He switched to jiu-jitsu instead.

During a 1902 bear hunt, Roosevelt's assistants captured and tied a bear to a tree, suggesting he shoot it. Finding this unsportsmanlike, Roosevelt refused to shoot the defenseless animal, according to the U.S. National Park Service. This act of principle, widely reported in newspapers, became the inspiration for the creation of the popular *"Teddy Bear,"* forever linking his name to a symbol of compassion.

Roosevelt earned the nickname *"Trust Buster"* for his efforts to limit the power of monopolies. His actions were rooted in the belief that the government had a responsibility to ensure fairness and economic opportunity for all citizens, rather than allowing big business unchecked power. He targeted trusts he considered harmful to the public interest, seeking a "square deal" for both average citizens and honest businesses.

Roosevelt's commitment to conserving natural resources was driven by a long-term vision and a sense of stewardship for the environment. He dramatically expanded national parks and forests, not for short-term gain or political maneuvering, but to preserve these resources for future generations.

These examples demonstrate that while Roosevelt was a shrewd politician, he also made decisions based on a strong moral compass and a commitment to fairness and public welfare.

Both leaders and manipulators use many of the same techniques. They build relationships, leverage their influence, and maneuver politically to attain the outcome they desire. Both leaders and manipulators capitalize on others' egos, personal agendas, and individual strengths and weaknesses to achieve their own preferred outcome.

But while there are many similarities between leaders and manipulators, there is one glaring difference. Manipulators are trying to get people to do things to benefit the manipulator; leaders are trying to get people to do things to benefit the team. This difference is stark. The manipulator is trying to get a promotion or a better position for themselves. The manipulator is trying to set themselves up to look good in the eyes of their boss. The manipulator has one ultimate priority in every move they make: that priority is the manipulator.

But a leader puts themselves at the bottom of the priority list. The good of the mission and the good of the team outweigh any personal concern a true leader has for themselves.

Both attitudes eventually shine through and reveal themselves. Manipulators might fool some of the people some of the time, but they will not fool all the people all the time. True leaders are the same. While they might not get the credit they deserve because they deflect it to other team members, over time they will absolutely be recognized, admired and likely promoted for their leadership.

This does not mean the leader always triumphs over the manipulator in the immediate situation. Sometimes a manipulator plays a good hand, gets themselves noticed, winding up winning. But the win is short term. Sacrificing others for yourself never pans out in the long term. People eventually take notice of the fact that you are not looking out for the good of the team but are looking out for yourself. When people notice that they will not follow for long.

HOW DO YOU DO THIS?

To transition from a manipulative approach to effective leadership, focus on building trust, fostering open communication, and prioritizing the well-being of those you lead. This involves actively listening, demonstrating empathy, and setting clear expectations while empowering others to contribute their ideas. Ethical leadership emphasizes shared success and long-term growth rather than short-term gains achieved through manipulation.

Key Differences Between Leadership and Manipulation:

- **Motivation:** Leaders inspire action through shared goals and vision, while manipulators seek to control others for personal gain.
- **Communication:** Leaders communicate openly and honestly, fostering transparency, whereas manipulators use selective information and deceptive tactics.
- **Relationship Building:** Leaders build trust through genuine connection and respect, while manipulators exploit relationships for their benefit.
- **Decision Making:** Leaders consider the impact on all stakeholders, while manipulators prioritize their own interests.
- **Accountability:** Leaders take responsibility for their actions and outcomes, while manipulators often deflect blame.

Steps to Cultivate Ethical Leadership:

1. **Develop Self-Awareness:** Understand your own motivations and how your actions impact others. Reflect on your leadership style and identify areas for improvement.
2. **Practice Active Listening:** Pay attention to what others are saying, both verbally and nonverbally. Seek to understand their perspectives and concerns.
3. **Build Trust Through Transparency:** Be honest and open to your communication. Share information and decision-making processes with your team.

4. Empower Your Team: Delegate tasks effectively, provide support and resources, and encourage your team members to take ownership of their work.

5. Focus on Shared Success: Align your goals with the needs and aspirations of your team. Celebrate collective achievements and support individual growth.

6. Seek Feedback and Reflect: Regularly solicit feedback on your leadership style and be open to constructive criticism.

7. Lead with Integrity: Demonstrate ethical behavior in all your actions. Be consistent in your values and principles.

8. Set Clear Boundaries: Establish clear expectations and boundaries for acceptable behavior. Communicate these boundaries effectively.

"Manipulation erodes trust, the foundation of healthy relationships, and makes it incredibly difficult to rebuild once broken."
- *Yankee Doodle Dave*

LEADERSHIP CHALLENGE

In this week's lesson we learned about two very different leaders. During their timeframes, it would be very safe to say that both of those were respected by their people. It is very clear that the way President Woodrow Wilson and President Theodore Roosevelt led were greatly different.

When a good leader makes sacrifices and puts other people and the mission ahead of themselves, eventually that will be recognized, and people will want to follow that leader. Good leaders do the right thing for the right reasons. They work hard, support the team and lead with solid execution. In the long run, the reputation of a true leader far outweighs the glory-seeking manipulator, and in the end, the good leader, looking out for the mission and the team, will win.

Several strategies were discussed in this week's lesson discussing the difference between leaders and manipulators. Try to implement at least one of these tactics into your workplace. How can you put it into place to "Ensure You are a Better Leader Without Manipulation?"

*"When I manipulate people, I move them for my personal advantage.
When I motivate people, I move them for their personal advantage."
- John C. Maxwell*

Being Mindful of Our Inner Voices (Especially in Making Decisions)

"My dear brothers and sisters, take note of this; Everyone should be quick to listen, slow to speak and slow to become angry."

- James 1:19

HISTORICAL FIGURE:
Henry Ford, Founder of Ford Motor Company

Did you know that we have different voices inside us that help in the decision-making process? No, I am not talking about the medical diagnosis of multiple personality disorders and hearing voices. What I am talking about is as a leader grows, they learn to trust and learn to listen to inklings, feelings and developing a strong sense of oneself. Some people will call it an *"Inner Voice."*

To understand this *"Inner Voice"* concept please allow me to share a story of a leader who focused a lot on his intuition and his *"Inner Voice."* That leader was Henry Ford.

Henry Ford's decision to implement the assembly line was driven by his intuition and desire to make cars affordable for everyone. While he faced skepticism and resistance, his vision and willingness to experiment led to a revolution in mass production. This approach, though seemingly unconventional, allowed Ford to dramatically increase production efficiency and ultimately lower the cost of its vehicles.

Ford envisioned a car that was not just a luxury item but a practical and affordable means of transportation for the average person. This vision was a leap of faith, as most cars at the time were handcrafted and expensive.

The assembly line, a concept that wasn't entirely new, was refined and implemented by Ford in a way that was unprecedented. He believed that by breaking down the manufacturing process into smaller, repetitive tasks, he could significantly speed up production.

Faced with high employee turnover, Ford, in a hunch, doubled its workers' pay to $5 per day, a radical move at the time. This decision, fueled by intuition, resulted in a surge of applications, allowing him to select the best workers and improve productivity.

Ford's unconventional methods faced resistance from established industry practices, and his intuition was often met with skepticism. However, his unwavering belief in his vision and his willingness to experiment allowed him to overcome these challenges and bring about a transformation in the automotive industry.

Here is a short story of how Henry Ford was influenced by the President of the United States. In 1918, President Woodrow Wilson asked Henry Ford to run for a U.S. Senate seat in Michigan as a Democrat. President Wilson sought to ensure a Democratic majority in Congress to support his policies, particularly his efforts to negotiate peace at the end of World War I. Henry Ford was seen as a popular candidate who could win the support of voters despite not being a career politician.

Henry Ford was very reluctant about entering into politics. He agreed to run for office but had a significant request. Henry would not actively campaign or spend any money on advertisements.

President Wilson agreed to Ford's request and endorsed his campaign. To boost Ford's chances, President Wilson publicly endorsed him and encouraged Michigan Democrats to support the industrialist. Ford also chose to run in the Republican primary, aiming for bipartisan support. He ended up losing the Republican nomination to his opponent.

Henry Ford's main opponent was Republican Truman H. Newberry. Newberry was a wealthy business executive and former Secretary of the Navy. Newberry ran an aggressive, well-funded campaign that spent thousands on advertising and publicly attacked Ford.

Despite his minimal campaigning, Henry Ford was defeated by Newberry in the 1918 general election by a relatively narrow margin of just over 2,200 votes.

Henry Ford was a leader who listened to his instincts. He listened primarily to his gut in making decisions. We happen to have more than one voice inside us; especially when it comes to making decisions. Please allow me to explain.

We are faced with decisions daily. These can vary from various subjects (what will I eat for lunch, how do I have a difficult conversation with a staff member, etc.). What I want to focus on are the decisions we must make in a professional setting. What I have discovered is that when you are forced to make a professional decision each person will have three voices (inklings, feelings or senses) that become prominent. Those are:

(1) VOICE IN THE HEART "EMOTIONS":

- Making decisions on emotions means basing your choices on how you feel now rather than carefully considering facts and logic. This can often lead to impulsive or potentially regrettable decisions.
- **Example**: Imagine the last time you were experiencing strong emotions (anger, excitement, fear or sadness). If a person is faced with a decision at that time, often our emotions will cloud rational thought. This is when you have people who allow their emotions to dictate their actions.

A classic story illustrating emotional decision-making is the biblical story of King Solomon's judgment. Two women claimed the same baby, and Solomon, faced with a seemingly impossible dilemma, proposed to cut the baby in half to divide it. One woman, overwhelmed by love and grief, begged him to give the baby to the other woman to save its life. This selfless act of love revealed her true motherhood, leading Solomon to reward her the child.

(2) VOICE IN THE GUT "INSTINCT":

- Making decisions on instinct means to base your choices primarily on your gut or intuition.
- This is done rather than carefully analyzing all available information and weighing options logically.
- It is essentially trusting your first immediate reaction to a situation to guide your decision-making process.
- **Example:** Imagine you are working in your work center. You have been asked to bring a new process created by Admin to your team. You are very familiar with this process. In fact, this is something you have been doing for a very long time. Instinctively you know if you do things your way it will get done and it might even be faster.
- **Another situation:** The situation of asking questions or reading a manual on how to assemble something. Maybe the thought is that I can do this faster and rely on my previous knowledge on my own instead of asking. If we make decisions solely on our gut, intuition or previous experiences; we are limiting our potential to grow.

(3) VOICE IN THE BRAIN "LOGIC":

- Making decisions on logic means basing choices on rational analysis and reasoning. Weigh carefully the pros and cons of each, based on facts and evidence. This means it is not based on emotions or personal bias. This helps a person arrive at the most sensible decision possible.

- **Example:** You have been tasked with completing a project. One thing that you could do is analyze data on past project performance or employee performance reviews to determine which team member is best suited for the project. This gathering of information and identifying patterns, helps formulate a reasoned choice based on evidence rather than personal preference.

In the Sherlock Holmes stories, a prominent example of decision-making with logic is found in *The Adventure of the Speckled Band.* Holmes uses deductive reasoning to identify the source of a mysterious illness and ultimately solve the murder. By carefully observing details, such as a bell rope that doesn't connect to a bell, he deduces it was used to summon someone to the victim's room. This logical deduction, along with other observations, leads him to the solution of the crime.

"It is important to be aware of a person's emotion, logic and instinct. Spend time in a quiet place to evaluate your situation."
- Yankee Doodle Dave

LEADERSHIP CHALLENGE

This week we learned about Henry Ford and how he would listen to his "Inner Voice" when making decisions. The next time you are placed in a situation where you need to make a professional decision, take a moment to be mindful of yourself and decide which "Inner Voice" you should follow.

a.   Is this a situation that you are very emotional about?

b.   Is it something that you simply feel instinctively about?

c.   Is this something where you have rationally applied analysis to the situation?

In business it is important to consider emotion, however most decisions are not based on them. Emotions can drive creativity and passion, but they can also lead to impulsive or irrational choices. Conversely relying solely on logic can sometimes stifle innovation and creativity.

When faced with a difficult professional situation I put myself in a quiet place where I can be alone with my thoughts; and there will be no interruptions.

Then I listen to each of the voices provide their advice. The quieter I remain, the louder the other voices appear. At some point, one of the voices becomes louder than all the others. That is the one that I listen to.

Here is my challenge for you:

At some point you will be posed with a difficult professional situation. Stop for a moment and try to embrace this concept. Put yourself in a quiet space with no interruptions. While you are there shut off the outside world and all the distractions.

Then all you need to do is remain quiet and really listen. Listen to your inner dialogue of logic, emotion and instinct. Sometimes people have a great deal of difficulty making decisions. Putting a system like this in place will not only help you but it will help your organization.

Can you share a personal example of this?

____

____

____

____

____

____

____

____

____

____

____

____

____

____

____

____

____

*"We are dangerous when we are not conscious of our responsibility
for how we behave, think and feel."
- Marshall R. Rosenberg*

Why Is Humility Considered a Cornerstone for Leadership?

"Humble yourselves, then, under God's mighty hand, so that He will lift you up in his own good time. Leave all your worries with Him, because he cares for you."
 - 1 Peter 5: 6-7

HISTORICAL FIGURE:
Frances Xavier Cabrini, Italian American Sister

There are several instances in history of leaders expressing unique levels of humility. One example that I would like to share with you happens to be that of Saint Cabrini. She was also known as Frances Xavier Cabrini or Mother Cabrini.

Please allow me to address something fundamental before I lose you (the reader's attention). The main concept of the book is about Leadership Development and follows American leaders through history. Frances Xavier Cabrini was born in Sant'Angelo Lodigiano, Italy (about 20 miles from Milan) in 1850. She became an American citizen in 1909 while in Seattle, Washington.

Mother Cabrini demonstrated exceptional humility in her leadership, particularly in her work with immigrants and the poor. She led by example, often performing tasks that others might consider menial, and encouraged her followers to do the same. Her humility was not just a personal trait but a cornerstone of her leadership style, fostering a spirit of service and shared sacrifice among her followers.

Mother Cabrini wasn't afraid to get her hands dirty. She was known to scrub floors, even in her habit, and perform other physically demanding tasks. There was no work she considered beneath her. This showed her commitment to the work and her willingness to share in the hardships of those she served.

She saw her role as one of service, constantly encouraging her sisters to be humble and to focus on spiritual growth through acts of service and self-denial.

Mother Cabrini faced skepticism and doubt about her ability to lead, particularly as a woman in a male-dominated field, but she persevered, demonstrating humility by not letting these challenges deter her from her mission.

Sister Cabrini was never afraid to stand up for what she believed was right. There is a wonderful example of this when she was founding a hospital in Chicago. She suspected the property measurements were wrong and felt as if she was being cheated. She and her sisters used shoestrings tied together to remeasure the property in the middle of night. When they found the measurements were incorrect, Cabrini adjusted the contract to her advantage.

There is another example of her confronting the Archbishop of New York. Despite being a newly arrived immigrant, Cabrini was not intimidated by authority. When the Archbishop of New York suggested she return to Italy, she refused and proceeded with her mission. Later a Roman prelate told her that missionaries were typically men. For those that may not know, a Roman prelate is a high-ranking member of the Roman Catholic Church who holds a position of authority. This could be anyone like bishops, archbishops, patriarchs, abbots and cardinals.

She famously said, *"If the mission of announcing the Lord's Resurrection to His Apostles had been entrusted to Mary Magdalene, it would seem a very good thing to confide to other women an evangelizing mission."*

She encouraged her followers to be humble, reminding them that pride could hinder their spiritual understanding. She also emphasized the importance of honesty, loving criticism and providing encouragement after addressing faults.

Mother Cabrini, also known as Saint Frances Xavier Cabrini, was canonized on July 7, 1946. Pope Pius XII canonized her in a ceremony in Rome. She is the patron saint of immigrants. Her feast day is celebrated on November 13th. She was the first American citizen to be declared a saint by the Catholic Church.

Cabrini approached obstacles with trust in God and a willingness to surrender to His will, believing that her strength came from her faith rather than her own abilities.

Mother Cabrini's humility wasn't just a personal virtue; it was a powerful leadership tool that allowed her to inspire and mobilize others to address the needs of the marginalized and contribute to the betterment of society.

Humility is the quality of being modest or respectful in one's self-assessment and behavior. It involves recognizing and accepting one's limitations, valuing others' contributions, and maintaining a sense of perspective.

HOW DO YOU DO THIS?

In leadership, humility has such a vital purpose. A leader lacking humility might display behaviors like being overly self-promoting, refusing to accept feedback, taking all the credit for team successes. They could also display being dismissive of concerns, and prioritizing their own agenda above the team's goals. They essentially exhibit arrogance and a lack of respect for others on their team.

Key Characteristics of a Non-Humble Leader:

- **Excessive Self-Praise:** Constantly talking about their own achievements and downplaying the contributions of others.

- **Difficulty Accepting Feedback:** Becoming defensive when criticized or offered constructive suggestions.
- **Micromanaging:** Not trusting team members to make decisions and constantly monitoring their work due to a lack of faith in their abilities.
- **"Know-It-All" Attitude:** Not seeking input from others because they believe they have all the answers.
- **Lack of Accountability:** Avoiding responsibility for mistakes and blaming others.
- **Dominating Conversations:** Not giving others a chance to share their thoughts or perspectives.
- **Using "I" Statements Excessively:** Focusing on personal achievements and rarely using "we" to acknowledge team efforts.

Negative Impacts of a Non-Humble Leader:
- **Low Team Morale:** Employees may feel undervalued and disengaged when their leader takes all the credit.
- **High Turnover:** Team members may leave due to frustration with a leader who does not value their contributions.
- **Poor Collaboration:** Difficulty building a cohesive team environment where people feel comfortable sharing ideas openly.
- **Damaged Reputation:** A leader perceived as arrogant may lose trust and respect from colleagues and stakeholders.

The humble leader works in the opposite direction. They are someone who actively listens to others, readily acknowledges their contributions, is open to feedback, admits their mistakes, prioritizes team success over personal glory, and empowers others to grow by valuing their ideas and perspectives, essentially putting the needs of the team first while remaining authentic and transparent in their interactions.

Key Characteristics of a Humble Leader:

- **Active Listening:** They actively seek out different viewpoints and genuinely listen to what others have to say.
- **Acknowledgement of Others' Contributions:** They openly recognize and appreciate the efforts of their team members.
- **Open to Feedback:** They are receptive to constructive criticism and use it to improve their leadership.
- **Ability to Admit Mistakes:** They are not afraid to acknowledge when they are wrong and take responsibility for their actions.
- **Focus on Team Success:** They prioritize the collective goals of the team over individual achievements.
- **Empowering Others:** They encourage growth and development by providing opportunities for team members to take ownership and contribute.
- **Authenticity:** They present themselves genuinely and transparently in their interactions with others.
- **Self-Awareness:** They understand their strengths and limitations and are not afraid to ask for help when needed.

"A humble person does not think less of themselves, they think of themselves less often."

- Yankee Doodle Dave

LEADERSHIP CHALLENGE

This week's lesson told the story of Mother Cabrini (later gaining Sainthood). She consistently demonstrated humility in her leadership. In this week's lesson there were several techniques to help you as a leader *"Place Humility as a Cornerstone in Your Leadership."*

I wish to extend a challenge to my fellow leaders this week. What techniques do you plan to use to ensure that you can place humility as a cornerstone in your leadership?

____

____

____

____

____

____

____

____

____

____

____

____

____

"The difference between a good leader and a great leader is humility."
- John C. Collins

Leaders Follow Through on Commitments

*"Commit your actions to the Lord,
and your plans will succeed."*
                                        - Proverbs 16:3

HISTORICAL FIGURE:
James Polk, 11th President of the United States

In our daily lives we are faced with various forms of commitment—professionally, personally, spiritually and even financially. Taking care of one's commitments is a task of any good leader. Let me paint a clear visual of this by describing a popular event in history.

According to some historical perspectives, James K. Polk stands out as a leader who consistently fulfilled his commitments. President James Polk was the 11th President of the United States, serving from 1845 to 1849. Elected in 1844, he laid out a four-part agenda and achieved every one of his key promises during his single term in office.

The first part of his agenda was the acquisition of the Oregon Territory. Polk successfully negotiated with Great Britain to settle the long-standing dispute over the Oregon Territory, securing a vast area for the United States.

Secondly, it covered the acquisition of the California and New Mexico Territories. President Polk pursued the annexation of California and New Mexico, eventually achieving this goal through the

Mexican American War and subsequent treaty. Despite the campaign slogan *"Fifty-Four Forty or Fight!,"* Polk pursued a diplomatic solution with Great Britain through the *Oregon Treaty of 1846*, establishing the boundary at the 49th parallel and securing significant territory for the U.S. without war.

Next, he focused on the re-establishment of an Independent U.S. Treasury. He fulfilled his promise to restore the Independent U.S. Treasury system. Polk supported lower tariffs and achieved this with the *Walker Tariff of 1846*. He successfully re-established the Independent Treasury System, separating government funds from private banks to create a more stable financial environment.

The fourth part of the agenda supported and oversaw the annexation of Texas. Texas then became the 28th state in December 1845. This increased tensions with Mexico.

He is renowned for his commitment to fulfilling his campaign promises during his single term in office. He entered the presidency with a clear agenda, focused on achieving the expansionist goals of *Manifest Destiny* and strengthening the American economy. Polk's success in achieving his stated goals during his presidency is often highlighted as a significant example of a president following through on his commitments.

After fulfilling his promises and declining to run for a second term, the exhausted James Polk returned to his home in Tennessee. Tragically, his relentless work ethic and the immense stress of the presidency had taken a heavy toll on his health. He died of cholera just 103 days after leaving office, marking the shortest retirement of any U.S. president.

The story of James Polk is often cited as an example of extreme follow-through and ambition. His unwavering determination to see his goals realized in a single term, at the cost of his own health, had a massive and permanent impact on the territorial size of the United States.

This story emphasizes personal follow-through on commitment, once made, often requires dedication and perseverance to see it through, even if it leads to unforeseen challenges or requires significant personal sacrifice.

HOW DO YOU DO THIS?

Have you ever worked at an organization where maybe your supervisor over promised and under delivered?

Maybe there was a staff member who consistently showed up late and did the absolute minimum just to maintain their job.

The idea of following through on commitments is something that unfortunately not everyone does. To effectively follow through on commitments, leaders should prioritize clear communication, establish accountability, lead by example, and be adaptable. This involves setting clear goals, tracking progress, and fostering a culture where commitments are taken seriously.

Here's a more detailed look:

1. Set Clear Goals and Expectations:

- **Be Specific:** Clearly define what needs to be achieved, when it needs to be done, and the expected outcomes.
- **Communicate Effectively:** Ensure everyone understands their roles and responsibilities in fulfilling the commitment.

2. Establish Accountability:

- **Track Progress:** Regularly monitor progress towards commitment, identifying any obstacles or delays.
- **Provide Feedback:** Offer constructive feedback, both positive and areas for improvement, to keep individuals on track.
- **Address Issues:** Proactively address any problems or conflicts that arise, preventing them from derailing the commitment.

3. Lead by Example:

- **Be Reliable:** Demonstrate commitment by consistently following through on your own promises and deadlines.
- **Inspire Others:** Your actions will motivate your team to prioritize commitments and work towards shared goals.

4. Be Adaptable:

- **Stay Flexible:** Be prepared to adjust plans as needed due to changing circumstances or new information.
- **Maintain Focus:** While adapting, ensure that the overall vision and purpose of the commitment remain clear.

5. Foster a Culture of Commitment:

- **Recognize Achievements:** Celebrate milestones and acknowledge successes to reinforce the importance of following through.
- **Promote Teamwork:** Encourage collaboration and open communication to build a sense of shared responsibility for commitments.
- **Address Concerns:** Create a safe space for team members to voice concerns or challenges related to commitments, facilitating problem-solving.

LEADERSHIP CHALLENGE

In this week's lesson we learned about President James Polk and how he delivered on practically everything he campaigned on. An example of following through on commitments.

Here is my challenge to you. Over the next week you may be faced with a myriad of personal, professional, spiritual and even financial commitments.

Which concepts do you plan to put in place in your department (work center) to help you follow through with your commitments?

____

____

____

____

____

"It was character that got us out of bed, commitment that moved us into action, and discipline that enabled us to follow through." - Zig Ziglar

"Without commitment you will never start. More importantly, you will never finish."

- Yankee Doodle Dave

Instead of Casting Blame, Take Ownership of Your Mistakes

"Whoever conceals their sins does not prosper, but the one who confesses them finds mercy. Blessed is the one who always trembles before God, but whoever hardens their heart falls into trouble."

- Proverbs 28: 13-14

HISTORICAL FIGURE: President Ronald Reagan – Japanese Internment Camps & the Iran-Contra Affair

This week I would like to bring up a situation in leadership for you to think about. I simply call it "Instead of Casting Blame, Take Ownership of Your Mistakes." Let me explain with a few short stories concerning President Ronald Reagan.

During World War II, President Franklin D. Roosevelt signed Executive Order 9066. This authorized the internment of over 120,000 Japanese Americans. This was solely based on their ancestry without a trial.

For years, Japanese American activists and their allies fought for a formal apology and reparations. This was due to the immense suffering and loss caused by their families placed in internment camps.

In 1988, President Ronald Regan signed the *Civil Liberties Act*. This offered a formal apology and provided a symbolic payment of $20,000 to each surviving internee.

In his speech upon signing the act, Reagan stated, "*We gather here today to right a grave wrong. The internment was based solely on race*" and called the action "*just that: a mistake.*" Clearly, while he was not president at the time, the government as an institution had failed.

The act was a significant moment in U.S. history, with Reagan's signature acknowledging the government's leadership failure. Reagan was in charge and took ownership of this mistake.

The next story involving President Reagan involves what was called the *Iran-Contra Affair*.

The *Iran-Contra Affair* was a political scandal during the Reagan administration involving the secret sale of arms to Iran, despite a U.S. arms embargo, and the diversion of profits from those sales to support the Contra rebels in Nicaragua. This occurred while the U.S. government was prohibited by Congress from funding the Contras.

The Reagan administration secretly sold arms including missiles to Iran to secure the release of American hostages held in Lebanon by pro-Iranian groups.

The profits from these arms sales were then diverted to support the Contras, a right-wing rebel group fighting the leftist Sandinista government in Nicaragua.

This covert operation violated U.S. law, specifically the *Boland Amendment*, which prohibited funding the Contras. It also went against the arms embargo on Iran.

The scandal came to light in 1986 and led to investigations, public backlash, and a decline in Reagan's approval ratings. Several individuals, including Lieutenant Colonel Oliver North (USMC), were indicted, though some convictions were later overturned.

The *Iran-Contra Affair* remains a significant example of the dangers of unchecked executive power and the complexities of foreign policy decisions. It also highlighted the importance of congressional oversight and accountability in government actions.

During the *Iran-Contra Affair*, President Ronald Reagan publicly acknowledged and took ownership of the mistakes made by his administration, despite claiming to be unaware of certain actions at the time.

In a March 4, 1987, address, President Reagan stated, *"I take full responsibility for my own actions and for those of my administration. As angry as I may be about activities undertaken without my knowledge, I am still accountable for those activities."*

During his 1987 State of the Union address, President Reagan stated, *"We did not achieve what we wished, and serious mistakes were made in trying to do so."*

This public acknowledgement was a significant moment in the scandal. It is widely considered a demonstration of his willingness to accept accountability for his administration's actions.

HOW DO YOU DO THIS?

Leaders can take ownership of mistakes by acknowledging them, apologizing, learning from them, and taking corrective action. This involves being transparent, admitting faults, and focusing on solutions rather than placing blame. By demonstrating vulnerability and a commitment to improvement, leaders can foster trust and build a stronger team culture.

Here's a more detailed breakdown:

1. Acknowledge the Mistake:

- **Be Upfront:** Don't try to hide or downplay the mistake. Leaders should openly admit when they've made an error.

- **Use "I" Statements:** Focus on personal responsibility rather than deflecting blame.

- **Be Specific:** Name the mistake clearly and concisely.

2. Apologize Sincerely:

- **Express Regret:** A genuine apology demonstrates remorse and acknowledges the impact of the mistake on others.

- **Focus on the Impact:** Explain the mistake's effect on the team or organization.

3. Learn and Improve:

- **Analyze the Cause:** Understand what led to the mistake to prevent future occurrences.

- **Seek Solutions:** Focus on fixing the problem and implementing preventative measures.

- **Share Lessons Learned:** Use the experience as a teaching moment for the team.

4. Take Corrective Action:

- **Fix the Problem:** Take concrete steps to rectify the situation and minimize negative consequences.

- **Follow Through:** Ensure that promised actions are completed and deadlines are met.

5. Foster a Culture of Ownership:

- **Be a Role Model:** Take ownership of mistakes, set an example for your team.

- **Encourage Vulnerability:** Create an environment where team members feel comfortable admitting errors and seeking help.

- **Promote Learning:** Emphasize mistakes are opportunities for growth and improvement.

LEADERSHIP CHALLENGE

In this week's lesson we followed the story of President Ronald Reagan and how he took ownership during the signing of the *Civil Liberties Act* and the *Iran Contra Affair.* There were several concepts that can help leaders take ownership of their mistakes.

Which concepts do you plan to put in place in your department (work center) to help you take ownership of your own mistakes?

____

____

____

____

____

____

"There is no one else to blame. The leader must acknowledge mistakes and admit failures, take ownership of them and develop a plan to win." - Jocko Willink

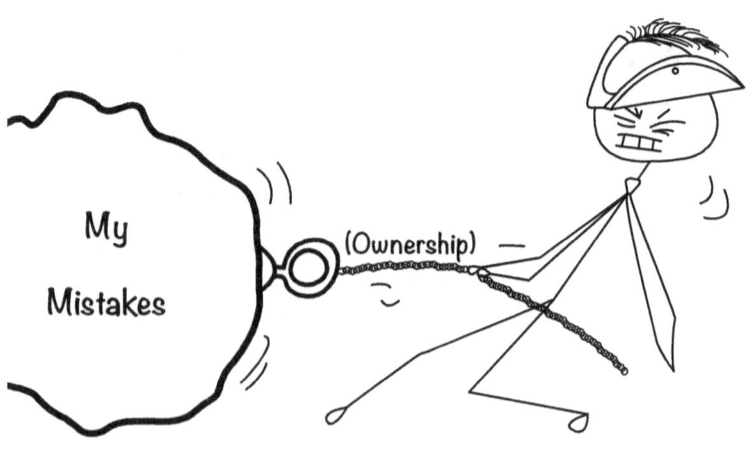

Difference Between Having People on Your Team and Having the Right People on Your Team

"If either of them falls down, one can help the other up. But pity anyone who falls and has no one to help them up. Also, if two lie down together, they will keep warm. But how can one keep warm alone? Though one may be overpowered, two can defend themselves. A cord of three strands is not quickly broken."

- Ecclesiastes 4:10-12

HISTORICAL FIGURE:
President Abraham Lincoln - Team of Rivals Concept

As an HR professional it is safe to say that I am in the people business. I understand people and what effects they can bring to a company. Some people would say (I have even said) that a company's number one asset is their people. I would like to take that concept and dig a little deeper on that. A company's number one asset is not just people; but it is the *"right people."*

To further illustrate this point I would like to share another short story.

During the turbulent period leading up to and throughout the Civil War, Lincoln faced immense challenges. He understood the gravity of the situation and the necessity of assembling a cabinet that could effectively navigate the political and military complexities of the time. Instead of surrounding himself solely with allies, he made the unconventional decision to include his three main political rivals for the 1860 Republican presidential nomination—William Seward, Salmon Chase, and Edward Bates—in his cabinet.

These men were formidable politicians with strong personalities and differing opinions. For example, Seward initially viewed himself as a more qualified candidate for the presidency than Lincoln. Yet, Lincoln's political genius and his capacity to understand and manage differing perspectives allowed him to harness their talents for the greater good of preserving the Union.

This decision demonstrates several key aspects of having the "right people" on your team. Lincoln recognized the value of having diverse viewpoints and experiences at the table, even if those views initially clashed with his own. He prioritized competence and expertise, choosing individuals he believed could contribute significantly, regardless of their prior opposition to him.

Despite the initial animosity, Lincoln's leadership style, characterized by his kindness and ability to connect with individuals, gradually built strong professional and even personal relationships within his cabinet.

President Lincoln understood the concept of strength in challenging assumptions. By having individuals with differing opinions and even criticisms, Lincoln could ensure decisions were thoroughly vetted and challenged, leading to more robust outcomes.

The "*Team of Rivals*" approach is a testament to Lincoln's political genius and serves as a powerful example of how effective leaders can leverage diverse talent and navigate potentially challenging relationships to achieve monumental goals.

Lincoln understood that a diversity of opinions would lead to better-informed decisions. He deliberately created an environment where robust discussion and debate were encouraged. This forced his ideas to be challenged and refined before being implemented. Lincoln was not intimidated by opposing views and was confident enough to manage strong personalities for the greater good.

While challenges existed, such as disagreements and animosity between cabinet members, Lincoln's skillful management, including his diplomacy and ability to mediate disputes, was a crucial factor in the successful functioning of his administration during the *Civil War*. He had the confidence to bring together individuals with differing views, and his empathy and collaborative style helped bridge divides and focus on the common goal of preserving the Union.

HOW DO YOU DO THIS?

To build a strong and effective team, leaders should focus on selecting individuals with the right skills, fostering a collaborative environment, and ensuring clear communication and expectations. This involves understanding each member's strengths, delegating tasks effectively, and creating a culture where team members feel valued and heard.

Here's a more detailed look at how leaders can ensure they have the right team members:

1. Selecting the Right People:

- **Identify Essential Skills and Attributes:** Leaders should clearly define the necessary skills and personality traits for each role within the team.
- **Assess Candidates Thoroughly:** Go beyond resumes and interviews, using practical exercises and assessments to gauge skills and cultural fit.
- **Look for Diversity:** A diverse team brings a wider range of perspectives and experiences, which can lead to more creative solutions and better problem-solving.
- **Prioritize Character and Values:** Choose individuals who demonstrate integrity, honesty, and a strong work ethic.
-

2. Fostering a Positive Team Environment:

- **Promote Open Communication:** Encourage team members to share ideas, concerns, and feedback openly and honestly.

- **Build Trust and Rapport:** Leaders should actively build relationships with team members, getting to know them personally and professionally.
- **Encourage Collaboration and Teamwork:** Facilitate opportunities for team members to work together, share knowledge, and leverage each other's strengths.
- **Recognize and Reward Contributions:** Acknowledge and appreciate individual and team achievements to boost morale and motivation.

3. Defining Clear Roles and Expectations:

- **Establish Clear Goals and Objectives:** Ensure everyone understands the team's overall goals and how their individual contributions fit into the bigger picture.
- **Delegate Tasks Effectively:** Assign tasks based on individual strengths and provide the necessary support and resources for successful completion.
- **Provide Regular Feedback:** Offer constructive feedback on performance, both positive and areas for improvement, to help team members grow.
- **Address Conflicts Constructively:** Leaders should be prepared to mediate and resolve conflicts within the team, ensuring a positive and productive atmosphere.

"You do not need just anyone on your team. You need the Right people on your team."
- Yankee Doodle Dave

LEADERSHIP CHALLENGE

In this week's lesson we discussed President Abraham Lincoln and his *"Team of Rivals"* approach. He understood the importance of surrounding himself with the right people. He did not surround himself with people that simply agreed with him. President Lincoln understood that if you are willing to listen to different perspectives you will be able to make the best decisions for the country, even if it meant disagreeing with his advisors.

There are several benefits of having the right people on your team. This can lead to increased productivity, improved communication, stronger trust and collaboration and a more positive and engaging work environment. These teams often demonstrate higher morale, greater loyalty, and a willingness to support each other.

Here is my challenge to everyone.

In this week's lesson there are several concepts that leaders can take to ensure they have the right person on their team. Which concepts do you plan to put in place to ensure that you do in fact have the right people on your team?

____

____

____

____

____

____

"If you get the best people on your team, you've got plenty of time to do the things you like to do and can add more value, too." - Jack Welch

How Do You Deal with Stress?
(Potato, Egg or a Coffee Bean)

"Do not be anxious about anything, but in everything by prayer and supplication with thanksgiving let your requests be made known to God."

- Philippians 4:6

HISTORICAL FIGURE:
Woodrow Wilson, 28th President of the United States

The Leadership Development topic today deals with Stress. We all face it; it enters our lives all the time. In fact, it is not if it happens, but more likely when stress happens how you act. In this week's lesson I want to begin by sharing a short story about the effects of stress and the toll it took on one of our presidents.

Woodrow Wilson was the 28th President of the United States and served from 1913 to 1921. He was a pivotal figure in *World War I*. President Wilson experienced significant physical and possibly a mental health decline during his presidency. This was particularly towards the war's conclusion and during subsequent peace negotiations.

President Woodrow Wilson's health led to a constitutional change. The frail President Wilson had a history of health issues, but stress related to promoting the League of Nations led to a series of strokes in 1919. The partially incapacitated Wilson remained in office until 1921. Eventually, the 25th Amendment, ratified in 1967, allowed for constitutional measures to deal with temporary or permanent incapacity of the President in office.

According to accounts from those closest to Woodrow Wilson his illness seemed to change his personality in a few unusual ways. The president became testy and suspicious of those around him, to even include his allies. He was particularly convinced the French were spying on him. The episode took place while Wilson was staying at the Hôtel de Prince Murat during the Paris Peace Conference. At that time, he was already facing intense and difficult negotiations with French leaders like Georges Clemenceau, who had fundamentally different ideas about the post-world war.

Wilson became obsessed with the idea that he was surrounded by French spies and that the furniture was somehow bugged. These were the signs of the cognitive effects of the flu. This led to extreme shifts in his personality and delusions.

It is important to understand that the United States entered *World War I* on April 6, 1917. The United States officially ended its involvement in *World War I* with the *Knox-Porter Resolution,* signed into law on July 2, 1921. President Wilson was in office and served as Commander in Chief for that entire time. It is very safe to say that stress and illness had a great impact on him.

It is important to know that President Wilson did have some pre-exiting medical issues before coming into office. He had a history of health issues, including suspected strokes, according to the University of Arizona Libraries. These earlier episodes, characterized by weakness in his limbs and difficulty with dexterity, may have been precursors to the more severe health crises he faced later. Stress is thought to have exacerbated these conditions.

In October 1919, Wilson suffered a major ischemic stroke that left him partially paralyzed on his left side and with a possible visual impairment in his right eye. This stroke significantly hampered his ability to effectively lead and negotiate, coming at a crucial time when the ratification of the *Treaty of Versailles* and the question of American membership in the *League of Nations* hung in the balance.

The full extent of Wilson's illness and disability was largely concealed from the public, Congress, and even from Wilson himself. This was a decision reportedly made by his wife and personal physician, Dr. Cary Grayson. Some historians believe that this concealment and Wilson's incapacitated state may have contributed to the U.S. Senate's refusal to ratify the *Treaty of Versailles* and join the *League of Nations.*

There's evidence to suggest that his illnesses, including the effects of his strokes, potentially contributed to changes in Wilson's personality and behavior. Some sources mention an increase in his stubbornness and a potential difficulty in compromising during the peace negotiations. Some historians also suggest that his previous strokes may have made him more driven and less inclined to recreation.

Despite his declining health and against medical advice, Wilson embarked on a relentless speaking tour across the country to garner public support for the *League of Nations.* This strenuous effort ultimately took a toll on his health, culminating in his collapse and later, the debilitating stroke, notes the American Association of Neurological Surgeons (AANS).

In essence, the immense pressures of leading the country through *World War I*, followed by the demanding peace process and the Spanish flu pandemic, significantly impacted Woodrow Wilson's physical and possibly mental health. His stroke, in particular, hindered his ability to effectively lead during a crucial period of American history.

It is clear that stress had an effect on President Wilson. I would like to share with you a story of how stress can impact our surroundings.

The story begins with a wise chef who wanted to teach his young apprentice a valuable lesson about how different people react to challenges and stress. The chef asked the young apprentice to describe what he was holding (a potato, an egg and some coffee beans). This is what the apprentice said:

- The potato is very firm and strong.
- The egg is very fragile, needing to be contained in its shell.
- The coffee beans are small, hard and have a nice aroma.

The chef then took each item and placed them into separate boiling pots of water (one for the potato, one for the egg and one for the coffee beans). The boiling water affected both the egg, the potato and the coffee beans over time.

- The potato, which started off as firm, gradually softened and became mushy under the heat.
- The egg on the other hand, though initially fragile, with its shell hardened on the inside transformed and became solid.
- The coffee beans were unique. After they were exposed to the boiling water, they changed the water and created something brand new.

The chef looked at the apprentice and simply said, "Which one are you?"

The chef then explained to his apprentice that just like the potato and the egg, people can react differently to stressful situations.

In some situations, like the potato, people may appear strong but crumble under pressure. Then there are others, like the egg, that may seem vulnerable but can become stronger when faced with adversity. The coffee bean changes the hot water. The very circumstance that brings the adversity, the pain and hardship changes into something wonderful. If you are like the coffee bean, when things are at their worst, you improve and change the situation around you for the better.

The concept behind the story deals with stress. It is not the circumstance that defines us, but how we choose to respond to it. When we are faced with adversity, we can choose to be like the potato and have it weaken us. Or we can choose to be like the egg and grow stronger from the experience. Or we can choose to be like the coffee bean and positively influence those around us when we are faced with stress.

HOW DO YOU DO THIS?

Leaders manage stress by prioritizing self-care, maintaining healthy boundaries, and fostering a supportive team environment. Strategies include practicing mindfulness, exercising, and seeking support when needed. Additionally, leaders can proactively reduce stress by delegating tasks, setting clear expectations, and managing their time effectively.

Strategies for Managing Leadership Stress:

- **Prioritize Self-Care:** Engage in activities that promote well-being, such as exercise, mindfulness, and hobbies, ensuring they have time for rest and rejuvenation.
- **Maintain Boundaries:** Establish clear boundaries between work and personal life to prevent burnout and maintain a healthy worklife balance.
- **Build a Strong Team:** Foster a supportive and communicative team environment where members feel comfortable seeking help and sharing their concerns.
- **Delegate Effectively:** Share the workload and delegate tasks to empower team members and reduce individual stress levels.
- **Practice Mindfulness and Meditation:** These techniques can help leaders manage stress, improve focus, and increase resilience.
- **Seek Support:** Don't hesitate to seek support from mentors, coaches, or therapists when facing overwhelming stress.

- **Set Realistic Goals and Expectations:** Avoid setting unrealistic goals that can contribute to unnecessary stress.
- **Communicate Openly:** Create an environment where team members feel comfortable discussing their concerns and challenges.
- **Time Management and Prioritization:** Effective time management and prioritization can help leaders reduce workload and improve focus.
- **Embrace Healthy Habits:** Prioritize healthy eating, regular exercise, and sufficient sleep to improve overall well-being and reduce stress.
- **Recognize and Address Burnout:** Be aware of the signs of burnout and take steps to address them before they escalate.

"We all have stress in our lives. That is not going to go away. It is what you do with it that matters. Can you let the stress affect you, so you influence everyone around you positively?"

- Yankee Doodle Dave

LEADERSHIP CHALLENGE

Here is my challenge to you:

This week's lesson dealt with two stories. We first learned about President Woodrow Wilson and how stress directly affected him during his presidency.

Then there was the story of the potato, the egg or the coffee bean. This outlined how stress will ultimately affect us; but we choose how we will affect others.

No matter where you are we are bombarded with stress. It can happen with our families, our work, our church and even our finances. Unfortunately, stress is a part of life that we as leaders need to learn to deal with.

In the upcoming week it is safe to say that each of you may face some sort of stress.

When you do, will you face it like the Potato, the Egg or the Coffee Bean?

What Is Gratitude and
Why Is Practicing It Important?

"Rejoice always, pray continually, give thanks in all circumstances; for this is God's will for you in Christ Jesus."
- Thessalonians 5: 16-18

HISTORICAL FIGURE:
Admiral Elmo "Bud" Zumwalt, 19th Chief of Naval Operations

Today, I would like to share a small Leadership Development class with you dealing specifically with gratitude. More importantly, why is gratitude important?

Life happens and sometimes it is the smallest of things that can derail a positive attitude. We know the grind of life can be hard and even thankless at times. Why should we act surprised by this? Getting worked up over a simple inconvenience does not make our lives easier.

The story that I want to share with you today deals with a situation where gratitude was found and much appreciation was given. The story is about a fine Naval leader, Admiral Elmo "Bud" Zumwalt, Jr. He served as the Chief of Naval Operations from 1970 to 1974. He was known for demonstrating gratitude towards his Sailors.

Zumwalt's gratitude drove his implementation of revolutionary personnel reforms, encapsulated in his "Z-grams." These included improving living conditions, promoting equality for minorities and women, and eliminating burdensome regulations. These initiatives reflected his appreciation for the dedication and potential of every sailor and aimed to create a more inclusive and fulfilling Navy experience for all.

His gratitude extended to the sacrifices made by veterans, particularly those exposed to Agent Orange during the *Vietnam War*. He tirelessly advocated for these veterans and their families, even leading a pro-bono study that challenged established findings and ultimately influenced the recognition of the link between Agent Orange and various health issues, leading to improved benefits for affected veterans.

Zumwalt's gratitude for the service of individuals was deeply intertwined with his belief in the importance of humanity and service to others. He actively encouraged an environment of respect and recognized the importance of leadership that truly cared for sailors and their well-being.

His children emphasized that his "humanity" was a core aspect of his legacy, inspiring a culture of care that continues in the Navy today. Sailors serving on the *USS Zumwalt*, a ship named in his honor, are reportedly dedicated to upholding his legacy of innovation and concern for others.

Admiral Zumwalt's efforts played a major role in the founding of the National Marrow Donor Program (NMDP) in July 1986. He became the first chairman of the organization's board of directors and dedicated himself to the cause. Admiral Zumwalt developed this program largely because his son, Elmo Zumwalt III, developed cancer that was believed to be caused by exposure to Agent Orange during the *Vietnam War*. The tragedy drove the Admiral to advocate for a bone marrow registry to help veterans with Agent Orange-related cancers find matching donors.

In essence, Admiral Zumwalt's gratitude was more than just a personal trait; it was a fundamental aspect of his leadership philosophy, driving significant positive changes in the U.S. Navy and impacting the lives of countless service members and veterans.

Admiral Elmo R. Zumwalt, Jr.'s deep sense of gratitude was not merely a personal sentiment but also a powerful force that shaped his leadership, reforms, and legacy within the United States Navy and beyond. His gratitude stemmed from a profound belief in the dignity and worth of every individual and the importance of creating an environment where all service members could flourish.

HOW DO YOU DO THIS?

Leaders can show gratitude by expressing sincere appreciation for their team's contributions, both publicly and privately, and by recognizing their efforts in a meaningful way. This can involve verbal praise, handwritten notes, or even providing opportunities for professional development and advancement.

Here's a more detailed breakdown:

Verbal and Written Appreciation:

- **Saying "Thank You":** Regularly express gratitude for specific contributions and efforts, both individually and as a team.
- **Handwritten Notes:** Personalized notes of thanks can be particularly meaningful and memorable.
- **Public Acknowledgement:** Recognize team achievements and individual contributions in team meetings or companywide communications.

Meaningful Recognition:

- **Highlighting Individual Efforts:** Spotlight specific contributions and how they helped the team or organization achieve its goals.
- **Celebrating Milestones:** Acknowledge birthdays, work anniversaries, project completions, and other significant achievements with small tokens of appreciation.

- **Providing Professional Development:** Invest in your team's growth by offering training, mentorship, and opportunities for advancement.
- **Flexible Work Options:** Offering flexible work arrangements is a meaningful way to show appreciation for employee loyalty.

Creating a Culture of Gratitude:

- **Prioritizing Employee Goals:** Have regular conversations with employees about their professional goals and how you can help them achieve them.
- **Actively Listening:** Pay attention to what your team is saying and value their input.
- **Empowerment and Trust:** Give your team members opportunities to take ownership of their work and make decisions.
- **Advocating for Your Team:** Speak up on behalf of your team members, recommending them for opportunities and support.

LEADERSHIP CHALLENGE

This week we learned about the gratitude that Admiral Zumwalt showed towards the Sailors and veterans within the United States Navy.

By consistently practicing these strategies, leaders create a positive and appreciative work environment where team members feel valued and motivated.

"Be a beacon of light. Allow your gratitude to shine bright and bring gratitude into the lives of others."

- Yankee Doodle Dave

Gratefulness is a feeling of thankfulness or appreciation for what's good in life. It can also mean feeling thankful for the kindness received from others. Examples of gratefulness:

Feeling thankful for food, family, and friends
Feeling thankful for help from healthcare workers
Feeling thankful for a kind gesture from a stranger

How does this apply to being thankful for having coffee spilled on me or a car cutting me off? I am glad you asked.

The coffee spilled on me (**Good**)! Now I can spend a few more minutes with my family and let them know I love them as I get a new shirt.

The driver cut me off (**Good**)! Now I can ensure that I am more of an attentive driver.

My boss asked me to work late (**Good**)! Now I will make more money for my family.

Here is my challenge to you this week. Instead of letting life dictate how you are supposed to feel and act in a situation. I challenge you to show gratitude in the face of inconvenience. Especially when things are difficult, hard and inconvenient, simply say "Good" and be thankful for that opportunity. I challenge each of you to share a moment when you did use this technique.

____

____

____

____

"Gratitude is not a limited resource, nor is it costly. It is abundant as air. We breathe it in but forget to exhale." - Marshall Goldsmith

Integrity—Doing the Right Thing Even When No One Is Looking

"The integrity of the righteous will guide them. But the perversity of the unfaithful will destroy them."

- Proverbs 11:3

HISTORICAL FIGURE:
John Adams, 2nd President of the United States

A leader's actions are extremely important as they directly influence team morale, productivity and the overall organizational success. Behaviors set the team tone. This ends up motivating that team and ultimately shaping the company culture.

Doing the right thing even when no one is looking is a good definition for integrity. In today's lesson I would like to share a short story that discusses integrity.

To understand this situation, you must examine the events that took place on March 5, 1770, in Boston, Massachusetts. The event was referred to as the *Boston Massacre.* This is where British soldiers fired into a crowd of civilians, killing five and wounding several others. It's significant because it intensified colonial anger and resistance towards British rule, becoming a key event leading to the American Revolution.

The most famous example of John Adams displaying integrity is his decision to defend the British soldiers involved in the *Boston*

Massacre, even though it was an unpopular and risky move. John Adams served as the defense attorney along with his colleague Josiah Quincy, Jr. They believed in upholding the rule of law and ensuring everyone, including those perceived as enemies, had access to a fair trial. This act, despite potentially damaging his reputation and career, demonstrated his unwavering commitment to justice and the principles of the legal system.

John Adams believed that even those accused of heinous crimes deserved a fair trial and the opportunity to present a defense.

Defending the British soldiers, who were seen as oppressors by many colonists, could have negatively impacted his legal practice and political standing. Adams' decision was not driven by personal gain or popularity but by his strong belief in justice and the importance of due process. Despite the backlash, Adams persevered, arguing that even those he disagreed with deserved a fair trial.

Adams successfully defended Captain Preston, the British officer, and most of the soldiers, securing acquittals for some and manslaughter convictions for others.

John Adams' actions during the *Boston Massacre* trial demonstrate the importance of integrity and the rule of law. Despite the intense public backlash, Adams defended the accused British soldiers, believing that everyone deserved a fair trial and that justice should be upheld regardless of popular opinion. His courage in defending the soldiers, even when it risked his reputation, showcased his commitment to his principles and the fundamental right to a fair trial.

This event is often cited as a key example of Adams' integrity because it showed his willingness to prioritize principle over popularity, even in the face of significant personal risk. He believed that a just society was one where the law applied equally to all, regardless of their background or the prevailing public sentiment.

For Adams, the decision was a matter of principle. He believed that every person deserved a fair trial, regardless of how heinous their alleged crime was or how unpopular they were. This was his chance to prove that the American legal system would be based on the rule of law, not mob passions.

During the trial, Adams famously declared: *"Facts are stubborn things; and whatever may be our wishes, our inclinations, or the dictates of our passions, they cannot alter the state of facts and evidence."* He knew that securing justice for his clients would require a calm, evidence-based approach, even as public opinion raged against them.

Adams successfully convinced the jury to acquit most of the soldiers, arguing the crowd had provoked them. Although his practice suffered in the short term, Adams considered his defense of the soldiers *"one of the most courageous, generous and disinterested actions of my whole life, and one of the best pieces of service I ever rendered to my Country."*

It is very safe to say that the actions from a leader are scrutinized far heavier than the average employee. Think about this for a moment. If an employee does something wrong and gets in trouble, they are held accountable for their actions. Now imagine if a leader in a company did the same thing. More attention and spotlight are put on the leader. The leader's actions impact those around them. As leaders this is something that we need to remember. We must hold each other accountable and maintain the highest standards.

HOW DO YOU DO THIS?

Leaders demonstrate integrity by being honest, transparent, and accountable, keeping their promises, and upholding ethical principles. They lead, by example, to treat everyone with respect, and foster open communication.

Here's a more detailed breakdown:

1. Honesty and Transparency:

- **Be Truthful in Communication:** Share information openly and honestly, even when it's difficult.
- **Avoid Deception:** Don't withhold or distort information for personal gain.
- **Be Transparent About Decisions:** Explain the reasoning behind choices, especially when they impact others.
- **Encourage Open Dialogue:** Create a safe space for team members to express their opinions and concerns.

2. Accountability and Responsibility:

- **Take Ownership of Actions:** Admit mistakes and take responsibility for them, rather than deflecting blame.
- **Follow Through on Commitments:** Keep promises and deliver on time, demonstrating reliability and trustworthiness.
- **Hold Yourself Accountable:** Set high standards for yourself and consistently strive to meet them.

3. Ethical Principles:

- **Adhere to Company Values:** Align actions with organizational values, even when no one is watching.
- **Make Ethical Decisions:** Prioritize what is right and just, even if it's not the easiest path.
- **Respect Others:** Treat everyone with fairness, respect, and dignity.

4. Leading by Example:

- **Set a Positive Example:** Demonstrate the behaviors you want to see in others.
- **Be a Role Model:** Inspire others by living up to your values and principles.
- **Promote a Culture of Integrity:** Encourage ethical behavior throughout the organization.

LEADERSHIP CHALLENGE

This week we learned about President John Adams and how his presidency was an example of integrity.

Doing the "right thing" even when no one is looking is important at work because it demonstrates integrity. This is a key quality that builds trust with colleagues, enhances your reputation. It also shows a strong ethical foundation in your professional conduct, even when faced with situations where you might be tempted to act otherwise. It essentially means being honest, accountable, and reliable regardless of whether someone is directly observing your actions.

Here is my challenge to you for this coming week:

Identify one (1) area how you can display integrity "doing the right thing even when no one is looking" at work. When you have identified that business practice write it down.

Being Brave as a Leader

"Have I not commanded you? Be strong and coura-geous. Do not be afraid; do not be discouraged, for the Lord your God will be with you wherever you go."
- Joshua 1:9

HISTORICAL FIGURE:
President John F. Kennedy - PT-109 & Cuban Missile Crisis

The topic on today's leadership development deals with the concept of "Being Brave as a Leader."

There are two (2) specific examples that outline President Kennedy's courage and bravery. That would be the actions as a PT Boat Commander and his actions during the *Cuban Missile Crisis.*

On August 2, 1943, a young Lieutenant (junior grade) John F. Kennedy served as the commander of PT-109 boat. PT-109 was stationed in the Blackett Strait, south of Kolombangara Island when it was struck by a Japanese destroyer.

While patrolling in the Solomon Islands during *World War II*, Kennedy's PT boat, PT-109, was rammed and sunk by a Japanese destroyer.

After PT-109 was sunk by a Japanese destroyer, John F. Kennedy displayed exceptional leadership and bravery in rescuing his crew and ensuring their survival. When the PT-109 was sunk, Kennedy, despite an injured back, towed a badly burned crewman, Patrick McMahon. Kennedy towed him by clenching the strap of his life jacket in his teeth for over three miles to a small island. You read that correctly. Kennedy swam three (3) miles through the dark water with a life jacket strap clenched in his teeth towing an injured man, while he was suffering from a back injury.

After swimming to another island, Kennedy needed to send a message. Instead of using a conventional method, he ingeniously carved a distress message into a coconut shell and entrusted it to local Solomon Islanders. They helped deliver that message to Allied Forces.

Lieutenant junior grade Kennedy's bravery ultimately led to their rescue by Allied Forces. He personally saved the lives of 10 of his men. His bravery earned him the Navy and Marine Corps Medal and a Purple Heart.

The second event occurred when he was serving as the President of the United States. During the October 1962 *Cuban Missile Crisis*, Kennedy faced immense pressure to launch an immediate military strike against Cuba due to the Soviet missile deployments. Instead, he chose a path of diplomacy and negotiation, ultimately averting a potential nuclear war.

This decision, while unpopular with some, required immense courage and a willingness to stand against powerful forces to pursue a peaceful resolution. President John F. Kennedy's response to the *Cuban Missile Crisis* in October 1962 was a calculated strategy to de-escalate the crisis while securing the removal of Soviet nuclear missiles from Cuba. His leadership directly resulted in the avoidance of nuclear war, a strengthened image and improved U.S.-Soviet relations.

While Kennedy's initial approach to civil rights was cautious, he eventually proposed landmark legislation, demonstrating courage in the face of political opposition. *The JFK Library* established the *Profile in Courage Award* to honor individuals who demonstrate political courage, a quality Kennedy himself embodied.

The public was unaware of the extent of President Kennedy's medical conditions, which included Addison's disease (an autoimmune disorder), severe back pain from osteoporosis, and colitis. Many medical experts and historians believe that John F. Kennedy may have had celiac disease due to his lifelong gastrointestinal symptoms, which align with the condition's characteristics. From childhood, Kennedy was plagued by sickness. By his early 40s, when he became president, his health was so precarious that he took a daily cocktail of up to 12 different medications. He hid these conditions from the public while relying on crutches and a back brace to manage his deteriorating health while performing presidential duties.

When one thinks of bravery, so many thoughts and images come to mind. Some of those could be of a soldier courageously running across a battlefield. Yes, that is an example of being brave. For today's topic, I want to look at a different aspect of bravery.

"Being brave as a leader" means having the courage to make difficult decisions, stand up for what is right, and act on your principles even when it's unpopular or challenging. Oftentimes it will involve taking calculated risks and facing uncertainty while prioritizing the greater good over personal popularity. Being brave as a leader is about leading with integrity and authenticity, even when it means being vulnerable and facing criticism.

HOW DO YOU DO THIS?

A leader can demonstrate bravery by making tough decisions, facing difficult conversations, taking calculated risks, and admitting mistakes. It also involves being authentic, vulnerable, and encouraging others to speak up and challenge the status quo.

Here's a more detailed look:

1. Making Tough Decisions:

- **Addressing Underperforming Areas:** Courageous leaders are willing to make difficult choices like closing underenrolled programs or reallocating resources to more promising areas, even if it's unpopular.

- **Prioritizing Long-Term Goals:** They can make decisions that might be painful in the short term for the benefit of the organization in the long run.
- **Taking Calculated Risks:** This could involve launching new initiatives, entering new markets, or challenging established norms.

2. Facing Difficult Conversations:

- **Giving Feedback:** Courageous leaders don't shy away from delivering difficult feedback, even if it's not well received.
- **Addressing Performance Issues:** They address performance problems directly and constructively, even when it's uncomfortable.
- **Having Tough Talks:** They are willing to have difficult conversations with team members, superiors, or stakeholders, even when it involves conflict or potential disagreement.

3. Showing Vulnerability and Authenticity:

- **Admitting Mistakes:** Courageous leaders are willing to own up to their mistakes and learn from them, setting a positive example for their teams.
- **Being Open About Feelings:** They don't pretend to be perfect; they share their vulnerabilities and challenges with their team.
- **Demonstrating Humility:** They acknowledge their limitations and are open to feedback and different perspectives.

4. Encouraging Courage in Others:

- **Creating a Safe Space:** They foster an environment where team members feel comfortable speaking up, sharing ideas, and challenging the status quo.
- **Promoting Open Communication:** They actively encourage feedback and create opportunities for open dialogue.

- **Celebrating Courageous Acts:** They acknowledge and reward acts of bravery, both big and small, to reinforce a culture of courage.

5. Standing Up for What's Right:

- **Acting with Integrity:** They make decisions and take actions that align with their values, even when it's challenging.
- **Advocating for Change:** They are willing to challenge the status quo and advocate for positive change, even if it's unpopular.
-

LEADERSHIP CHALLENGE

In this weeks' lesson we learned about President John Kennedy and his examples of being brave as a leader. What does this mean for you as a leader?

Let me share a few scenarios with you.

"You don't need a title to lead. True leadership is not about being in charge. It is about being the reason someone did not give up."

- Yankee Doodle Dave

Scenario #1:

You are at your work center with your staff. Some employees who work directly for you are talking with one another next to you. They are talking loud enough for you to hear their conversation. They are gossiping about other staff members. You hear them go on and on about how these staff members are not pulling their weight and are extremely lazy.

As a leader, what do you do? Do you have the courage to step in and intervene?

Scenario #2:

You are in your work center with your staff. It is time to complete a performance review on your staff members. One of your staff members has been here for a long time. They are extremely loyal. You can always count on them being there when you need someone. However, their work performance is not as good. You have noticed lately that things are starting to slip, and many things seem to be forgotten.

You need to complete a performance review on this employee. Do you complete the performance review without addressing the recent decline in performance? Or do you have difficult conversations with them?

Here is my challenge to you. As leaders, how would you handle either of these situations? How would you use courage to deal with these scenarios?

Do you stand back and accept the behavior? Or do you have the courage to have a difficult conversation?

"Leaders must display their humanness. Those under their authority must be empowered & have the courage to engage in honest dialogue."
- Patrick Lencioni

Why You Need to Check Your Ego in Leadership?

"Let each of you look out not only for his own interests, but also for the interests of others."
- Philippians 2:4

HISTORICAL FIGURE:
Ulysses S. Grant, 18th President of the United States

Today's Leadership Development session is on our ego. More importantly, why do we need to check our ego in a leadership situation?

In leadership I am referring to "*ego*" as an individual's sense of self-importance, often manifesting as a strong need for recognition. It can also be a need for power, and validation, which can be detrimental if inflated. This can lead to arrogance, defensiveness, and a disconnect from the needs of the team when not kept in check. It is essentially the tendency to prioritize one's own perspective over others' when leading.

Let me share a story of ego and how this leader was able to check his personal ego.

Ulysses S. Grant's life provides a fascinating study in overcoming adversity, demonstrating resilience, and maintaining a humble demeanor despite achieving immense success and experiencing significant failures.

Grant faced numerous challenges early in his life, including struggles with alcoholism and business failures that left him in poverty before the *Civil War*. Despite being an unenthusiastic student and having a mediocre academic record at West Point, the outbreak of the *Civil War* presented an opportunity for him to apply his military talent.

Ulysses Grant's leadership during the *Civil War* was characterized by a clear vision, focus on essentials, and the ability to inspire his troops to fight bravely. He displayed humility in both success and defeat, taking responsibility for mistakes and giving credit to others. He was known for his calm and composed demeanor even during the most challenging situations.

Ulysses S. Grant was well known for his humility and lack of ego. This was a sharp contrast with his contemporaries and fueled his leadership style. This unassuming nature was evident in his mannerisms, his relationships with his soldiers and fellow officers.

When Grant met Robert E. Lee for the Confederate surrender, General Lee appeared in a pristine, full-dress uniform. Grant, by contrast, arrived in a mud-spattered, well-worn private jacket with only his lieutenant general's rank showing. He considered the uniform he wore sufficient for the purpose.

Rather than reveling in victory, Grant was compassionate toward the surrendering Confederate soldiers. He offered generous terms, allowing them to keep their horses for spring planting and simply return home. He forbade his own men from celebrating, telling them, *"The war is over; the Rebels are our countrymen again."*

Ulysses S. Grant was considered a celebrity, particularly after his *Civil War* victories. His victory in the *Civil War*, leading the Union to success, earned him immense popularity and trust among the Northern public and within the Republican party. It ultimately played a significant role in his election for the presidency in 1868.

Despite his military success, Grant's presidency was marked by scandals and economic challenges, including the *Panic of 1873*, which tarnished his reputation. Grant's loyalty to those who served him may have contributed to his inability to address corruption within his administration effectively. He faced financial ruin after his investment firm collapsed due to a pyramid scheme run by his partner. Facing bankruptcy and battling throat cancer, Grant channeled his perseverance and focused on writing his memoir. He completed the book, a detailed account of the *Civil War*, just days before his death, securing his family's financial future. The memoir, *Personal Memoirs of Ulysses S. Grant*, became a bestseller and is considered a literary and historical masterpiece.

Throughout his life, Grant demonstrated a remarkable ability to overcome personal and professional setbacks, highlighting the importance of humility, perseverance, and learning from mistakes. His willingness to accept responsibility for failures and maintain a calm demeanor in the face of adversity showcases his strong character and ability to keep his ego in check.

Grant's story serves as a testament to the power of resilience and the lasting impact that focusing on one's duty and the greater good can have, regardless of the challenges faced. Ulysses Grant's approach to leadership was characterized by a strong sense of purpose, integrity and a willingness to prioritize the objective over personal accolades.

HOW DO YOU DO THIS?

A leader can check their ego by prioritizing listening, fostering a culture of feedback, and maintaining a focus on the collective good rather than personal accolades. This involves actively seeking diverse perspectives, acknowledging the contributions of others, and recognizing that leadership is a privilege, not a right.

Here's a more detailed look:

1. Cultivating Self-Awareness and Humility:

- **Recognize Ego's Influence:** Understand that ego can lead to defensiveness, a need for constant validation, and difficulty accepting feedback.
- **Practice Humility:** Leaders should acknowledge their own fallibility, admit mistakes, and be willing to learn from others.
- **Seek Feedback:** Regularly ask for input from team members, both positive and negative, and be open to constructive criticism.
- **Reflect on Actions:** Take time for self-reflection to identify personal biases and ego-driven impulses.

2. Focusing on the Collective:

- **Value Diverse Perspectives** Actively seek input from team members with different backgrounds and experiences.
- **Prioritize Team Goals:** Shift the focus from personal achievements to the success of the entire team and organization.
- **Empower Others:** Encourage team members to contribute their ideas and take ownership of their work.
- **Celebrate Team Wins:** Recognize and celebrate the accomplishments of the team as a whole.

3. Leading with Integrity and Empathy:

- **Be a Role Model:** Demonstrate humility and a focus on the collective through your actions and behaviors.
- **Listen Actively:** Pay attention to what others are saying, both verbally and nonverbally.
- **Empathize With Others:** Try to understand the perspectives and feelings of your team members.
- **Be Approachable:** Create an environment where people feel comfortable sharing their thoughts and concerns.

"Ego is the one requirement that can destroy any relationship. Skip the 'E' and let it 'Go.'"

- Yankee Doodle Dave

LEADERSHIP CHALLENGE

Here is my challenge to you: This week we learned about President Ulysses S. Grant and how he learned to check his ego. There were several techniques provided to help leaders in the process of checking their ego. What techniques do you plan to use over the next week to help in checking your own ego?

*"Avoid having your ego so close to your position
that when your position falls, your ego goes with it."
- Colin Powell*

The Dangers of Vanity and Flattery in Leadership

"With flattery he will corrupt those who violate the covenant. But the people who know their God will firmly resist him."

- Daniel 11:32

HISTORICAL FIGURE:
General Douglas MacArthur, General of the Army

Have you ever known a person that was focused more on being likeable instead of leading the team? Perhaps this person spent their time saying what people wanted to hear instead of leading their people. Think about what that did to morale at the company.

General MacArthur was one of the most decorated U.S. military figures in history. He received numerous accolades throughout his military career. He was awarded the Medal of Honor for his defense of the Philippines in *World War II*. The story that I want to focus on regarding General MacArthur deals with this week's lesson. That is the dangers of vanity and flattery in leadership.

General Douglas MacArthur was known for his vanity, which manifested as a theatrical public presence, a belief in his own infallibility, and a tendency to prioritize personal glory over institutional loyalty. He cultivated a larger-than-life persona, often disregarding orders and protocols to pursue his own objectives, which sometimes led to conflict with civilian leadership.

His declaration, "*I shall return,*" after escaping from the Philippines in 1942 was a highly publicized and personal vow. His eventual landing was carefully orchestrated for the press, and he made sure to be photographed wading ashore with his men to symbolize his personal triumph.

During his time overseeing the occupation of Japan, MacArthur maintained an imperial demeanor. This led to historian William Manchester dubbing him the "American Caesar." He was also known to wear a Japanese kimono at his desk.

MacArthur was known for his self-promoting behavior, even while holding high military rank and responsibility. He often sought to associate himself with historical events and figures, presenting himself as a man of destiny.

He frequently challenged or disobeyed superiors, including Presidents Roosevelt and Truman, showcasing a disregard for the chain of command and civilian control over the military.

MacArthur's arrogance extended to his dealings with those he considered his inferiors, including junior officers and even civilians. This attitude often led to friction and conflict during his career.

Shortly after the Pearl Harbor attack in 1941, Japanese aircraft destroyed most of MacArthur's air force in the Philippines while the planes were on the ground. Though he had hours of warning after the Pearl Harbor attack, General MacArthur was slow to act, leading to a catastrophe he later downplayed.

In 1950, despite clear intelligence reports showing Chinese troops massing near the border, MacArthur was "hell bent on chasing the retreating North Koreans." His hubris directly led to a major defeat for U.S. Forces.

A well-known narcissist, MacArthur struggled to take responsibility for his mistakes. For instance, he publicly criticized his Australian troops during the New Guinea campaign and downplayed their contributions, later crediting Americans for the victory.

MacArthur cultivated a flamboyant public image, often appearing in public in his signature sunglasses, corncob pipe, and tailored uniform, further emphasizing his larger-than-life persona.

While his vanity and self-assuredness may have contributed to his successes, they also led to his eventual dismissal by President Truman during the *Korean War* due to insubordination. General MacArthur's vanity ultimately had a negative impact on his career.

HOW DO YOU DO THIS?

Leaders can avoid vanity and flattery by cultivating self-awareness, fostering open communication, and prioritizing genuine feedback and recognition over superficial praise. They should also be mindful of their own ego, seek diverse perspectives, and create a culture where honesty and constructive criticism are valued.

Here's a more detailed look at how leaders can navigate this:

1. Cultivate Self-Awareness:

- **Recognize Your Own Biases:** Understand everyone has an ego and flattery can be appealing. Be aware of your vulnerabilities and actively work to mitigate them.
- **Seek Feedback:** Regularly solicit feedback from trusted sources, including peers, subordinates, and mentors. This provides valuable insights into how their actions are perceived and whether they are susceptible to flattery.

2. Foster Open Communication:

- **Encourage Open Dialogue:** Create an environment where team members feel comfortable expressing their opinions, even if they are dissenting.
- **Listen Actively:** Pay close attention to what others are saying, both verbally and nonverbally. Avoid interrupting or dismissing feedback, even if it's challenging.

- **Be Transparent:** Share information openly and honestly with the team. This builds trust and reduces the likelihood of manipulative flattery.

3. Prioritize Genuine Feedback and Recognition:

- **Focus on Performance:** Recognize and reward employees based on their contributions and achievements, rather than on empty praise.
- **Be Specific:** When offering feedback, be clear and specific about what was done well and what could be improved.
- **Avoid Empty Praise:** Refrain from using generic compliments or exaggerated praise that is not based on concrete actions or results.

4. Manage Your Ego:

- **Be Humble:** Acknowledge you don't have all the answers; it is okay to ask for help.
- **Embrace Constructive Criticism:** View feedback as an opportunity for growth and improvement, rather than a personal attack.
- **Don't Take Yourself Too Seriously:** Remember that leadership is about serving others, not about personal glory.

5. Seek Diverse Perspectives:

- **Surround Yourself with Different Viewpoints:** Seek out people with diverse backgrounds, experiences, and opinions.
- **Challenge Your Own Assumptions:** Be willing to question your own beliefs and assumptions and consider alternative perspectives.
- **Avoid Echo Chambers:** Don't surround yourself with people who only tell you what you want to hear.

6. Create a Culture of Honesty and Constructive Criticism:

- **Lead by Example:** Demonstrate that you value honesty and constructive criticism by actively seeking and responding to feedback yourself.
- **Establish Clear Expectations:** Make it clear that honest feedback is expected and valued, and that flattery is not tolerated.
- **Address Flattery Directly:** If someone is attempting to flatter you, address it directly and explain that you prefer honest feedback.

By actively working to avoid vanity and flattery, leaders can create a more positive, productive, and ethical work environment.
Here's why leaders should be wary of flattery:

1. **It can be manipulative and deceptive:** Flattery is often insincere and can be used to influence a leader into making decisions that benefit the flatterer, not the organization.

2. **It can lead to poor decision-making:** Leaders who are easily flattered may be more likely to accept advice and ideas from those who flatter them, even if that advice is not in the best interest of the organization.

3. **It can damage a leader's reputation:** If leaders are seen as easily swayed by flattery, it can damage their reputation as competent and trustworthy leaders.

4. **It can undermine trust and create resentment:** Flattery can create a perception that leaders are more concerned with being liked than with making effective decisions.

5. **It can hinder true feedback and development:** Leaders who are constantly surrounded by flatterers may not hear the truth about their performance or the performance of their team, which can hinder their ability to learn and grow.

6. It can lead to favoritism and inequitable rewards: Leaders who are easily swayed by flattery may be more likely to reward flatterers with promotions or other benefits, even if they are not the best performers.

7. It can create a toxic work environment: A culture where flattery is the norm can create resentment and distrust among employees who feel they are not being recognized for their actual contributions.

In essence, leaders should strive for genuine feedback and recognition based on merit and performance, rather than succumbing to the allure of flattery, which can ultimately harm their leadership and the organization they lead.

"Flattery looks like friendship, just like a wolf looks like a dog."

- Yankee Doodle Dave

LEADERSHIP CHALLENGE

Here is my challenge to you: This week we learned about General Douglas MacArthur and his vanity. There were several techniques provided to help leaders in the process of understanding excessive flattery and vanity in leadership.

What techniques do you plan to use over the next week to help you understand your own excessive flattery and vanity in a professional setting?

Why Is Delegation Important in Leadership?

"Let every soul be subject to the governing authorities. For there is no authority except from God, and the authorities that exist are appointed by God."
- Romans 13:1

HISTORICAL FIGURE:
Lyndon B. Johnson, 36th President of the United States

Have you ever worked with someone who was a bit of a control freak? They needed to be in control as much as possible and had a great deal of difficulty letting go. Unfortunately, the concept of delegating is something that many people struggle with.

Have you ever heard or maybe you yourself have uttered some of these phrases:

"It is easier to take care of this on my own."

"It would take more time to explain so I might as well do this by myself."

"No one here can do this. It is up to me to make it happen."

I am just as guilty as the next person for wanting to take care of things on my own.

This short story outlines our 36th President, Lyndon B. Johnson (LBJ). He was renowned for his hands-on approach and famously intimidating style known as the "Johnson Treatment." What was the "Johnson Treatment" you say? Allow me to explain.

Standing at 6 feet 4 inches tall, Johnson would often use his imposing physical stature to dominate those he was trying to persuade. The "Johnson Treatment" was a combination of flattery, bargaining, and intimidating tactics that involved getting uncomfortably close to a person. A favorite tactic was to tower over a seated colleague, whispering in their ear and refusing to let them leave until he had won them over.

Johnson was a master legislator who used his imposing physical presence to intimidate knowledge out of the political system to get what he wanted. This was highly effective in securing the passage of his Great Society and civil rights legislation

While masterful at corralling Congress, Johnson's intense, personal and often domineering style meant that many decisions flowed directly through him. His reliance on his own mastery of the process over aides or the Cabinet was a key feature of his presidency.

Johnson's leadership style was described as a wheel with the president as the hub. This meant that all key staff members would act as spokes reporting directly to the president. In fact, he never appointed a Chief of Staff, preferring to be in direct control of his entire staff.

There were a few consequences where LBJ's lack of delegation had a significant impact within the *Vietnam War*. The first had to deal with his micromanagement of military strategy. Johnson's controlling nature extended directly into military strategy. LBJ and his Secretary of Defense (Robert McNamara), famously micromanaged the bombing campaigns in Vietnam, hand-picking targets from Washington.

Another consequence was his restrictive rules of engagement placed on military forces. Johnson implemented restrictive rules of engagement that some historians argue prevented the military from using its full force. Critics contend this strategy unnecessarily prolonged the war and cost countless American lives. There was an intent to minimize civilian casualties and prevent escalation with China or the Soviet Union.

The third consequence was that Johnson was very dismissal and not open to differing opinions. Johnson often disregarded dissenting opinions, especially those that challenged his commitment to the war. He famously rejected advice from Undersecretary of State George Ball, who warned that escalation would lead to an unwinnable, costly war. Instead, Johnson would listen to his aides that favored greater military commitment.

Johnson's leadership style is seen as a double-edged sword. It was instrumental in passing landmark legislation but was also unsustainable. This was particularly the case during the *Vietnam War*. It eventually contributed to his political downfall.

The attitude and demeanor that Johnson showed had a significant impact on his staff and his administration. Johnson's demanding and volatile style led to high turnover rates among his staff. For example, only two of his twelve top staffers in 1964 remained with him by 1968.

The disconnect between Johnson's public optimism about Vietnam and the reality on the ground—especially following the 1968 Tet Offensive—led to a "credibility gap" with the American public. As casualties mounted and the war's progress stalled, his approval ratings plummeted making him deeply unpopular. The escalating cost and public backlash of the *Vietnam War* drew funding and attention away from Johnson's ambitious domestic programs. Those were facing criticism and urban unrest. The *Vietnam War* ultimately overshadowed his legislative achievements.

Faced with dwindling public support Johnson announced in March 1968 that he would not seek another term. His legacy became deeply intertwined with the failure in Vietnam.

The story of President Lyndon B. Johnson and his initial struggles with delegation serves as a cautionary tale about the importance of recognizing one's limitations and the benefits of empowering others.

Delegation is crucial in leadership because it empowers team members, builds trust, and allows leaders to focus on higher-value tasks. It also fosters growth, development, and innovation within the team. By effectively delegating, leaders can maximize team productivity, improve efficiency, and drive overall organizational success.

HOW DO YOU DO THIS?

Effective delegation is a critical leadership skill. It involves assigning tasks and responsibilities to team members, empowering them to take ownership, and fostering their growth. To delegate effectively, leaders should carefully assess their team's strengths, provide clear instructions, offer support, and communicate openly.

Here's a breakdown of how leaders can work at delegation:

1. Identifying and Preparing for Delegation:

- **Assess Team Strengths:** Understand each team member's skills, experience, and areas for development.

- **Identify Tasks for Delegation:** Determine which tasks are suitable for delegation, considering their complexity, frequency, and alignment with team members' capabilities.

- **Define Clear Expectations:** Clearly articulate the task's objectives, desired outcomes, and deadlines.

- **Provide Necessary Resources:** Ensure the team member has the tools, information, and support needed to complete the task successfully.

- **Set Realistic Timelines:** Establish clear deadlines and milestones for the delegated task.

2. Empowering and Supporting Delegation:
- **Communicate Effectively:** Provide clear and concise instructions, explaining the "why" behind the task and its significance.
- **Trust Your Team:** Empower team members by giving them autonomy and ownership of their delegated tasks.
- **Offer Guidance and Support:** Regularly check in with team members, provide feedback, and offer coaching to help them overcome challenges.
- **Encourage Open Communication:** Create a safe space for team members to ask questions, share concerns, and provide feedback.
- **Recognize and Appreciate Efforts:** Acknowledge and celebrate successes to boost morale and reinforce a culture of appreciation.

By mastering delegation, leaders can empower their teams, foster growth, and drive organizational success.

Here's a more detailed look at why delegation is important:

1. Empowering Team Members:
- Delegation allows team members to take ownership of tasks, gain responsibility, and develop their skills.
- It fosters a sense of trust and autonomy, which can boost morale and motivation.
- By giving team members, the opportunity to learn and grow, delegation can help them develop into future leaders.

2. Focusing on Strategic Goals:
- Delegation frees up leaders' time and energy, allowing them to focus on higher-level strategic planning, decision-making, and leadership activities.
- This allows leaders to focus on long-term goals and vision, rather than getting bogged down in day-to-day operations.

3. Building Trust and Fostering a Positive Culture:

- Delegation demonstrates a leader's confidence in their team's abilities, which builds trust and strengthens relationships.
- It creates a culture of empowerment, where team members feel valued and capable.
- A positive culture can lead to improved morale, engagement, and overall team performance.

4. Improving Efficiency and Productivity:

- Delegation helps optimize the team's productivity by aligning tasks with individual strengths and capabilities.
- It can reduce workload and prevent burnout for leaders and team members.
- By allowing team members to take ownership of their work, delegation can lead to more efficient and effective outcomes.

5. Fostering Growth and Innovation:

- Delegation provides team members with opportunities to learn new skills, gain experience, and develop their expertise.
- It leads to new ideas, approaches, and solutions, fostering a culture of innovation.
- By empowering team members to take initiative and make decisions, delegation can lead to better products, services, and processes

LEADERSHIP CHALLENGE

Here is my challenge to you:

This week we learned about President Lyndon B. Johnson and his difficulty with delegation. If we are honest, there are many leaders out there that have an issue with this. There were several techniques provided to help leaders in effective delegation.

Can you identify this in yourself? What techniques do you plan to use over the next week to help with effective delegation?

____

____

____

____

____

____

*"Don't tell people how to do things, tell them what to do
and let them surprise you with their results." - George S. Patton*

"The people in your company were hired for a specific reason. Let them do what you hired them to do. Delegate to them in order so they can be successful."

- Yankee Doodle Dave

Why Leaders Need to Be Able to Make Decisions

"Trust in the Lord with all your heart; do not depend on your own understanding. Seek his will in all you do, and he will show you which path to take."
- Proverbs 3:5

HISTORICAL FIGURE:
Colonel Joshua Chamberlain - Battle of Gettysburg

Making tough decisions, especially when they are unpopular or have significant consequences, is a key leadership skill. Leaders need to weigh options, consider risks, and make decisions that are in the best interest of the team and the organization.

A famous story about a leader who was put in a situation where he had to make a difficult decision occurred during one of our nation's most famous battles, *the Battle of Gettysburg*. Listen to this famous story of Colonel Joshua Lawrence Chamberlain, who led the 20th Maine Volunteer Infantry to defend the Union's left flank at Little Round Top, July 2, 1863.

Before we get to that famous day it is important that you understand a little about the man. Who was Colonel Joshua Lawrence Chamberlain? Chamberlain was a distinguished professor of rhetoric and modern languages at Bowdoin College in Brunswick, Maine. He was a gifted academic, fluent in nine languages, and a superb intellectual.

Chamberlain took a sabbatical from Bowdoin College to go to war. Some of the colleagues at Bowdoin College opposed this. They wrote letters to the Governor of Maine to try and prevent Chamberlain from getting a military commission.

Joshua Lawrence Chamberlain was the son and grandson of military men. There was military experience in his family dating back to the Revolutionary War and the War of 1812. Joshua had a call to serve his nation and was deeply interested in joining the military. Joshua Chamberlain joined the Army in August 1862 when he was appointed the rank of lieutenant colonel.

The Battle of Gettysburg was a turning point in the *Civil War*. On the third day, the Union Army, particularly Colonel Joshua Chamberlain's 20th Maine Regiment, was positioned on the extreme left flank and facing relentless attacks. With ammunition depleted and the Confederate forces pressing hard, Chamberlain faced a dire situation. Rather than retreat or surrender, he made the daring decision to order a bayonet charge.

Colonel Chamberlain yelled out to his troops, *"Fix bayonets!"*

The charge, executed with bayonets fixed, was a shock to the Confederate soldiers, who were not expecting such a counterattack. It halted their advance, allowed the Union to regroup, and ultimately contributed to the Union victory at Gettysburg.

Chamberlain understood that his 20th Maine Regiment was responsible for holding Little Round Top. This was a position of immense strategic importance on the Union flank.

The charge broke the Confederate attack. This prevented a catastrophic collapse of the Union left flank and ended up preserving a key position on the battlefield.

The 20th Maine Regiment captured more than 100 Confederate soldiers, including a substantial number on Little Round Top and more during a subsequent advance on nearby Big Round Top.

For his actions, Chamberlain was presented with the Congressional Medal of Honor in 1893.

This story highlights the importance of Chamberlain's decision that required immense courage and a willingness to take a calculated risk in the face of overwhelming odds. He adapted his tactics to specific circumstances, recognizing that a conventional approach would not work.

Chamberlain's leadership inspired his troops to follow him into a seemingly suicidal charge.

Chamberlain's actions at Gettysburg solidified his reputation as a war hero and continued his post-war prominence as a public figure. This even included him serving as the Governor of Maine and the President of Bowdoin College.

HOW DO YOU DO THIS?

Leaders need to be able to make decisions because their choices directly impact the organization's direction, resource allocation, problem-solving, and overall success. Effective decision-making builds confidence, reduces ambiguity, and fosters trust among team members, ultimately leading to increased productivity and a more effective workplace.

Here's a more detailed look at why decision-making is crucial for leaders:

1. Strategic Direction and Resource Allocation

- Leaders make decisions that shape the organization's long-term vision and goals.
- They determine how resources (time, money, personnel) are allocated to achieve strategic objectives.
- Effective allocation maximizes productivity and ensures the organization's success.

2. Problem-Solving and Risk Management:

- Leaders face challenges and obstacles that require timely and informed decisions.

- They need to assess risks and opportunities, make calculated choices to manage potential negative outcomes and capitalize on opportunities.

3. Building Confidence and Trust:
- Decisive leaders inspire confidence and motivation in their teams.
- Clear direction and decisive actions help eliminate ambiguity, allowing teams to focus on execution.
- When leaders make sound decisions, they build trust creating an engaged workforce.

4. Improving Productivity and Efficiency:
- Effective decision-making accelerates projects and improves overall productivity.
- When decisions are made quickly and efficiently, employees can start work sooner, reducing delays and improving workflow.

LEADERSHIP CHALLENGE

In essence, decision-making is the cornerstone of effective leadership. It's the process through which leaders guide their teams, navigate challenges, and ultimately achieve organizational goals.

Here is my challenge to you.

This week we learned about Colonel Joshua Chamberlain and his decision that occurred at *the Battle of Gettysburg.* There were several techniques provided to help you make decisions.

What techniques do you plan to use over the next week to help with effective decision-making?

____

____

____

____

____

____

____

"In any moment of decision, the best thing you can do is the right thing, the next best thing is the wrong thing, and the worst thing you can do is nothing."
- Theodore Roosevelt

"Nothing happens until someone makes a decision."

- Yankee Doodle Dave

Leaders Need to Be Able to Navigate Uncertainty

"In their hearts humans plan their course, but the Lord establishes their steps."

- Proverbs 16:9

HISTORICAL FIGURES:
Meriwether Lewis and William Clark - Lewis & Clark Expedition

The most successful leaders learn to tolerate uncertainty. This provides a healthy blend of stability and agility for their teams along with the ability to adopt productive strategies to move forward. In other words, they embrace uncertainty rather than resist it.

The 1804 journey of Lewis and Clark is an American historic story illustrating the navigation of uncertainty! Meriwether Lewis & William Clark embarked on an expedition to explore the newly acquired Louisiana Purchase, a vast and largely unknown territory. The Lewis & Clark Expedition traveled over 8,000 miles. The journey took them from Camp Wood, near present-day Hartford, Illinois, to the Pacific Ocean and back. This entire journey lasted over two and a half years.

Faced with uncharted rivers, challenging terrains, and unknown indigenous populations, they had to constantly make decisions with incomplete information. Their success hinged on their ability to learn from each encounter, adapt their plans, and maintain a flexible approach. This story highlights the importance of resilience, adaptability, and the willingness to embrace the unknown when charting a course into the uncertain future.

The Louisiana Purchase, bought by the United States from France in 1803, was a vast and largely unexplored region. President Jefferson commissioned the expedition to map the territory, assess its resources, and establish relations with its inhabitants.

Lewis and Clark faced numerous uncertainties with their journey. They didn't know the exact course of the Missouri River, the nature of the Rocky Mountains, or the best route to the Pacific Ocean. The party encountered diverse Native American tribes, many of whom had never interacted with Europeans. Understanding their customs and building trust was crucial for their safety and success. They had to rely on the land for food, supplies, and shelter, constantly facing the uncertainty of finding food, navigable waterways, and suitable campsites. They had to contend with extreme weather conditions, including harsh winters and unpredictable storms.

Lewis and Clark needed to be adaptable for several reasons to achieve success. They constantly adjusted their plans based on new information and changing circumstances. The party faced hardships and setbacks, but they persevered and continued their journey. Lewis and Clark's strong leadership and ability to inspire their crew were essential for maintaining morale and focus. They actively sought knowledge from the indigenous peoples they encountered, learning about the land, its resources, and its inhabitants.

There is an interesting story that occurred during their expedition. In August 1806 during a hunting expedition, a crew member by the name of Pierre Cruzatte, who happened to be very nearsighted, shot Captain Meriwether Lewis.

Lewis was wearing buckskins, and in the dim light, Cruzatte mistook him for an elk.

Meriwether Lewis was shot in the buttock and instantly recognized it was Cruzatte. He called out to Cruzatte.

Cruzatte realized his mistake, initially hid and then claimed they were under attack by Native Americans.

Captain Lewis later examined the bullet and confirmed it was from Cruzatte's gun. He ended up recording the incident in his journal along with his recovery a month later in September.

Despite the many challenges, Lewis and Clark successfully navigated the Louisiana Territory, reaching the Pacific Ocean and returning valuable information about the newly acquired land. The story of Lewis and Clark provides a powerful example of how to navigate uncertainty. It demonstrates the importance of adaptability, resilience, and the willingness to embrace the unknown when charting a course into the future.

Leaders need to navigate uncertainty because it's a crucial skill for effectively guiding teams and organizations, especially in today's dynamic and unpredictable world. It is quite possible that Captain Lewis could never have predicted he would be shot in his buttock. His leadership was able to navigate that situation along with whatever else came his way. Uncertainty can create anxiety and stress, but leaders who can embrace and navigate it can turn these challenges into opportunities for innovation, collaboration, and growth.

Here's a more detailed look at how leaders can navigate uncertainty:

1. Embrace Flexibility and Adaptability:

- **Adjust to Changing Circumstances:** Be prepared to adjust plans, realign teams, and renew commitment as needed.
- **Encourage Experimentation:** Create an environment where teams feel comfortable testing new ideas and approaches.
- **Don't Be Afraid to Change Course:** Situations can change rapidly, and leaders should be willing to adapt their strategies.

2. Maintain Open and Transparent Communication:

- **Share Information:** Keep teams informed about the situation, decisions being made, and any potential changes.
- **Be Honest and Transparent:** Acknowledge when information is limited or when decisions are difficult.
- **Communicate Frequently:** Regular updates help reduce anxiety and build trust.

3. Lead with Empathy and Emotional Support:

- **Acknowledge Stress:** Recognize that uncertainty can be stressful and provide support to team members.
- **Offer Emotional Support:** Be available to listen, offer encouragement, and show understanding for individual experiences.
- **Develop a System:** Encourage connection and collaboration within teams to foster a sense of belonging.

4. Make Incremental Decisions and Focus on the Present:

- **Break Down Large Decisions:** Divide complex problems into smaller, manageable steps to reduce overwhelm.
- **Focus on the Immediate Tasks:** Help teams stay grounded by focusing on what needs to be done in the present moment.
- **Celebrate Small Wins:** Acknowledge progress and achievements, even during challenging times.

5. Reinforce Purpose and Core Values:

- **Connect to the Bigger Picture:** Remind teams of the organization's mission and values to maintain a sense of direction.
- **Focus on Long-Term Goals:** Ensure that shortterm decisions align with the overall strategic vision.
- **Stay Grounded in Purpose:** Reinforce the reasons for the work being done, even when facing uncertainty.

By implementing these strategies, leaders effectively navigate uncertainty, build stronger teams, and position their organizations for success in the face of change.

LEADERSHIP CHALLENGE

Here is my challenge to you:

This week we learned about navigating 8,000 miles on horseback over a two-and-a-half-year journey. Everything about this was uncertain and facing the unknown.

What they did is a lost skill.

When was the last time you were faced with embarking on a trip? Perhaps it was one for business or even pleasure. In today's age we have an entire industry that aids people in having successful trips. If you took that trip by car did navigation assistance (either from the car or via the phone) help you? Of course it did.

"In moments of uncertainty do what you understand, not what you feel. God's truth will always lead you to the right path."

- Yankee Doodle Dave

Being able to navigate uncertainty is something that leaders will need to face.

It might be economic shifts, technological changes and evolving market demands.

There were several techniques provided this week to help navigate uncertainty.

What techniques do you plan to use over the next week to help with navigating uncertainty?

"The goal of leadership is not to eradicate uncertainty but rather to navigate it."
- Andy Stanley

Leaders Need to Be Resilient

"Fear not, for I am with you; be not dismayed, for I am your God; I will strengthen you. I will help you; I will uphold you with my righteous hand."

- Isaiah 41:10

HISTORICAL FIGURE:
Staff Sergeant Ronald Shurer, II, Medal of Honor Recipient

Resilience is defined by the capacity to withstand or to recover quickly from difficulties or to display a certain sense of toughness.

When one thinks of resilience or toughness, thoughts often lead to the military and then ultimately to that of the Special Forces. There is one story of resilience and extreme toughness that I want to share involving a specific Soldier.

Staff Sergeant Ronald J. Shurer, II, deployed with Combined Joint Special Operations Task Force in Afghanistan from November 2007 to May 2008 in Operation Enduring Freedom. He was serving as a Senior Medical Sergeant (Army Medic) for Special Operational Detachment Alpha 3336, Special Operations Task Force-33. He was part of an assault element inserted by helicopter into a location in Afghanistan.

As the assault element moved up a near-vertical mountain toward its objective, it was engaged by fierce enemy machine gun, sniper, and rocket-propelled grenade fire.

The lead portion of the assault element that included the ground commander, sustained several casualties and became pinned down on the mountainside. Staff Sergeant Shurer and the rest of the trailing portion of the assault element were likewise engaged by enemy machine gun, sniper, and rocket-propelled grenade fire.

As the attack intensified, Staff Sergeant Shurer braved enemy fire to move to an injured Soldier and treat his wounds. Having stabilized the injured Soldier, Staff Sergeant Shurer then learned of the casualties among the lead elements.

Staff Sergeant Shurer fought his way up the mountainside, under intense enemy fire, to the lead element's location. Upon reaching the lead element, he treated and stabilized two more Soldiers. Finishing those lifesaving efforts, Staff Sergeant Shurer noticed two additional severely wounded Soldiers under intense enemy fire. The bullet that had wounded one of these Soldiers had also impacted Staff Sergeant Shurer's helmet. With complete disregard for his own life, Staff Sergeant Shurer again moved through enemy fire to treat and stabilize one Soldier's severely wounded arm.

Shortly thereafter, Staff Sergeant Shurer continued bravely weathering enemy fire to get to the other Soldier's location to treat his lower leg, which had been almost completely severed by a high-caliber sniper round. After treating the Soldier, Staff Sergeant Shurer began to evacuate the wounded, carrying and lowering them down the sheer mountainside.

While moving down the mountain, Staff Sergeant Shurer used his own body to shield the wounded from enemy fire and debris caused by danger-close air strikes. Reaching the base of the mountain, Staff Sergeant Shurer set up a casualty collection point and continued to treat the wounded. With the arrival of the medical evacuation helicopter, Staff Sergeant Shurer, again under enemy fire, helped load the wounded into the helicopter. Having ensured the safety of the wounded, Staff Sergeant Shurer then regained control of his commando squad and rejoined the fight. He continued to lead his troops and emplacing security elements until it was time to move to the evacuation landing zone for the helicopter.

Staff Sergeant Shurer ultimately saved the lives of eight other Soldiers despite being wounded 37 times. For his actions, he received the *Congressional Medal of Honor* on October 1, 2018, during a ceremony at the White House.

Resilience is crucial in leadership because it allows leaders to navigate challenges and uncertainty, bounce back from setbacks, and inspire their teams to do the same. Resilient leaders are better equipped to make sound decisions under pressure, adapt to change, and foster a positive and productive work environment, ultimately contributing to organizational success.

Here's a more detailed look at why resilience is important in leadership.

1. Navigating Change and Uncertainty:
- Resilient leaders are adept at navigating turbulent times and adapting to new situations, whether it's technological advancements, market fluctuations, or unforeseen global events.
- They are more likely to embrace change and see it as an opportunity for growth and innovation.

2. Inspiring Confidence and Motivation:
- Resilient leaders inspire confidence in their teams by demonstrating their own ability to bounce back from challenges and setbacks.
- They create a positive and supportive work environment where employees feel valued and motivated to contribute their best.

3. Fostering a Culture of Resilience:
- Resilient leaders model the behaviors that inspire resilience in others, creating a culture where employees are encouraged to persevere and learn from failures.

- They provide a safe space for employees to take risks and innovate, knowing that setbacks are part of the learning process.

4. Enhancing Decision-Making:
- Resilient leaders are better equipped to make sound decisions under pressure, as they can stay calm, focused, and clear-headed even in challenging situations.
- They can also better assess risks and opportunities, making more informed decisions that benefit the organization.

5. Improving Team Performance:
- Resilient leaders are more likely to foster a high-performing team, as they create an environment where employees feel supported, motivated, and empowered.
- Teams led by resilient leaders are more likely to adapt to change, recover from setbacks, and achieve their goals.

6. Building Stronger Relationships:
- Resilient leaders are better able to build strong relationships with their teams by demonstrating empathy, understanding, and support.
- They are also more likely to be approachable and open to feedback, fostering trust and respect within the team.

In essence, resilience is a fundamental skill for leaders in today's dynamic and challenging world. It allows them to not only survive difficult times but to thrive and lead their organizations toward sustainable success.

HOW DO YOU DO THIS?
Leaders enhance their resilience by focusing on personal well-being, cultivating a growth mindset, and building strong social connections. This involves prioritizing self-care, embracing challenges as

learning opportunities, and fostering supportive relationships with colleagues and mentors.

Resilient leaders understand the importance of taking care of themselves physically, mentally, and emotionally. This includes getting enough sleep, eating a healthy diet, exercising regularly, and finding time for relaxation and hobbies.

- **Cultivate a Growth Mindset:** Resilient leaders view challenges as opportunities for learning and growth, rather than threats. They are not afraid to take risks and embrace failure as a valuable learning experience.

- **Focus on What You Can Control:** Leaders can also focus on what they can influence, rather than dwelling on things outside their control.

- **Increase Self-Awareness:** Understanding one's strengths, weaknesses, and emotional responses is crucial for resilience.

- **Embrace a Curious Mindset:** Leaders who adopt a curious mindset are more open to new perspectives and ideas, making them better equipped to adapt to change.

- **Acknowledge What You Don't Know:** Humility allows leaders to recognize their limitations and seek guidance from others, fostering a collaborative environment.

- **Adaptability:** Resilient leaders adapt to changing circumstances and embrace new ideas.

- **Emotional Intelligence:** Leaders with high emotional intelligence effectively manage their own emotions and understand the emotions of others, fostering a more positive and supportive work environment.

- **Decision-Making Under Pressure:** Resilient leaders can make sound decisions even in high-pressure situations.

"Resilience isn't just bouncing back. It is moving forward even after you have been knocked down."

- Yankee Doodle Dave

LEADERSHIP CHALLENGE

Here is my challenge to you:

This week we learned about the grit and resilience of Staff Sergeant Ronald Shurer, II. Staff Sergeant Shurer's actions were unbelievable. What he endured is something that the average person will fortunately not ever have to endure.

The average leader must deal with a sense of resilience. In the workplace this can refer to the capacity to effectively cope with and adapt to challenges, stress, and setbacks. This ultimately deals with productivity and well-being. Resilience also deals with bouncing back from adversity and learning from those experiences. Resilient employees are better equipped to handle change, manage stress and maintain positive relationships with colleagues. There were several techniques provided to develop resilience.

What techniques do you plan to use over the next week to help you and your staff become more resilient?

"Resilience is the antidote to complacency. It is the mindset that allows you to push beyond your limits and achieve greatness,"
- David Goggins

Why Mistakes Are Important

"Whoever conceals their sins does not prosper, but the one who confesses and renounces them finds mercy. Blessed is the one who always trembles before God, but whoever hardens their heart falls into trouble."
- Proverbs 28:13-14

HISTORICAL FIGURE:
President James Buchanan - Role Leading to the Civil War

This week's lesson deals with the topic of why mistakes are important. It has become a cultural norm to emphasize success and perfection, leading to a stigma around failure. Mistakes can be seen as a reflection of incompetence or carelessness. I would like to take a very different approach to mistakes.

Let's start with what the word really means. The etymology of the word "mistake" in the context of archery, and particularly its connection to religious concepts like "sin," is rooted in the idea of "missing the mark." Both the Greek and Hebrew words that are often translated as "sin" have this archery-related meaning, indicating a failure to hit the intended target. The English word "mistake" itself, through Old Norse, ultimately comes from the idea of "taking" something in error, which also reflects a failure to hit the mark.

The definition of incompetence is not having or showing the necessary skills to do something successfully. Understanding the basic definitions would lead one to realize that making a mistake is not necessarily incompetence.

To further illustrate this concept let me share a famous story that deals with this concept of making mistakes. President Buchanan served in office from 1857-1861. He assumed office during a time of escalating tensions between the North and South over the issue of slavery.

Two days after his inauguration, the Supreme Court, in a decision influenced by Buchanan, ruled that enslaved and free African Americans were not citizens and lacked the right to sue for their freedom. The court also deemed the *Missouri Compromise* unconstitutional, further escalating tensions.

Violence erupted in Kansas as pro-slavery and anti-slavery forces vied for control of the territory. Buchanan, attempting to please the South, supported the pro-slavery *Lecompton Constitution*, deepening the national divide.

In 1859, Abolitionist John Brown's attempt to spark a slave uprising at Harpers Ferry further intensified the conflict, solidifying the belief in the South that the North was plotting their destruction.

Following Abraham Lincoln's election in 1860, Southern states began seceding from the Union. Buchanan, while disagreeing with secession, believed the Federal government lacked the authority to prevent it. His inaction and indecisiveness in the face of this crisis are widely criticized by historians. President Lincoln inherited a huge mess when he assumed office due to James Buchanan's lack of leadership.

In 1860, there was a corruption scandal involving President James Buchanan's Secretary of War, John Floyd. This all centered on a "sweetheart deal" for the sale of Fort Snelling military reservation and the mishandling of Indian trust bonds. The affair, which broke in the final months of President Buchanan's administration, further eroded public trust during the escalating secession crisis.

Many historians and scholars rank Buchanan among the worst presidents in U.S. history due to his inability to address the slavery crisis and prevent the *Civil War*. Buchanan's perceived bias towards the South and his refusal to acknowledge differing perspectives alienated a significant portion of the Northern population and exacerbated sectional tensions. In a time demanding strong leadership to navigate the complex issue of slavery and preserve the Union, Buchanan faltered, ultimately leaving the nation on the brink of war for his successor to inherit.

Examining historical mistakes helps individuals and societies learn from past errors and avoid repeating them. This process promotes growth, adaptation, and the development of more effective solutions to current and future challenges. Acknowledging historical injustices and reflecting on past decisions, including those of leaders like Buchanan, are essential for fostering a more equitable and inclusive society. Studying history provides a deeper understanding of the causes and consequences of events, equipping individuals with a broader perspective to analyze present-day challenges and make more informed decisions.

While it's important to recognize that the *Civil War* was the result of decades of complex issues and cannot be solely blamed on one individual, it is important to note that Buchanan's actions, and inactions, during his presidency are considered by most historians to have been a prime contributing factor in the coming of the *Civil War*. Understanding these mistakes provides valuable insight into the critical events that led to this defining moment in American history.

Mistakes are valuable opportunities for learning and growth, fostering creativity and resilience. They help us develop a growth mindset, overcome fear of failure, and build resilience. By embracing mistakes we can learn from them, adapt our approaches, and become better versions of ourselves, both personally and professionally.

Here's a more detailed look at why mistakes are good:

1. Learning and Growth:
- **Valuable Insights:** Mistakes reveal what works and what doesn't, providing valuable insights for improvement.
- **Reflecting and Adapting:** Each mistake offers a chance to reflect, analyze the cause, and adapt our approach for future attempts.
- **Continuous Learning:** Embracing mistakes allows us to view life as a continuous learning journey, fostering a growth mindset.
- **Fear of Failure:** Mistakes help us overcome the fear of failure and build confidence in our ability to learn and adapt.

2. Fostering Creativity and Innovation:
- **Thinking Outside the Box:** When we make mistakes, we are often pushed to think creatively and explore alternative solutions. Mistakes can lead to new ideas and approaches, fueling innovation and creative problem-solving.
- **New Perspectives:** Mistakes open our minds to new perspectives and approaches, allowing us to see problems from different angles.

3. Building Resilience:
- **Resilience:** Learning to cope with failure and bounce back stronger builds resilience and emotional fortitude.
- **Dealing with Disappointment:** Mistakes can teach us how to manage disappointment and navigate setbacks in a healthy way.
- **Motivational:** Learning from mistakes can be a powerful motivator, pushing us to strive for improvement and achieve our goals.

4. Personal Development:
- **Realistic Expectations:** Mistakes can help us develop a realistic understanding of our abilities and skills.

- **Self-Compassion:** Embracing mistakes can foster self-compassion and understanding, reducing self-criticism.
- **Strengthening Relationships:** Admitting mistakes and taking ownership of them can build trust and strengthen relationships.
- **Embracing Vulnerability:** Showing vulnerability by admitting mistakes can create a more relatable and human image, and foster trust and understanding.

HOW DO YOU DO THIS?

To foster an environment where staff feel comfortable making mistakes, it's crucial to create a psychologically safe space, encourage open communication, and view mistakes as learning opportunities. This involves leaders demonstrating vulnerability, acknowledging their own mistakes, and providing regular feedback loops to help employees understand the importance of learning from errors.

Here's a more detailed breakdown of how to create such an environment:

1. Encourage Open Communication and Psychological Safety:

- **Lead by Example:** Leaders should openly acknowledge their own mistakes and share the lessons learned. This demonstrates that it is safe to make mistakes.
- **Promote a Blameless Culture:** Avoid assigning blame and instead focus on understanding the root cause of the mistake.
- **Create a Safe Space for Sharing Mistakes:** Ensure employees feel comfortable admitting mistakes without fear of repercussions.
- **Foster a Growth Mindset:** Encourage employees to view mistakes as opportunities for learning and improvement.
- **Make Mistake Sharing Part of the Culture:** Host meetings where team members can discuss missteps and lessons learned.
- **Communicate Clearly:** Ensure employees understand expectations and processes to minimize the likelihood of errors.

2. Focus on Learning and Improvement:

- **View Mistakes as Learning Opportunities:** Emphasize that mistakes are valuable for growth and innovation.
- **Encourage Feedback and Reflection:** Provide opportunities for employees to share their experiences and reflect on mistakes.
- **Establish Processes for Learning from Mistakes:** Implement feedback loops, and team retrospectives to analyze mistakes and identify areas for improvement.
- **Commitment to Continuous Employee Training:** Provide consistent training to equip employees with the skills and knowledge needed to avoid errors.
- **Analyze Situations and Identify Root Causes:** Help employees understand why mistakes occur and how to prevent them in the future.

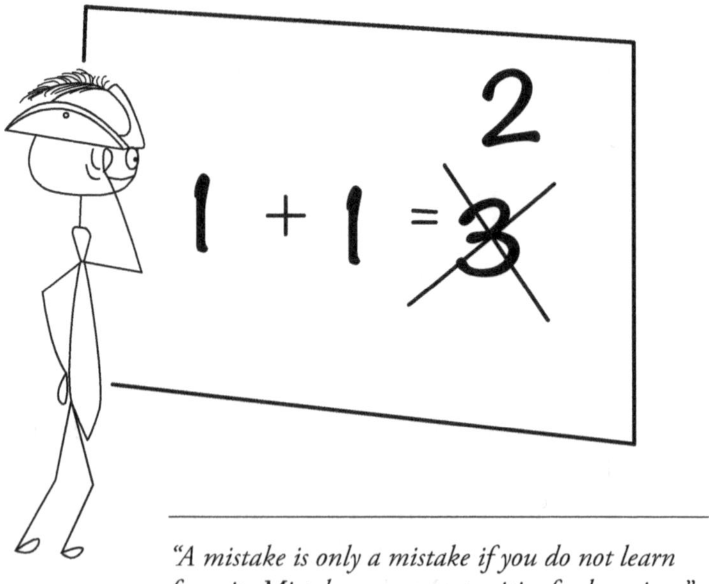

"A mistake is only a mistake if you do not learn from it. Mistakes are opportunities for learning."

- Yankee Doodle Dave

LEADERSHIP CHALLENGE

Here is my challenge to you:

This week we learned about President James Buchanan's role and how that contributed towards our nation going into the *Civil War*.

What is the culture like in your organization? Is it acceptable for people to make mistakes? Or do you have a cultural norm of not making mistakes where there is a focus on avoidance and emphasizing on perfection? Is there a culture of punishing errors and possibly reduced innovation and learning?

The idea of creating an environment where mistakes are acceptable is against a social norm.

There were several techniques that have been provided to help you create an environment where staff members feel comfortable making mistakes.

What techniques do you plan to use over the next week to create an environment that permits or allows mistakes?

____

____

____

____

____

____

____

____

"To learn to succeed, you must first learn to fail."
- Michael Jordan

Leaders Inspire Greatness

"Great is the Lord, and greatly to be praised in the city of our God, in the mountain of his holiness."
- Psalms 48:1

HISTORICAL FIGURE:
Eleanor Roosevelt, Former First Lady, Diplomat and Activist

Leaders should be able to inspire their team members to achieve their full potential and contribute to the organization's goals. There are numerous leaders through history who have inspired their people (team, staff or entire organization) to endure hardship and create greatness.

Here is a story that outlines a significant historical figure who inspired greatness.

She was born in New York, NY, on October 11, 1884. From an early age she preferred to be called by her middle name, Eleanor. Through her father, she was the niece of President Theodore Roosevelt. In 1905, she married the future President Franklin D. Roosevelt. She was the longest serving first lady of the United States. Her husband served four terms.

Eleanor was a strong voice for human rights, particularly for marginalized groups. She championed the rights of women, African Americans, Asian Americans, and refugees. She was instrumental in the formation and early work of the United Nations, particularly in drafting the *Universal Declaration of Human Rights*. Eleanor faced personal challenges, including a difficult childhood and her husband's illness, but she persevered and found strength in her public service.

She is widely remembered for her inspiring actions and words that encouraged and empowered others throughout her life. She believed good leaders inspire confidence in their followers, but *great* leaders inspire people to have confidence in themselves. This philosophy guided her approach to advocating for others, particularly during her time as First Lady and at the *United Nations*.

Eleanor served as the chair of the *UN Human Rights Commission*. In that role, she played a crucial role in drafting the *Universal Declaration of Human Rights*. This monumental achievement advocated for equal rights and dignity for all individuals, regardless of gender, race, religion, language, or political beliefs, inspiring global human rights movements.

Eleanor dedicated her life to social reform and diplomacy, focusing on critical issues like education, healthcare, equal employment, and childcare. She gave voice to the concerns of laborers during the *Great Depression* and continued to speak out for women and children's issues.

Eleanor constantly encouraged courage and resilience of others. Her famous quote, *"You gain strength, courage, and confidence by every experience in which you really stop looking fear in the face,"* exemplifies her belief in overcoming challenges and building inner strength.

There is a wonderful story of Eleanor Roosevelt that is not as common, but her efforts inspired many. In March 1941, First Lady Eleanor Roosevelt flew with the Tuskegee Airmen's chief civilian flight instructor, Charles "Chief" Anderson, at the Tuskegee Army Air Field in Alabama. This ended up being an event that provided crucial national visibility and support for the program and helped dismantle stereotypes about Black people's ability to fly. Despite Secret Service objections, Roosevelt's flight, captured in famous photographs and video, demonstrated her strong personal support for the program in its early stages of development. This helped convince her husband to use his influence to advance the integration of the country's aviation forces.

Roosevelt's flight brought significant national media attention to the Tuskegee program and the abilities of Black pilots. The event served as a powerful counter-narrative to the racist views and flawed Army reports that claimed Black people couldn't operate complex machinery like aircraft. Upon her return, Roosevelt lobbied her husband, President Roosevelt, to support the integration of the Armed Forces' aviation branches. This was a move that eventually led to the activation of the 99th Pursuit Squadron, the first all-Black military aviation unit.

She encouraged others to confront their fears and pursue their dreams, reminding them that they have the capacity to overcome adversity. She believed in inspiring women to recognize their true influential potential. Eleanor encouraged women to awaken to their power and influence, urging them to accept the responsibility that comes with that power.

Through her words and actions, Eleanor Roosevelt served as a powerful role model, demonstrating the impact one person can have in advocating for a more just and equitable world. She inspired greatness with all those whom she encountered.

Leaders inspire others because doing so fosters higher team engagement, motivation, and productivity, leading to increased success and a positive work environment. Inspired employees are more likely to exceed expectations, contribute beyond their role, and build a strong sense of collective purpose.

Here's Why Inspirational Leadership is Crucial:

- **Increased Engagement and Motivation:** Inspired employees are more likely to be engaged and motivated, leading to improved work quality and overall team performance.
- **Improved Productivity:** Inspired individuals are often more productive and willing to go the extra mile, contributing to overall organizational success.
- **Higher Job Satisfaction:** When employees feel inspired and valued, they are more likely to have higher job satisfaction and a greater sense of belonging.
- **Reduced Turnover:** Inspired and engaged employees are less likely to leave the organization, leading to lower turnover rates and reduced recruitment costs.
- **Positive Work Culture:** Inspirational leaders create a positive and supportive work environment where employees feel valued and encouraged to reach their full potential.
- **Collective Success:** Inspiring leaders help employees overcome challenges and work together to achieve collective goals, leading to a more successful and thriving organization.
- **Longlasting Legacy:** Inspiring leaders contribute to a positive and lasting influence on people, organizations, and society, leaving behind a legacy of success and positive change.

HOW DO YOU DO THIS?

Inspirational leaders cultivate qualities like authenticity, strong communication, and empathy to motivate and guide their teams. They inspire by leading by example, empowering their team, and fostering a positive and inclusive environment. Inspirational leadership also involves having a clear vision, passion, and the ability to articulate that vision effectively.

Here's a more detailed look at how leaders become inspirational:

1. Authenticity and Vulnerability:

- **Inspirational Leaders Are Genuine and Transparent:** Sharing details about themselves to build trust and connection with their team.
- **They Are Willing to Be Vulnerable:** Admit mistakes and take responsibility for their actions.

2. Strong Communication Skills:

- **Listening:** Inspirational leaders are skilled listeners, valuing the input and perspectives of their team members.
- **Clear Vision:** They articulate a compelling vision for the future, making it easy for others to understand and get on board with.
- **Effective Communication:** They use language that inspires and motivates, not just to inform but to create a sense of purpose and shared goals.
- **Storytelling**: They use storytelling to connect with their audience on an emotional level and make their message more memorable.

3. Empowerment and Support:

- **Delegation:** They empower their team members by delegating tasks and providing the resources and support they need to succeed.
- **Recognition and Appreciation:** They acknowledge and appreciate the contributions of their team, fostering a sense of value and belonging.
- **Openness to Feedback:** They are open to feedback and actively seek input from their team, creating a culture of continuous improvement.

4. Leading by Example:

- **Embodying Values:** They live by the values they espouse, demonstrating integrity and ethical behavior in all their actions.

- **Hard Work and Dedication:** They lead by example, demonstrating a strong work ethic and dedication to their goals.
- **Positive Attitude:** They maintain a positive and optimistic outlook, even in challenging situations, inspiring their team to persevere.

5. Cultivating Emotional Intelligence:

- **Empathy:** They understand and empathize with the feelings and experiences of their team members.
- **Self-Awareness:** They are aware of their own emotions and how they impact others, using this awareness to build stronger relationships.
- **Self-Regulation:** They manage their emotions effectively, remaining calm and composed under pressure.

"If your actions inspire others to dream more, learn more and do more and become more…you are a Leader!"

- Yankee Doodle Dave

LEADERSHIP CHALLENGE

Here is my challenge to you:

This week we learned about Eleanor Roosevelt's ability to inspire greatness in others. Her impact was felt across the globe and affected numerous generations.

Perhaps you may not be in a situation to provide such a massive impact. You can make an impact on your staff at your organization. Inspiring others in the workplace might be focusing on creating a positive environment, communicating effectively and showing genuine appreciation. As a leader, you could lead by example, encourage growth, and foster collaboration to motivate your colleagues to do their best work.

There were several techniques that have been provided to help you create greatness in others. What techniques do you plan to use over the next week to achieve that goal?

"Good leaders inspire people to have confidence in their leader.
Great leaders inspire people to have confidence in themselves."
- Eleanor Roosevelt

Leaders Know How to Listen

"The way of a fool is right in his own eyes, but a wise man listens to advice."

- Proverbs 12:15

HISTORICAL FIGURE:
President William McKinley - His Listening Ability

This week I want to discuss the concept of leaders understanding how to listen. To illustrate this point I want to share a story.

President William McKinley was the 25th President of the United States, from 1897-1901.

McKinley's presidency saw rapid economic growth. He rejected free silver in favor of keeping the nation on the gold standard and raised protective tariffs. He signed the *Dingley Tariff* in 1897 to protect manufacturers and factory workers from foreign competition and securing passage of the *Gold Standard Act of 1900*.

Strange as it may seem, President McKinley was known for his listening ability, although not in the way one might typically imagine a charismatic, publicly eloquent leader.

There is a story about William McKinley that illustrates his listening ability long before he became our president. During the *Civil War*, McKinley earned the nickname "Coffee Bill" for his bravery and care for his fellow soldiers. As a commissary sergeant in the 23rd Ohio Volunteer Infantry, the 19-year-old McKinley was responsible for his regiment's supplies. At the bloody Battle of Antietam in 1862, he drove a wagon of hot coffee and rations directly to the front line while under heavy fire. The men were so revived by the food and coffee that an officer said it was *"like putting a new regiment in the fight."* He took time out to talk to the soldiers, and it is often told how he cared for his troops. His superior officer, Rutherford B. Hayes (a future president), praised his actions, and McKinley was promoted to second lieutenant.

He was described as someone who kept *"his ear so close to the ground that it was full of grasshoppers,"* implying a keen awareness of public opinion. This was demonstrated when he was undecided about how to handle Spanish possessions besides Cuba. He took a tour across the country and grasped the imperialist sentiment, subsequently annexing the Philippines, Guam, and Puerto Rico.

Unlike presidents who might engage in dramatic public speeches, McKinley preferred to concentrate on private meetings with senators and congressmen, listening attentively to their concerns and viewpoints.

While not a *"bully pulpit"* orator, he understood the power of listening and then shaping public discourse. He would edit the remarks of visiting delegations to his home during the 1896 presidential campaign, making sure to weave in his preferred themes while also allowing them to speak their minds.

In his 1896 campaign, he was the first president to actively engage with the media by holding press conferences and traveling across the nation to speak with voters. This suggests an effort to connect directly with the electorate and understand their perspectives.

Therefore, while he might not have been an outwardly expressive orator, McKinley's reputation as a good listener stemmed from his focus on understanding public sentiment, his tactful approach to political negotiations, and his innovative ways of engaging with the media and voters to gauge and subtly influence opinions.

The story of President McKinley focuses on his listening skills.

Some of those skills were: patience and tact, listening to public opinion, prioritizing outcomes, preparing and delivering effective messages, building connections and support, and focusing on understanding.

To move forward I want to truly ensure that you (the reader) grasp the difference between hearing and listening. Allow me to share a scenario with you:

> You are home and the football game is on with your favorite team playing. They are down by three points. They have the ball. It is the fourth quarter and there are less than two (2:00) minutes on the clock. There are no timeouts left. The winner of this game advances to the playoffs. You are literally sitting on the edge of your seat.
>
> At this time, your significant other comes into the room and needs your attention. They begin to talk to you and ask for your input on something.
>
> They keep looking at you and simply asking *"Are you listening to me?"*

That is the question. Are you hearing them or are you listening to them? Let's understand the difference between those two things.

HEARING: This is the passive physiological process of perceiving sounds.

Sound waves are collected by the outer ear, travel to the middle ear, and then on to the inner ear, where they are converted to electrical impulses. Those impulses are then transmitted to the brain via the auditory nerve. This is where they are processed and interpreted as sound.

This is a passive, involuntary and automatic function of the body. You do not have to put forth effort to make this happen.

Example: Simply being in a room where music is playing; your ears are receiving the sound waves without you consciously trying to do so.

LISTENING: This is an active cognitive process that involves paying attention and understanding the meaning of those sounds.

Listening to something is where you would hear with thoughtful attention, giving consideration and making a sincere effort to understand the meaning.

In a conversation, listening truly means that one person is trying to understand what the other person is saying and responding accordingly.

In essence, you can hear sounds without listening, but you cannot listen without hearing. Listening involves both hearing and actively processing the information to comprehend its meaning.

Listening is a crucial leadership skill because it fosters trust, improves communication, and enhances decision-making. Leaders who listen actively are better equipped to understand their team's perspectives, address concerns, and create a positive work environment.

Here's a more detailed look at why listening is so important in leadership:

1. Building Trust and Relationships:

- **Demonstrates Care and Respect:** When leaders actively listen, they show that they value their team members' opinions and concerns. This builds trust and loyalty.
- **Enhance Communication:** Effective listening fosters open and honest communication.
- **Creates a Supportive Environment:** A leader who actively listens creates a space where employees feel comfortable sharing ideas, concerns, and feedback.

2. Improving Decision-Making:

- **Access to Diverse Perspectives:** Listening allows leaders to gather information from different sources, leading to more well-rounded and informed decision-making.

- **Identifying Potential Problems:** By actively listening, leaders can detect issues early on and address them proactively.
- **Fostering Innovation:** A culture of listening encourages employees to share new ideas and solutions.

3. Enhancing Leadership Effectiveness:

- **Improved Employee Morale:** When employees feel heard and valued, their morale and engagement increase.
- **Increased Productivity:** A positive work environment and strong relationships lead to better productivity and overall innovation.
- **Reduced Conflict:** Active listening can help resolve conflicts by promoting understanding and finding common ground.

4. Becoming a Better Communicator:

- **Understanding Needs:** Effective listening helps leaders understand the needs and motivations of their team members, allowing them to tailor their communication accordingly.
- **Improving Clarity:** Listening helps ensure that messages are clear and understood.
- **Building Rapport:** Active listening helps build strong relationships and rapport with team members.

HOW DO YOU DO THIS?

To listen effectively as a leader, focus on actively receiving information, engaging with the speaker, aligning your understanding with theirs, and learning more about the situation. This involves giving full attention, demonstrating that you're hearing, checking for understanding, and asking open-ended questions.

Here's a more detailed breakdown:

1. Receive (Giving Full Attention):

- **Be Present:** Minimize distractions and focus solely on the speaker.

- **Make Eye Contact:** Demonstrates engagement and attentiveness.
- **Remove Barriers:** Ensure a comfortable and open environment for communication.

2. Engage (Demonstrating You're Hearing):

- **Verbal Cues:** Use phrases like "I hear you," or "I see what you mean."
- **Non-Verbal Cues:** Nodding, smiling, and appropriate body language show that you're engaged.
- **Encourage the Speaker:** Use "mm" or other encouraging noises to show you're following.

3. Align (Checking for Understanding):

- **Paraphrase and Reflect:** Summarize what you've heard to confirm your understanding.
- **Clarify Misunderstandings:** Ask questions to ensure you're on the same page.
- **Correct Misalignments:** If needed, clarify any misunderstandings to ensure everyone is aligned.

4. Learn More (Asking Open-Ended Questions):

- **Inquire About Details:** Ask clarifying questions for more information.
- **Show Commitment to Exploration:** Engage in a conversation to better understand.
- **Don't Assume Agreement:** Focus on learning more, even if you don't agree.

Additional Tips for Effective Listening:

- **Defer Judgment:** Refrain from judging the speaker's ideas until you fully understand their perspective.
- **Be Empathetic:** Try to understand the speaker's feelings and motivations.

- **Be Mindful of Your Own Internal Monologue:** Avoid thinking about your response while the speaker is talking.
- **Focus on the Speaker's Needs:** Adjust your communication style to meet their needs.
- **Seek Feedback:** Create an environment where others feel comfortable offering feedback.

LEADERSHIP CHALLENGE

Here is my challenge to you:

This week we learned about President William McKinley and his ability to listen. We went on to further examine the concepts of hearing and listening.

Effective listening in the workplace involves actively focusing on the speaker, understanding their message, and responding thoughtfully. This includes paying attention, showing engagement through body language, and asking clarifying questions. It is about creating a supportive environment where everyone feels heard and valued.

There were several techniques that have been provided to help you effectively listen.

"Most people do not listen to understand. They listen with the intent to reply."

- Yankee Doodle Dave

What techniques do you plan to use over the next week to listen effectively?

"I'm a very strong believer in listening and learning from others."
- Justice Ruth Bader Ginsburg

Humility and Pride in Leadership

"When pride comes, then comes disgrace, but with humility comes wisdom."

- Proverbs 11:2

HISTORICAL FIGURE:
Benjamin Franklin – List of 13 Virtues – "Humility"

This week we will discuss the topic of Humility and Pride in Leadership. I would like to share a famous story that discusses a person who did not listen.

A well-known story about Benjamin Franklin's humility involves his friend pointing out his pride and prompting him to add "humility" to his list of virtues. Franklin recognized that pride was a difficult trait to overcome and decided to actively work on cultivating humility. He even created a system to track his progress in practicing humility, along with his other virtues.

The humorous anecdote he recounts involves his first journey back to Boston. About seven months after leaving Boston for Philadelphia in 1723, Franklin returned home. He was determined to impress the city with his apparent success.

He arrived "in a new suit, a new watch, and with plenty of coins in his pocket," ready to show off his success to the people who knew him as an apprentice. This was a stark contrast to his struggling beginnings as a young runaway.

While attempting to show off his importance, Franklin encountered Cotton Mather, a respected Bostonian. Cotton Mather was a former adversary of Franklin's growing up.

In his pride, Franklin was so engrossed in his posturing that he failed to notice a low ceiling beam. Mather saw what was coming. *"Stoop! Stoop!"* Mather warned him.

Franklin, too busy with his proud posturing, ignored the advice and walked headfirst into a low-hanging beam. He hit his head so hard he nearly fell over.

Mather, with a wry smile, offered a memorable quip: *"Let this be a caution to you not always to hold your head so high. Stoop, young man, stoop—as you go through this world—and you'll miss many hard thumps."*

Franklin took the lesson to heart, and it inspired a lifelong attempt to temper his pride. However, his funny, self-aware conclusion reveals his humorous skepticism that anyone can ever truly escape their own ego.

This additional story highlights Franklin's self-awareness and dedication to self-improvement. A Quaker friend pointed out to Franklin that he was often perceived as proud and overbearing in his conversations. He even provided specific examples of this behavior, according to a blog post on *Ben Franklin Circles*.

Benjamin Franklin, rather than becoming defensive, acknowledged the validity of the criticism and decided to address his pride.

He added "humility" to his list of thirteen virtues that he was consciously working on developing. He saw humility to improve his interactions with others and become a better person. His list of thirteen virtues was a means for him to aim for moral perfection. Here are those thirteen virtues: Temperance, Silence, Order, Resolution, Frugality, Industry, Sincerity, Justice, Moderation, Cleanliness, Tranquility, Chastity, and Humility.

Franklin's pursuit of humility was a lifelong endeavor; he even joked that if he ever truly achieved humility, he would likely be proud of it. Benjamin created a system to track his progress on all thirteen virtues, including humility. He would focus on one virtue per week, keeping a record of his successes and failures in a notebook. This systematic approach to self-improvement is a testament to his dedication and self-awareness.

Franklin found immense advantages in his change of behavior, which not only improved his rhetorical skills but also increased his influence in civic matters.

In a poignant moment at the Constitutional Convention, the elderly Franklin urged the delegates to doubt their own infallibility, acknowledge their differing views, and act in the public good.

Franklin's own struggle and eventual embrace of humility demonstrate a profound self-awareness and an enduring understanding that true wisdom often involves a willingness to be open to others' ideas and to concede when one is incorrect.

Benjamin Franklin's approach to humility offers valuable lessons in self-improvement and interpersonal relationships. He recognized humility as a crucial virtue and actively worked to cultivate it. This demonstrated the importance of self-awareness, continuous effort, and a focus on understanding others. His practice of humility also highlighted the benefits of listening more and speaking less. This ultimately led to more effective communication and stronger relationships.

HOW DO YOU DO THIS?

To avoid excessive pride, leaders should cultivate humility by actively seeking feedback, acknowledging mistakes, and prioritizing the needs of others. They should also be mindful of the dangers of hubris, engage in self-reflection, and foster a culture of openness and collaboration within their teams.

Here's a more detailed look at how leaders can avoid excessive pride:

1. Embrace Humility:

- **Seek Feedback:** Actively solicit feedback from team members, peers, and mentors to gain a more realistic perspective on their performance and identify areas for improvement.
- **Acknowledge Mistakes:** Be willing to admit when they are wrong and take responsibility for their actions.
- **Practice Gratitude:** Recognize and appreciate the contributions of others, rather than taking all the credit for success.
- **Focus on Service:** Shift the focus from personal achievements to the needs and development of their team and organization.

2. Cultivate Self-Awareness:

- **Reflect on Performance:** Regularly assess their actions and decisions, consider both successes and failures, identify patterns and areas where pride may influence behavior.
- **Challenge Assumptions:** Be willing to question their own beliefs and assumptions and consider alternative perspectives.

3. Foster a Culture of Openness:

- **Encourage Dissent:** Create an environment where team members feel comfortable sharing their opinions and challenging the leader's ideas.
- **Listen Actively:** Pay attention to what others are saying, both verbally and nonverbally, and demonstrate genuine interest in their perspectives.

4. Remember the Dangers of Hubris:

- **Self-Sabotaging:** Excessive pride can lead to poor decision-making, strained relationships, and ultimately, failure.
- **Trust:** It can damage trust and respect among team members, making it difficult to build a strong and effective team.

By actively practicing these strategies, leaders can avoid the pitfalls of excessive pride and cultivate a leadership style that is both effective and inspiring.

LEADERSHIP CHALLENGE

Here is my challenge to you:

This week we learned about the story of Benjamin Franklin and his list of thirteen (13) Virtues. He saw humility as something that was so important that it had to be worked on constantly.

Excessive pride, also known as arrogance or hubris, in the workplace can manifest as an inflated sense of self-importance, a disregard for others' opinions, and a reluctance to admit to mistakes. This can negatively impact team dynamics, productivity, and overall company culture. While healthy pride in one's work is beneficial, excessive pride can be a detrimental trait.

There were several techniques provided to help you deal with excessive pride in the workforce.

What techniques do you plan to use to create an environment that is free of excessive pride?

____

____

____

____

____

"Dear God, We pray for humility in our hearts. May we approach life with a humble, always willing to learn and grow. This we pray in your Holy name, Amen."

- Yankee Doodle Dave

Importance of Vulnerability in Leadership

"Trust in the Lord with all your heart and lean not on your own understanding; in all your ways acknowledge him, and he will make your paths straight."
- Proverbs 3: 5-6

HISTORICAL FIGURE:
Alexander Hamilton - "Reynolds Pamphlet"

Today we are going to learn a little about another leader who is responsible for many of the freedoms we have today. That leader is Alexander Hamilton. Alexander Hamilton was a pivotal figure in the founding and development of the United States.

The topic of this week's lesson deals with the importance of vulnerability in leadership. Although Hamilton provided numerous critical elements in establishing our country, I want to discuss his vulnerability as a leader. Hamilton was a complex figure with a strong public image, but one instance where he displayed significant vulnerability was during the *Reynolds Affair*.

In the 1790s, Hamilton, then Secretary of the Treasury, became entangled in an extramarital affair with Maria Reynolds

Alexander Hamilton's vulnerability began early in his childhood. There was immense loss and instability in the West Indies. When he was a boy, his father, James, abandoned his family. His mother, Rachel Faucette, died of yellow fever in 1768 when Hamilton was just 13, leaving him and his brother destitute. After their mother's death, both Alexander and his brother were taken in by a cousin, who later committed suicide. Hamilton also lost his aunt, uncle, and grandmother. Growing up, Hamilton was exposed to public shame because his parents were not married. After being orphaned, he was dependent on others for survival and advancement, which fostered a powerful need to prove his worth.

These early traumas created a deep insecurity that drove many of Hamilton's most visible—and at times, self-destructive—behaviors throughout his life. Hamilton was known for being obsessed with his reputation and personal honor, which is a key reason he wrote the *Reynolds Pamphlet* admitting to his extramarital affair. He valued his political reputation so highly that he confessed to adultery to disproving accusations of financial corruption.

The Federalist Papers, were crucial in persuading states to ratify the Constitution, and he served as the first Secretary of the Treasury, laying the foundation for the nation's financial system. His contributions extended to shaping the nation's economic policies, including the establishment of a national bank and the implementation of a system of tariffs and taxes.

When her husband, James Reynolds, discovered the affair, he blackmailed Hamilton, threatening to expose him unless he made payments. Hamilton paid these sums to protect his reputation and family. However, when allegations of financial misconduct arose later, suggesting Hamilton was using public funds for these payments, he chose a highly unusual and vulnerable path.

To refute the corruption charges, Hamilton published the *Reynolds Pamphlet* in 1797. In this detailed document, he publicly admitted to the affair with Maria Reynolds and shared the letters and evidence to prove he was being blackmailed. This act, while demonstrating his innocence of financial impropriety, exposed his personal failings and caused immense humiliation to his wife, Eliza Hamilton, and damaged his reputation.

This public confession, considered the first major sex scandal in U.S. history, showcases a surprising moment of vulnerability for Hamilton, a man known for his ambition and pride. He essentially chose to expose a personal, shameful secret to defend his public integrity as a statesman, effectively sacrificing his chances of becoming president. Despite the personal cost, the *Reynolds Pamphlet* did successfully clear his name of the more serious corruption accusations.

The revelation of the affair, while clearing him of financial wrongdoing, severely damaged his public image and credibility. The scandal effectively ended any realistic hope Hamilton had of ever becoming President of the United States. The affair also deeply wounded his wife, Eliza, who had to endure the public knowledge of his infidelity.

His insecurity manifested in vicious verbal attacks against anyone he perceived as criticizing him. When his mentor George Washington issued mild rebukes, Hamilton would take great offense. This need to defend his honor also led to his habit of challenging rivals to duels for insults. This impulsive, foolhardy behavior eventually cost him his life in his duel with Aaron Burr. Hamilton's unrelenting drive was not just for public good but was also born from a fragile, emotional place. His desperate climb from poverty often left him feeling that no amount of success was ever truly enough to prove his worth.

What we can learn from Alexander Hamilton's ability to be vulnerable as a leader is that true leadership requires a degree of vulnerability. It also is the ability to acknowledge imperfections, learn from mistakes, foster meaningful relationships, compromise when necessary and connect with others on a human level.

Vulnerability is crucial in leadership because it builds trust, fosters open communication, and encourages innovation. By being authentic and admitting areas where they need help, leaders create a safe and inclusive environment where team members feel empowered to take risks, share ideas, and contribute to growth.

Here's a more detailed look at why vulnerability is important in leadership:

1. Building Trust and Authenticity:

- Leaders who are willing to show vulnerability demonstrate authenticity, making them more relatable and trustworthy to their teams.
- Authentic leaders encourage open communication and create a space where team members feel comfortable sharing their thoughts and ideas without fear of judgment.
- This, in turn, fosters deeper connections and stronger relationships within the team, as individuals feel more connected to their leader.

2. Encouraging Innovation and Problem-Solving:

- When leaders acknowledge their own limitations and are willing to seek help, they create an environment where others are encouraged to contribute their expertise and insights.
- This collaborative approach fosters innovation and allows for a wider range of solutions to be explored.

3. Boosting Employee Engagement and Morale:

- Vulnerability helps leaders create a more emotionally intelligent work environment, where individuals feel safe to express their emotions and share their challenges.
- This leads to increased employee engagement, as individuals feel more connected to their work and their team.

4. Fostering a Culture of Psychological Safety:

- Leaders who are willing to admit when they don't know something or have made a mistake create a psychological safety space where team members feel empowered to speak up, share ideas, and take risks.

- This can lead to a more innovative and collaborative work environment, where individuals feel comfortable taking on challenges and contributing to the team's success.
- By demonstrating vulnerability, leaders can create a sense of belonging and trust within the team, fostering a culture where individuals feel valued and supported.

HOW DO YOU DO THIS?

Being vulnerable is never easy. Most of us are hard-wired to keep our thoughts and feelings close to ourselves and not open. As a leader there is an absolute benefit for being vulnerable.

Leaders can cultivate vulnerability at work by acknowledging mistakes, seeking feedback, sharing personal experiences, and fostering open communication, creating a culture of trust and psychological safety. This allows for stronger connections with team members, improved problem-solving, and a more supportive work environment.

Here's How Leaders Can Show Vulnerability:

- **Acknowledge Mistakes:** Leaders can admit when they make errors and take responsibility for them, demonstrating a willingness to learn and grow.
- **Seek Feedback:** Asking for input from team members, especially those in lower-ranking positions, shows that leaders value their perspectives and are open to improvement.
- **Share Personal Experiences:** Sharing challenges, failures, or emotional stories can humanize leaders and build trust with team members.
- **Encourage Open Communication:** Creating a safe space where employees feel comfortable expressing their thoughts and concerns without fear of judgment is crucial for building a psychologically safe workplace.

Yankee Doodle Dave has an issue with this. Because he was unable to be vulnerable in his work center he could not rely on his teammates to help him out. He was unable to ask for help when he needed it.

It's okay to say, *"I don't know"* or *"I need help,"* as it opens the door for collaboration and shows that the leader is open to learning from others.

LEADERSHIP CHALLENGE

Here is my challenge to you:

This week we learned about the story of Alexander Hamilton and the *Reynolds Pamphlet*. This demonstrated his ability as a leader the importance of being vulnerable.

In sum, vulnerability in leadership is not a weakness, but a strength that transforms the work environment, boosts performance, and creates a culture of trust, innovation, and engagement.

Vulnerability in the workplace, when handled correctly can be a powerful leadership tool that fosters trust, connection, and innovation. It involves being authentic, transparent, and willing to show one's emotions and acknowledge weaknesses. By embracing vulnerability, leaders can create a safe environment for teams, encouraging communication and collaboration.

Several techniques were provided to help you create an environment that allows vulnerability in the workplace.

What techniques do you plan to use over the next week to create a safe environment that embraces vulnerability for you and your employees? What is one way you plan to be vulnerable working with your staff?

"To share your weakness is to make yourself vulnerable; to make yourself vulnerable is to show your strength."
- Brené Brown

Understanding One's Weaknesses and Strengths

"That is why, for Christ's sake, I delight in weaknesses, in results, in hardships, in persecutions, in difficulties. For when I am weak, then I am strong."
- 2 Corinthians 12:10

HISTORICAL FIGURE:
General George Washington

This week I am discussing the topic of understanding one's weaknesses and strengths. I would like to share a historical perspective to illustrate this topic.

The story that I would like to share is focused on the "Father of our Nation"—The First President of the United States. Of course I am talking about George Washington. This story takes places in Colonial America during the *Revolutionary War* (1775-1783). George Washington was appointed the commander of the *Continental Army* in 1775. A compelling historical narrative demonstrating the interplay of strengths and weaknesses can be found in the story of George Washington during the *American Revolutionary War*. While lauded as a strategic leader and a symbol of resilience, he also faced significant tactical challenges and personal limitations.

There were several "strengths" George Washington possessed in commanding the *Continental Army*. He had a remarkable ability to see the "big picture" and plan for the long term, which was crucial for maintaining the *Continental Army's* morale and ultimately winning the war. Despite facing numerous defeats and setbacks, Washington never lost sight of the goal of independence, inspiring his troops to continue fighting. General Washington was able to adjust his strategies based on the changing circumstances of the war, learning from his mistakes and evolving his approach. He inspired loyalty and dedication from his troops, even during periods of hardship and low morale.

There is an amazing story about George Washington that describes an amazing strength in character and fighting spirit. During the battle on July 9, 1755, Washington was in the thick of the fighting, and despite his horse being shot out from under him twice and his coat being pierced by bullets, he remained uninjured.

Washington himself described his survival as a miracle, believing he was protected by God's providence, a sentiment echoed in his letter to his brother.

Fifteen years after the battle, Washington and his physician, Dr. Craik, encountered a sachem from one of the tribes that fought against the British. The sachem's name was Chief Red Hawk. Chief Red Hawk was identified as the leader of the Native forces, and recounted how he specifically gave orders to shoot George Washington.

Chief Red Hawk stated he shot at Washington eleven times, but every single shot missed its intended target.

Believing that a higher power was protecting Washington, the warriors ceased fire, and the commander himself became convinced of Washington's divine protection.

This story was later recounted, solidifying the legend that Washington was fated to be a great leader. Many in the young American nation later viewed this event as proof of destiny's hand, believing that God had protected Washington to ensure the future birth of the United States.

George Washington's weaknesses included his limited tactical skill, particularly early in the *Revolutionary War.* This led to repeated dangers and a history of losing more battles than he won. He was also an awkward and embarrassed public speaker, as evidenced by his nervous delivery of his first address to Congress. Additionally, his appointment as commander was political, and he initially had limited military experience. This lack of experience resulted in him having to do extensive on-the-job training. There are also several noted weaknesses with General Washington's charge. While a strong strategist, Washington sometimes struggled with the finer details of battlefield tactics. George Washington is considered to have been a poor military tactician early in the *Revolutionary War*, most notably during the New York and New Jersey campaign in 1776. His cautious approach, while understanding given the circumstances, sometimes hindered his ability to seize opportunities or respond decisively to enemy movements.

General Washington battled with self-doubt, depression, and anger, which he often had to manage to maintain his leadership role. Prior to the war, Washington's military experience was primarily in frontier warfare, and he lacked formal training in European-style warfare, which sometimes put him at a disadvantage, according to *Washington Crossing Historic Park*.

In essence, Washington's story highlights that even a great leader can have weaknesses. Recognizing and addressing these limitations while leveraging strengths is vital for success, even in the face of seemingly insurmountable challenges.

Here's a more detailed look at why this understanding is important:

Leveraging Strengths:
- **Maximizing Potential:** Knowing your strengths allows you to focus your efforts on activities where you naturally excel, leading to greater impact and satisfaction.
- **Career Advancement:** Identifying your strengths helps you narrow down career options, highlight your unique skills to employers, and ultimately lead to more fulfilling work.

- **Personal Growth:** By recognizing your strengths, you can set ambitious goals and pursue opportunities that align with your natural talents.
- **Building Confidence:** When you are aware of your strengths and can utilize them effectively, your self-esteem and confidence naturally increase.

Addressing Weaknesses:

- **Identifying Areas for Improvement:** Understanding your weaknesses allows you to pinpoint areas where you may need additional support or training.
- **Developing Mitigation Strategies:** Knowing your weaknesses enables you to develop strategies to compensate for them, either by seeking help from others or by finding alternative approaches.
- **Avoiding Pitfalls:** Being aware of your weaknesses can help you avoid situations or tasks where you are likely to struggle, preventing frustration and setbacks.
- **Promoting Self-Acceptance:** Acknowledging your weaknesses can be a sign of strength and self-awareness, fostering a more realistic and accepting view of yourself.

In essence, understanding your strengths and weaknesses is a fundamental aspect of self-awareness, which is crucial for personal and professional development. It allows you to make informed decisions, set realistic goals, and navigate challenges with greater confidence.

HOW DO YOU DO THIS?

Understanding one's strengths and weaknesses involves honest self-reflection, seeking feedback, and analyzing past experiences to identify areas of excellence and areas needing improvement. It's a continuous process of self-discovery that allows for personal and professional growth.

Here's a breakdown of how to understand your strengths and weaknesses:

1. Self-Reflection:

- **Consider Past Experiences:** Think about situations where you excelled and received positive feedback. What skills were you using?
- **Analyze Tasks You Enjoy:** What activities come naturally to you? What do you find yourself drawn to?
- **Identify Areas of Struggle:** What tasks do you find challenging or avoid? What feedback have you received that highlights areas for improvement?

2. Seeking Feedback:

- **Talk to Trusted Individuals:** Ask friends, family, or colleagues for their honest opinions on your strengths and weaknesses. They may offer insights you haven't considered.
- **Review Performance Evaluations:** Look for patterns in past feedback from employers or mentors. What areas have they consistently pointed out for development?

3. Using Assessments:

- **Take Personality or Skills Assessments:** Tools like Strengths-Finder can provide insights into your natural tendencies and areas where you might excel.
- **Use SWOT Analysis:** This framework can help you identify your strengths, weaknesses, opportunities, and threats.

4. Focusing on Growth:

- **Turn Weaknesses Into Opportunities:** Recognize that weaknesses are not fixed and can be improved with effort.
- **Develop a Plan for Improvement:** Set specific goals and create a plan to address your weaknesses.

- **Seek for Support:** Don't hesitate to ask for help from mentors, coaches, or colleagues as you work on developing your weaknesses.

By consistently reflecting on your experiences, seeking feedback, and actively working on self-improvement, you gain a deeper understanding of your strengths and weaknesses, ultimately leading to greater personal and professional success.

"Sometimes our greatest strength comes when we understand our greatest weakness."
- Yankee Doodle Dave

LEADERSHIP CHALLENGE

Here is my challenge to you:

This week we learned about the story of General Washington in the *Revolutionary War* and the importance of understanding your strengths and weaknesses. In summary, vulnerability in leadership is not a weakness, but a strength that can transform the work environment, boost performance, and create a culture of trust, innovation, and engagement.

Understanding your strengths and weaknesses in the workplace is crucial for personal and professional growth. Self-awareness, facilitated by tools like performance reviews, self-assessments, 360-degree feedback, helps individuals focus on their strengths and develop areas needing improvement. This knowledge enables better job performance, increased productivity, and enhanced career satisfaction.

There were several techniques that have been provided to help you understand the importance of strengths and weaknesses in the workplace.

What techniques do you plan to use over the next week to identify your strengths and weaknesses?

____

____

____

____

____

"Sometimes you don't realize your own strength until you come face to face with your greatest weakness." - Susan Gale

Leaders Make Informed Decisions

"If any of you lacks wisdom, let him ask God, who gives generously to without reproach, and it will be given to him."

- James 1:5

HISTORICAL FIGURE:
Warren Buffet - Acquisition of See's Candies

Making informed decisions means choosing after carefully considering available information, options, and potential consequences. It's about using knowledge and understanding to make choices that are well-reasoned and likely to lead to positive outcomes, rather than relying on chance or incomplete information.

This week I would like to share a story that illustrates making an informed decision. It involves two very well-known names. Those are Warren Buffett and See's Candies.

Warren Buffett is primarily known as one of the world's most successful investors and philanthropists. He is the chairman and CEO of Berkshire Hathaway, a multinational conglomerate holding company. Buffett's investment success, particularly his long-term, value-oriented approach, has earned him the nickname *"The Oracle of Omaha."* He is also known for his philanthropic efforts, including his pledge to donate the vast majority of his wealth to charitable causes.

See's Candies is known for its high-quality, delicious chocolates and candies, made with Mary See's original recipes and fresh, high-quality ingredients. They are also recognized for their commitment to tradition, taste, service, and quality, with a focus on maintaining the original recipes and avoiding preservatives. Additionally, See's is known for its iconic black and white shops, its large-scale production of lollipops, and its history with famous personalities like Lucille Ball and Cher.

Warren Buffett and See's Candies seemed like two completely different things from two different worlds. Strange as it may seem, but both those worlds collided. One of the most famous examples of Warren Buffett making an informed decision is his acquisition of See's Candies in 1972. While initially hesitant about the purchase price, Buffett was eventually persuaded by Charlie Munger to recognize the intangible value of the brand and the strength of its competitive advantage.

Buffett and Munger saw beyond the immediate financial statements to understand the deeper qualities of See's Candies. The company possessed a strong brand reputation, customer loyalty, and pricing power that allowed it to raise prices without losing business. This was a shift in their thinking, as their prior investment strategy was more focused on finding bargains based on financial metrics alone.

See's ability to raise prices consistently without sacrificing sales volume revealed a crucial competitive advantage that Buffett later termed an *"economic moat."* This pricing power was a result of the brand's strength and the emotional connection customers had with See's chocolates. Buffett's investment in See's demonstrated a deepened understanding of businesses with a durable competitive advantage.

Instead of prioritizing short-term gains or rapid expansion, Buffett chose to preserve See's quality and focus on slow and steady growth. He recognized that sacrificing quality to increase sales would jeopardize the brand's value and undermine its competitive advantage. This long-term approach, driven by a deep understanding of the business, paid off significantly over time.

See's Candies had minimal capital requirements and generated high cash returns, allowing Berkshire Hathaway to redeploy the excess cash into other attractive investments. This showcased Buffett's expertise in capital allocation, where cash generated by one profitable business could be strategically deployed to fuel growth in other areas.

In short, the story of See's Candies demonstrates how Buffett's informed decisions, guided by a focus on intangible assets, pricing power, long-term potential, and strategic capital allocation, contributed to Berkshire Hathaway's remarkable success.

There are several takeaways that we can have from this story. Warren Buffett's success stems from a disciplined approach to making informed decisions, extending beyond finance. Some of those principles are patience, discipline, independent thinking, continuous learning, emotional control and learning from your mistakes.

HOW DO YOU DO THIS?

Leaders make informed decisions by gathering and analyzing information, defining clear objectives, evaluating alternatives, considering stakeholder input, and reflecting on past decisions. They also need to balance data with intuition, consider the context, and be adaptable to changing circumstances.

Here's a more detailed breakdown:

1. Define the Problem and Objectives:

- Clearly articulate the issue at hand and the desired outcome.
- Understand the root cause and the impact of the problem.
- Establish specific, measurable, achievable, relevant, and time-bound (SMART) goals.

2. Gather and Analyze Information:

- Collect relevant data and insights from various sources, including market trends, customer feedback, and financial metrics.
- Seek expert opinions and diverse perspectives to avoid biases.
- Use data analytics tools and techniques to identify patterns and trends.

3. Evaluate Alternatives:

- Generate multiple potential solutions or options.
- Assess the risks, benefits, and long-term consequences of each option.
- Consider using decision-making frameworks or matrices to compare options.

Good leaders must make informed decisions to effectively lead. This involves gathering all relevant information, analyzing it thoroughly, and then choosing the best course of action based on that analysis. Informed decision-making minimizes risks, maximizes opportunities, and leads to better outcomes for the organization.

Here's a more detailed breakdown:

- **Gathering Information:** Good leaders don't jump to conclusions. They take the time to collect data and insights from various sources, including team members, experts, and relevant research.
- **Analyzing Information:** Once the information is gathered, it needs to be analyzed to identify patterns, trends, and potential implications. This step helps in understanding the situation and making well-reasoned judgments.
- **Considering Alternatives:** Instead of settling for the first solution that comes to mind, explore different options and evaluate their potential consequences before making a choice.

By following these steps, leaders can develop strong decision-making skills and improve their overall effectiveness.

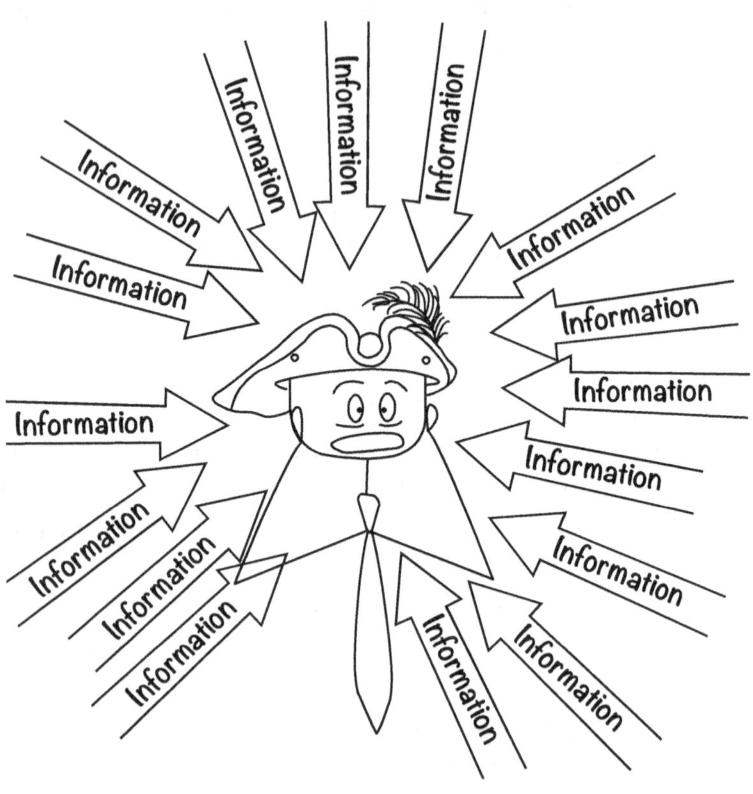

"Withholding information that would allow someone to make an informed decision is betrayal. Lying through omission is still lying."

- Yankee Doodle Dave

LEADERSHIP CHALLENGE

In the story of Warren Buffett and his acquisition of See's Candies he made plenty of informed decisions.

In summary, informed decision-making involves a structured process of gathering information, analyzing options, and assessing potential outcomes before making a choice. It is a process that moves beyond impulse or guesswork by grounding decisions in facts and data.

Making informed decisions in the workplace involves a systemic approach to gathering and analyzing information to choose the best course of action. It is critical for achieving organizational goals and minimizing potential risks.

There were several techniques provided to help you understand the importance of making informed decisions.

What techniques do you plan to use to help you make informed decisions?

Leaders Are Intrinsically Motivated

"Whatever you do, work at it wholeheartedly as though you were doing it for the Lord and not merely for people."

- Colossians 3:23

HISTORICAL FIGURE:
Albert Einstein, Theoretical Physicist

There are two (2) types of motivation that leaders can exercise. Those are: Intrinsically Motivated and Extrinsically Motivated.

Extrinsic motivation is where individuals are motivated to perform an activity to earn a reward or avoid punishment. Intrinsic motivation is where individuals perform an activity for their own sake and personal rewards. Intrinsic motivation is the driving motivation behind engaging in an activity for its inherent satisfaction, pleasure and enjoyment rather than external rewards or recognition. It is the feeling of being drawn to a task because it is personally fulfilling, interesting and challenging.

Albert Einstein was born in Germany in 1879. He was granted American citizenship on October 1, 1940. He previously renounced his German citizenship due to the rise of the Nazi party and the persecution of Jewish people.

When Albert Einstein was four or five years old, he was sick in bed. His father gave him a magnetic compass. He was deeply impressed and fascinated by the compass needle's ability to consistently point north, guided by an invisible force. This experience sparked a sense of wonder and curiosity about the unseen forces governing the world and the mysteries of the universe.

His compass was inscribed with the following words *"holy zeal."* This was a critical moment in his life. This was a key moment that ignited his passion for science and his lifelong pursuit of understanding the universe. He later stated that he pursued his studies in theoretical physics with a *"holy zeal"* at home, sometimes even skipping school to learn what truly motivated him.

Einstein wasn't limited by formal schooling and actively tailored his learning, including studying theoretical physics masters in his own time. He sought out challenging material and developed a unique perspective that allowed him to approach problems differently and find creative solutions. During this time, he did not seek external rewards. His motivation was not primarily driven by external rewards like fame or recognition, but rather the internal satisfaction of understanding the physical world.

Einstein's intrinsic motivation meant he was not easily swayed by the prevailing scientific dogma. His mathematics professor, Hermann Minkowski, once called Einstein a *"lazy dog."* Yet, years later, Minkowski developed a geometric representation of Einstein's special theory of relativity.

In developing his theory of general relativity, Einstein demonstrated a genius for reconciling two common-sense principles by discarding a third, long-held belief in absolute measurements of space and time. This came from a deeply personal, intuitive grasp of physics.

For the last three decades of his life, Einstein pursued a fruitless search for a unified field theory that would combine gravity and electromagnetism. He was driven by an aesthetic and intellectual need to unify the forces of nature, a pursuit he found profoundly necessary, even as others found it a quixotic, dead-end quest.

Intrinsic motivation, driven by internal factors like passion and purpose, is crucial for effective leadership as it fosters a more engaged, productive, and resilient team. Intrinsically motivated leaders inspire others through their commitment and enthusiasm, creating a positive work environment and encouraging innovation. They are more likely to develop a transformational leadership style, focusing on long-term goals and fostering a sense of purpose among their team members.

Here's a more detailed look at the importance of intrinsic motivation in leaders:

1. Enhanced Engagement and Productivity:

- Intrinsically motivated leaders are passionate about their work and inspire similar passion in their teams.
- This passion translates into increased engagement, with team members feeling more connected to their work and motivated to perform at their best.
- When leaders are intrinsically motivated, they tend to create a positive work environment that fosters creativity, innovation, and a sense of accomplishment.

2. Fostering a Transformational Leadership Style:

- Intrinsic motivation often leads to a transformational leadership style, where leaders inspire and motivate their teams to achieve a shared vision.
- They focus on empowering their team members, fostering a sense of ownership, and encouraging them to develop their skills and abilities.
- This approach leads to higher levels of employee engagement, satisfaction, and ultimately, better performance.

3. Resilience and Long-Term Focus:

- Intrinsically motivated leaders are driven by a deeper sense of purpose and meaning, making them more resilient in the face of challenges.
- They are less likely to be derailed by setbacks and are more focused on achieving long-term goals, inspiring their teams to persevere through difficult times.
- Their passion and commitment can be contagious, creating a culture of perseverance and determination within the team.

4. Building Trust and Connection:

- Leaders who are driven by intrinsic motivation are more likely to build strong relationships with their team members based on trust and mutual respect.
- They are more attuned to the needs and motivations of their team members, fostering a sense of belonging and connection.
- This sense of connection can lead to increased collaboration, open communication, and a more supportive work environment.

5. Promoting the Culture of Growth and Development:

- Intrinsically motivated leaders are often invested in the growth and development of their team members.
- They create opportunities for learning, skill development, and career advancement, fostering a culture of continuous improvement.
- This focus on growth and development not only benefits individual team members but also contributes to the overall success of the organization

HOW DO YOU DO THIS?

Leaders can foster intrinsic motivation by focusing on purpose, autonomy, and mastery for themselves and their teams. This involves creating a work environment where employees feel connected to a meaningful purpose, have autonomy over their work, and have opportunities to develop their skills and expertise. Leaders should also cultivate a culture of trust, recognition, and continuous learning to support intrinsic motivation.

Here's a more detailed breakdown:

1. Purpose and Meaning:

- **Connect Work to a Larger Mission:** Leaders can help employees understand how their daily tasks contribute to the organization's overall goals and values.
- **Share the "Why":** Explain the reasons behind changes and decisions, fostering a sense of understanding and ownership.
- **Highlight Impact:** Emphasize the positive impact of employees' work on others, whether it's customers, colleagues, or the broader community.

2. Autonomy and Empowerment:

- **Delegate Effectively:** Give employees clear responsibilities and freedom to make decisions within their roles.
- **Encourage Ownership:** Foster a sense of accountability and pride in their work.
- **Provide Support, Not Control:** Offer guidance and resources while allowing employees to find their own solutions.

3. Mastery and Growth:

- **Offer Opportunities for Learning:** Provide training, mentorship, and challenging projects that allow employees to develop new skills.
- **Recognize Progress:** Acknowledge and celebrate achievements, both big and small, to build confidence and motivation.
- **Encourage Continuous Improvement:** Foster a mindset of growth and development, where employees are always striving to improve their performance.

By focusing on these key areas, leaders can create a workplace where intrinsic motivation thrives, leading to increased engagement, productivity, and overall success.

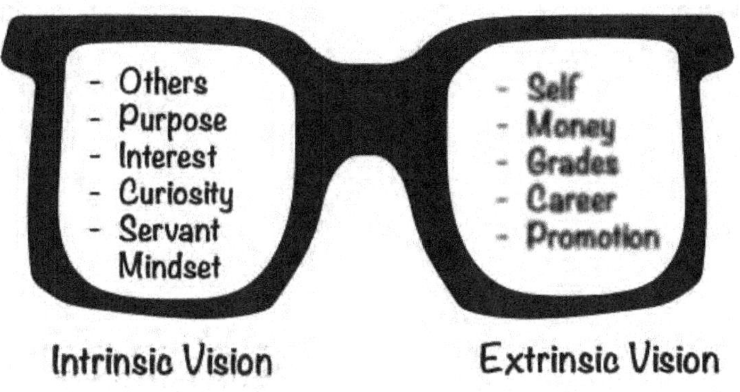

"Pay attention to what life looks like when you look at life through my glasses. Focus on the Intrinsic Vision, and all those other things on the Extrinsic side will fall into place."

- Yankee Doodle Dave

LEADERSHIP CHALLENGE

Here is my challenge to you:

In the story of Albert Einstein, we learned that he was Intrinsically Motivated. In summary, Intrinsic Motivation is the drive to engage in activities for the inherent satisfaction, enjoyment, or challenge they provide, rather than for external rewards or pressures. This stems from internal desires and leads to a deeper engagement with tasks, fostering creativity, persistence, and a sense of fulfillment.

Making informed decisions in the workplace involves a systemic approach to gathering and analyzing information to choose the best course of action. It is critical for achieving organizational goals and minimizing potential risks.

There were several techniques provided to help you understand the difference between extrinsically and intrinsically motivated.

What techniques do you plan to use over the next week to help you find your intrinsic motivation?

____

____

____

____

____

____

____

____

____

____

____

____

____

It's Important to Have a Clear Vision

"And the Lord answered me, and said, 'Write the vision, and make it plain upon tables, that he may run that readeth it.'"

- Habakkuk 2:2

HISTORICAL FIGURE:
Helen Keller, American Author

Leaders with a vision have a clear idea of what they want to achieve and the steps they need to get there. They can articulate this vision in a way that motivates and inspires others.

Vision is crucial for setting long-term goals and aligning the team's efforts towards achieving them. For example, a non-profit leader who outlines a strategic plan to eradicate a social issue and regularly communicates this vision to volunteers and donors can effectively galvanize support and resources toward the cause.

This is an incredible story of an American leader who displayed enormous perseverance and creativity. Her name is Helen Keller. Allow me to share a powerful illustration of the difference between physical sight and having a vision.

Helen Keller lost both her vision and her hearing at a young age. Her life was full of challenges, but she didn't let her disabilities define her. She learned to communicate, earned a college degree, became a writer, a lecturer and an activist.

Keller's vision propelled her to achieve these things. She had a clear sense of what she wanted to accomplish, and her determination allowed her to overcome the barriers in her path.

Helen Keller's experience resonates with everyone. Having a vision allows individuals to pursue their goals, overcome challenges, and make a meaningful impact on the world. In essence, her story is a testament to the idea that true vision extends beyond physical sight. It's about having a clear purpose, setting goals, and using that vision to navigate life's journey, regardless of the obstacles encountered.

Helen Keller co-founded the American Civil Liberties Union (ACLU) in 1920 alongside Jane Addams, Crystal Eastman, and other social activists. She used her platform to advocate for various social and political causes beyond disability rights. Many of those causes were women's suffrage, workers' rights, and racial justice. Driven by a belief in collective good and interconnected struggles against oppression, Keller's activism for civil liberties and social change was extensive and continued throughout her life.

Helen Keller was a multifaceted activist who championed a wide array of progressive causes.

She supported the rights of workers and unionism, and was an associate of the socialist Eugene Debs. Keller was a vocal advocate for women's suffrage, believing that women's needs were just as genuine as men's. An early supporter of the NAACP, she used her voice to condemn racism and lynching, connecting the struggle for disability rights to the fight for racial justice.

A clear vision is crucial for leaders as it provides direction, motivates teams, and ensures everyone is working towards the same goals. Without a clear vision, efforts can become disjointed, and the organization may lack focus and purpose, hinder progress and potentially lead to failure. A strong vision inspires, aligns, and guides decision-making, ultimately driving success.

Here's a more detailed look at why a clear vision is so important:

- **Provides Direction:** A clear vision acts as a roadmap, guiding the organization towards a desired future state. It helps leaders and their teams understand where they are going and what they need to do to get there.
- **Motivates and Inspires:** A compelling vision can inspire employees, fostering a sense of purpose and commitment. When people understand the "why" behind their work, they are more likely to be engaged and motivated.
- **Aligns Efforts:** A shared vision ensures that everyone is working towards the same goals, minimizing confusion and maximizing efficiency. This alignment is crucial for effective teamwork and coordinated action.
- **Facilitates Decision-Making:** When faced with choices, a clear vision provides a framework for decision-making, to help leaders choose the best path based on the overall goals.

HOW DO YOU DO THIS?

A leader can cultivate a clear vision by focusing on long-term goals, understanding core values, and communicating effectively. This involves envisioning the desired future state, aligning it with organizational values, and inspiring others to work towards it.

Here's a more detailed breakdown:

1. Define the Vision:

- **Set Clear Goals:** Establish specific, measurable, achievable, relevant, and time bound (SMART) goals that align with the overall vision.

2. Communicate the Vision:

- **Be Clear and Concise:** Express the vision in a way that is easily understood by everyone, avoiding jargon and complex language.

- **Tell a Compelling Story:** Use narratives and examples to illustrate the vision and connect it to people's emotions and aspirations.
- **Lead by Example:** Demonstrate commitment to the vision through actions and behaviors, inspiring others to follow.

3. Execute the Vision:

- **Prioritize and Plan:** Break down the vision into actionable steps and create a roadmap for achieving the goals.
- **Adapt and Learn:** Be flexible and willing to adjust the vision and plans as needed, based on feedback and changing circumstances.
- **Celebrate Successes:** Acknowledge and celebrate milestones along the way to maintain motivation and momentum.

By focusing on these aspects, leaders can develop and communicate a clear vision that inspires, motivates, and guides their teams towards a shared future.

"Vision has to do with your deepest desires and what connects you to that desire."

- Yankee Doodle Dave

LEADERSHIP CHALLENGE

Here is my challenge to you:

In the story of Helen Keller, we learned that she lost both her sight and her hearing; however, she led a life that had a clear vision.

In summary, a clear vision in the workplace provides direction, purpose, and alignment, leading to increased employee engagement, productivity, and overall success. It acts as a roadmap during times of change, guiding decisions and fostering a sense of shared purpose. A clear vision helps employees understand how their daily tasks contribute to the larger organizational goals.

There were several techniques that have been provided to help you understand the importance of establishing a clear vision.

What techniques do you plan to use over the next week to ensure that you have a clear vision in your work center?

"Vision without action is a dream. Action without vision is simply passing the time. Action with vision is making a positive difference."
- Joel Barker

The Buck Stops with You; Leaders Are Accountable

*"So, whoever knows the right thing to do
and fails to do, for him it is sin."*

- James 4:17

HISTORICAL FIGURE:
Harry S. Truman, 33rd President of the United States

There are several examples to further illustrate the concept of accountability.

Allow me to share a story about Harry S. Truman, the 33rd President of the United States from 1945 to 1953. He was the 34th vice president in 1945, he assumed the presidency upon the death of Franklin D. Roosevelt that year.

On April 12, 1945, Vice President Harry S. Truman was summoned to the White House and told by Eleanor Roosevelt that President Franklin D. Roosevelt had died. Having been Vice President for only 82 days, Truman was shocked and overwhelmed, famously telling reporters, *"I felt like the moon, the stars, and all the planets had fallen on me."*

This moment marks the beginning of a president thrust into power while feeling profoundly unprepared but who rose to the challenge by embracing accountability.

Roosevelt's inner circle had largely kept Truman in the dark, and Truman was not in FDR's confidence. The former haberdasher, with only a high-school education, was excluded from key meetings and received no briefing on the major issues. The term "haberdasher" is not used in modern conversations. For those that may not be aware of what that may be, a haberdasher would be a person who primarily deals in men's clothing. Most crucially, he was completely unaware of the Manhattan Project, the top-secret mission developing an atomic bomb.

The sudden death of FDR, whom the public had worshiped for years, meant Truman had to immediately handle immense responsibilities with little preparation, including:

- The closing stages of World War II in Europe and the Pacific.
- The decision of whether to use the atomic bomb on Japan.
- The beginning of the Cold War and mounting tensions with the Soviet Union.
- The transition from a wartime economy to a peacetime one.

Despite his initial shock and unease, Truman was a student of history who knew the enormity of the role he was about to fill. He decided to "face the music" and approach the presidency with a sense of humility and absolute responsibility.

Harry S. Truman is renowned for his commitment to accountability, famously displaying "*The Buck Stops Here*" desk sign. This motto symbolized his willingness to accept responsibility for all decisions made during his presidency, both successes and failures. A prominent example of this is his decision to use atomic bombs on Japan.

President Truman famously said, *"The blood is on my hands."*

Truman's presidency also saw him tackle the challenges of the *Cold War, the Korean War* and the beginnings of the *Civil Rights Movement*, all while maintaining a focus on integrity and responsibility.

The phrase *"the buck stops here"* originated from the slang expression *"pass the buck."* This highlighted Truman's rejection of shirking responsibility. He believed that the president must own the consequences of their decisions.

Truman's presidency was marked by a focus on integrity and accountability in both domestic and foreign policy. He believed that leaders must be held responsible for their actions and that transparency and honesty were essential to good governance.

President Truman's emphasis on accountability served as an example for others, inspiring leaders to embrace responsibility and avoid passing the buck. In essence, Truman's story of accountability is a testament to the importance of taking ownership of one's actions and decisions, especially in positions of leadership. President Truman led by example and truly understood the concept of personal accountability.

Accountability is crucial in leadership because it fosters trust, improves performance, and strengthens team cohesion. When leaders demonstrate accountability, they set a positive example for their teams, encouraging them to take ownership of their work and contribute to a culture of responsibility. This, in turn, leads to better outcomes and a more productive work environment.

Here's a more detailed look at why accountability is so important:

1. FOSTERING TRUST AND CREDIBILITY:

- **Demonstrates Integrity:** When leaders admit their mistakes and take responsibility, it builds trust and credibility with their team members.
- **Reduces Ambiguity:** Clear accountability minimizes confusion and uncertainty, allowing team members to understand expectations and their roles.
- **Builds Confidence:** Accountability ensures that promises are kept, and commitments are followed through, leading to greater confidence in the leader's ability.

2. Improving Performance and Results:

- **Encourages Ownership:** Accountability encourages individuals to take ownership of their work and its outcomes, leading to increased motivation and better performance.

- **Drives Continuous Improvement:** When leaders and teams are held accountable, they are more likely to identify areas for improvement and strive for excellence.
- **Aligns Efforts:** Accountability helps align individual and team efforts with organizational goals, ensuring everyone is working towards the same objectives.

3. Strengthening Team Cohesion:

- **Promotes Collaboration:** When team members know they are accountable to each other, it fosters a sense of shared responsibility and encourages collaboration.
- **Reduces Conflict:** Clear expectations and accountability can minimize misunderstanding and conflicts that may arise from unclear roles or responsibilities.
- **Creates a Positive Culture:** A culture of accountability promotes a sense of fairness, respect, and mutual support, leading to a more positive and productive work environment.

4. Other Benefits:

- **Better Decision-Making:** Leaders who are accountable are more likely to make thoughtful and strategic decisions, as they know they will be held responsible for the outcomes.
- **Increased Employee Engagement:** When employees feel valued and accountable, they are more likely to be engaged and motivated in their work.
- **Improved Problem-Solving:** Accountability encourages a proactive approach to problem-solving, as individuals are more likely to be engaged and motivated in their work.

HOW DO YOU DO THIS?

Leaders demonstrate accountability by taking ownership of their actions and decisions, both successes and failures, and by fostering a culture of transparency and trust within their teams. This includes clearly communicating goals, following through on commitments, and admitting mistakes with a focus on learning and improvement.

Key Actions:

- **Taking Responsibility:** Leaders accept responsibility for their actions and decisions, rather than shifting blame.
- **Owning Up to Mistakes:** They acknowledge when they make mistakes, showing humility and a willingness to learn from them.
- **Fostering Transparency:** Leaders are open and honest about their plans, actions, and the reasons behind them.
- **Setting Clear Goals and Expectations:** They communicate goals and expectations clearly, ensuring everyone understands their roles and responsibilities.
- **Following Through on Commitments:** They do what they say they will do, building trust and reliability.

"People who can't communicate think everything is an argument. People who lack accountability think everything is an attack."

- Yankee Doodle Dave

LEADERSHIP CHALLENGE

Here is my challenge to you:

In the story of President Truman, we learned about his level of personal accountability. He was the one who stated that "*The Buck Stops with Him.*" He felt as if he was ultimately responsible and accountable.

In summary, accountability in the workplace means that all members of a work center are responsible for their actions, behaviors, performance, and decisions. It is about taking ownership of one's work and being answerable to the results, both good and bad. This includes fulfilling assigned tasks, maintaining quality work, collaborating effectively, and communicating with management. Accountability is not just about individual tasks, but also about the impact of one's actions on the team and the organization.

There were several techniques that have been provided to help you understand the concept of accountability in the work center.

What techniques do you plan to use over the next week to ensure that you build an environment that establishes accountability in your work center?

"A culture of accountability makes a good organization great and a great organization unstoppable."
- Henry Evans

Slow to Speak

"My dear brothers and sisters, take note of this: Every-one should be quick to listen, slow to speak and slow to become angry."

- James 1:19

HISTORICAL FIGURE:
Calvin Coolidge, 30th President of the United States

"*Slow to speak*" means to be cautious and deliberate in one's speech, taking time to consider what is said before speaking. It emphasizes the importance of listening attentively to others and carefully weighing one's words, rather than speaking impulsively or carelessly.

This week I would like to share a story about our 30th President of the United States, Calvin Coolidge. He served in office from 1923-1929. President Calvin Coolidge, known as *"Silent Cal,"* was famous for his slow and deliberate speech, a trait that gave rise to many anecdotes.

Raised in rural Plymouth Notch, Vermont, Coolidge learned the value of economical speech from his father. His quiet, frugal nature was a product of his modest, small-town roots.

Coolidge's reserved nature earned him the nickname *"Silent Cal,"* and shows that speaking less can be an advantage, particularly in politics. By carefully choosing words and sometimes remaining silent, he avoided rash statements or unnecessary controversies. In a world of constant communication, especially with the rise of social media, politicians can learn from Coolidge's example to be more deliberate and concise in their communication to avoid mistakes and maintain a positive public image.

President Coolidge himself noted, *"No man ever listened himself out of a job."*

His quietness suggests a strong emphasis on listening and absorbing information, rather than feeling pressured to constantly express opinions or dominate conversations. This skill can be invaluable in leadership, allowing for a better understanding of different perspectives before acting.

Coolidge believed in the power of speaking sparingly. He also understood that the words of a president carried enormous weight and should not be used indiscriminately.

On June 30, 1924, 16-year-old Calvin, Jr., was playing tennis on the White House court with his brother, John. He was not wearing socks and developed a blister on his toe. The blister became infected with a Staphylococcus albus bacteria, and the infection soon spread to his bloodstream.

As his condition worsened, he was taken to Walter Reed Hospital. At the time, antibiotics like penicillin had not yet been discovered. Despite the efforts of multiple doctors, they could do little to stop the advancing infection. He died a week later at age 16. The loss devastated the Coolidges. In his autobiography, the president wrote that "the power and the glory of the Presidency went with him."

Coolidge's restrained nature was a stark contrast to the flamboyant, freewheeling culture of the 1920s. Yet, his silent, frugal persona appealed to many Americans who saw him as respectable and responsible.

Calvin Coolidge's leadership style was often characterized by a philosophical dislike of excessive government and a focus on established principles like thrift, economy, and limited government intervention. His lack of pronouncements on every issue allowed the country to thrive under a period of economic prosperity, leading some to refer to it as *"Coolidge Prosperity."*

Despite his quiet demeanor, Coolidge understood the importance of public relations. He used methods like regular press conferences, photography, and radio addresses to connect with the public and project an image of a prudent, no-nonsense leader. He knew when and how to leverage the media to his advantage, despite his reserved nature.

Coolidge offered some wisdom regarding his approach to communication:

"If you don't say anything, you won't be called on to repeat it."
"I have never been hurt by what I have not said."

In essence, Calvin Coolidge's "silent" approach teaches the importance of thoughtful communication, strategic silence, and the power of listening, especially in the context of leadership and public life.

Leaders should be slow to speak to foster better communication, build trust, and encourage diverse perspectives within their teams. By listening more and speaking less, leaders can create a more inclusive environment where team members feel valued and empowered to contribute to their ideas, leading to better decision-making and stronger team cohesion.

Here's a more detailed explanation:

- **Encourage Active Listening:** When leaders are quick to speak, they may miss valuable insights and perspectives from others. Being slow to speak allows leaders to truly listen to what their team members are saying, both verbally and non-verbally, which can lead to a better understanding of the situation and the needs of the team.

- **Foster Trust and Respect:** When leaders demonstrate that they value the input of others by actively listening, it fosters a sense of trust and respect within the team. Team members are more likely to feel comfortable sharing their ideas and concerns when they know they will be heard and considered.
- **Reduce Assumptions and Errors:** Speaking too quickly can lead to assumptions and hasty decisions. By taking the time to listen and process information, leaders can avoid making mistakes based on incomplete or inaccurate information.

HOW DO YOU DO THIS?

A leader can demonstrate they are slow to speak by pausing before responding, asking clarifying questions, and actively listening to others. They can also show this through their non-verbal cues, like maintaining eye contact and nodding to show they are engaged, and by encouraging others to share their thoughts and ideas.

Here's a more detailed breakdown:

1. Pausing Before Speaking:

- **Taking a Moment to Reflect:** A leader can pause for a few seconds after someone finishes speaking before offering a response. This demonstrates that they are considering the information and not just reacting impulsively.
- **Using Pauses for Emphasis:** Pauses can also be used to draw attention to key points or allow time for the audience to process information.
- **Avoiding Filler Words:** Reducing filler words like "um," "like," and "you know" can help a leader sound more confident and thoughtful.

2. Asking for Clarifying Questions:

- **Ensuring Understanding:** Leaders can ask questions to confirm they understand the speaker's message, such as *"Can you clarify what you mean by...?"* or *"Could you elaborate on...?"*
- **Encouraging Deeper Thinking:** Thoughtful questions can also encourage others to think more deeply about their own ideas.
- **Paying Attention:** Leaders should try to truly listen to what others are saying, both verbally and nonverbally.
- **Providing Feedback:** Leaders can show they are listening by summarizing what they've heard, asking follow-up questions, and offering feedback.
- **Creating a Safe Space:** Creating a safe and open environment where team members feel comfortable sharing their thoughts and concerns is crucial for effective listening.

4. Non-Verbal Cues:

- **Eye Contact:** Maintaining eye contact shows that the leader is engaged and paying attention.
- **Nodding:** Nodding can signal that the leader is following the conversation and understanding what is being said.
- **Body Language:** Open and attentive body language can further demonstrate active listening.

5. Encouraging Others:

- **Valuing Diverse Perspectives:** A leader who is slow to speak often values the input of others and encourages a variety of viewpoints.
- **Creating Space for Discussion:** They might use techniques like the "speak last" approach in meetings, allowing others to share their ideas before the leader offers their own.
- **Facilitating Dialogue:** Leaders can guide conversations without dominating them, ensuring that everyone has a chance to participate.

"When you are quick to listen and slow to speak, you are much less likely to become angry. Think before you speak, but don't speak everything you think."

- Yankee Doodle Dave

LEADERSHIP CHALLENGE

Here is my challenge to you:

In the story scenario I discussed how President Coolidge developed the nickname of *"Silent Cal"* and the importance of being slow to speak.

In summary, the concept behind *"slow to speak"* in a work center is strongly related to active listening and mindful communication. This is about cultivating the skills of active listening and mindful communication. It is a conscious choice to prioritize understanding and thoughtful response over impulsive reactions. It ultimately leads to improved communication, stronger relationships and better outcomes.

There were several techniques provided to help you understand the concept of "slow to speak."

What techniques do you plan to use over the next week to ensure that you cultivate active listening and mindful communication?

____

____

____

____

____

____

"Speak softly and carry a big stick; you will go far."
- Theodore Roosevelt

Leaders Are Relationship Builders

"Let no corrupting talk come out of your mouths, but only such as is good for building up, as fits the occasion, that it may give grace to those who hear."
- Ephesians 4:29

HISTORICAL FIGURE:
Thomas Jefferson, 3rd President of the United States

This week's lesson deals with the concept of relationship building. To explain this concept allow me to share a short story that involves Thomas Jefferson, the 3rd President of the United States.

Jefferson served as President of the United States from 1801-1809. Thomas Jefferson was lifelong friends with James Madison. Thomas Jefferson and James Madison shared a close and enduring friendship and political alliance spanning five decades. They met in 1776 and bonded over their shared intellect, passion for religious freedom, and love of learning. Jefferson became a mentor to Madison, and their relationship grew into one of the most impactful collaborations in American history. They were neighbors at Monticello and Montpelier, sharing interests in books, science, art, and agriculture. They supported each other through personal and political triumphs and challenges. Their friendship is described as a *"perfectly balanced friendship,"* according to Madison biographer Irving Brant.

The *Compromise of 1790* was a political agreement that resolved a deadlock in U.S. Congress.

This event demonstrates Jefferson's skill in finding common ground and fostering collaboration, even among political opponents. The compromise addressed two major issues of the time: Alexander Hamilton's plan for the federal government to assume state debts from the *Revolutionary War* and the debate over the location of the national capital. Southern states, including Virginia, opposed the debt assumption plan, fearing it would consolidate too much power in the federal government and potentially lead to higher taxes for them. Northern states opposed the relocation of the capital to the South.

To break the deadlock, Jefferson, Hamilton, and James Madison held a private dinner meeting. Madison agreed to support the assumption plan, albeit passively, and rallied some Southern votes. In exchange, Hamilton agreed to garner Northern support for locating the capital on the Potomac River and to lower Virginia's tax rate under the assumption plan. The compromise ultimately led to the passage of both *the Residence Act*, which established the capital in Washington, D.C., and the *Funding Act*, which included the assumption of state debts. While some historians debate the exact impact of the dinner meeting, it highlights Jefferson's willingness to engage in dialogue and negotiation to achieve a mutually beneficial outcome, showcasing a key aspect of his relationship-building skills in a political context.

Thomas Jefferson viewed relationships as essential for both political and personal life, but he was pragmatic in how he approached them. He cultivated friendships with both allies and opponents, though his political rivalries often complicated these dynamics.

Jefferson famously used social settings, like dinners, to build consensus and soften political adversaries. He understood that private, informal conversations were often more effective for negotiation than heated debates in a legislative chamber.

Thomas Jefferson was a keen observer of human nature and political motives. When dealing with his rival John Adams, he once noted that Adams "*is vain, irritable and a bad calculator of the force and probable effect of the motives which govern men,*" but also called him an honest and amiable man. This demonstrates his ability to assess the personalities of his political peers, even those he disagreed with.

He forged a powerful and enduring political alliance with James Madison. Their partnership was foundational to the Democratic-Republican Party, and their correspondence reveals a close personal friendship alongside their political collaboration.

Thomas Jefferson's experiences offer insights into building and maintaining relationships. Some of those lessons are importance of being a good listener; the power of dialogue and a shared purpose; the art of compromise, and prioritizing family.

Leaders need to be relationship builders because strong interpersonal connections foster trust, collaboration, and a positive work environment, ultimately leading to increased engagement; productivity; and success. By prioritizing relationships, leaders can create a culture where team members feel valued, supported, and motivated to achieve shared goals.

Here's why relationship building is crucial for leaders:

- **Increased Trust and Engagement:** Leaders invest time in building relationships, they foster trust and create a sense of belonging, which leads to higher levels of employee engagement and commitment.
- **Improved Teamwork and Collaboration:** Strong relationships facilitate open communication, collaboration, and the sharing of ideas, leading to more effective teamwork and problem-solving.
- **Enhanced Motivation and Productivity:** When employees feel connected to their leaders and colleagues, they are more likely to be motivated, productive, and invested in their work.

- **Positive Work Environment:** Relationship-focused leaders create a positive and supportive atmosphere where individuals feel comfortable, respected, and empowered to contribute their best.
- **Effective Change Management:** Strong relationships help leaders navigate change more effectively, as they can rely on the support and understanding of their team members.

HOW DO YOU DO THIS?

Leaders build relationships by fostering trust, open communication, and a sense of belonging within their teams. This involves demonstrating empathy, actively listening, and showing genuine care for their team members' well-being and professional development.

Here's a more detailed breakdown:

1. Cultivating Trust:

- **Consistency and Transparency:** Leaders build trust by being reliable, predictable, and open about their decisions and actions.
- **Honesty and Integrity:** Leaders who are honest and ethical in their dealings create a strong foundation for trust.
- **Following Through:** Leaders who keep their promises and commitments build confidence and reliability.

2. Encouraging Open Communication:

- **Active Listening:** Leaders try to truly listen to their team members, understanding their perspectives and concerns.
- **Creating a Safe Space:** Leaders foster an environment where team members feel comfortable sharing their thoughts and ideas, even if they differ from the leader's.
- **Regular Communication:** Leaders make themselves accessible and maintain regular communication with their team members, keeping them informed about important updates and changes.

3. Showing Empathy and Care:

- **Understanding Individual Needs:** Leaders take the time to understand each team member's strengths, weaknesses, and motivations.
- **Providing Support:** Leaders offer support and guidance to their team members, helping them overcome challenges and achieve their goals.
- **Recognizing Achievements:** Leaders acknowledge and appreciate the contributions of their team members, fostering a sense of value and belonging.

4. Fostering a Sense of Belonging:

- **Team Building Activities:** Leaders can organize activities that help team members connect with each other on a personal level.
- **Inclusivity:** Leaders ensure that all team members feel included and valued.
- **Shared Purpose:** Leaders help team members understand how their work contributes to the larger organizational goals, creating a sense of shared purpose.

LEADERSHIP CHALLENGE

"Building relationships is more than understanding others. It's about making people feel understood."

- Yankee Doodle Dave

In this week's lesson there was a story involving Thomas Jefferson and his ability to build relationships.

Several different concepts were discussed that can help leaders further build relationships in the workplace. By consistently practicing these behaviors, leaders can build strong, positive relationships with their team members, which in turn leads to increased motivation, engagement, productivity, and overall success.

What concepts do you plan to put in place to demonstrate how you will be able to be a "Leader Who Naturally Builds Relationships" and how you will display that as a team leader?

"Building relationships is not about transactions—it is about connections."
- Michelle Tillis Lederman

Openness to Criticism

*"He who listens to life-giving reproof
will dwell among the wise."*
- *Proverbs 15: 31*

HISTORICAL FIGURE:
Andrew Jackson, 7th President of the United States

This week's lesson deals with the concept of being open to criticism. Not being open to criticism is a common human trait, and it can stem from various psychological reasons.

Being open to criticism means being willing and able to receive feedback, even if it's negative, without becoming overly defensive or emotionally upset. It involves recognizing that criticism, particularly constructive criticism, can be a valuable tool for growth and improvement.

This week I'm sharing a story of someone who was not necessarily open to criticism. That leader is President Andrew Jackson.

Andrew Jackson, the 7th President of the United States, was a strong-willed figure known for his defiant approach to criticism and unwavering commitment to his own agenda. His presidency (1829-1837) saw significant expansion of executive power, often in the face of strong opposition.

Jackson, who rose from humble beginnings and achieved national fame as a military hero, cultivated an image as a champion of the *"common man."* He believed himself to be the people's tribune, defending their interests against established elites and special interests, including those in Congress. This self-perception fueled his strong sense of conviction and made him reluctant to yield to opposing viewpoints.

There are multiple aspects of evidence that suggest Andrew Jackson was not easily swayed by criticism. He often bypassed or defied Congress, using his veto power more frequently than any of his predecessors and dominating his cabinet. Jackson frequently replaced members who disagreed with his policies. Despite strong opposition and a Supreme Court ruling in favor of the Cherokee Nation, Jackson pressed forward with the forced removal of Native Americans from their ancestral lands, resulting in the tragic *Trail of Tears.* When South Carolina threatened to nullify federal tariffs, Jackson forcefully asserted the supremacy of the federal government, even threatening to use military force to ensure compliance. He waged a determined campaign against the *Second Bank of the United States,* viewing it as a symbol of aristocratic privilege. This battle ultimately led to the bank's demise and the transfer of federal funds to state banks, despite significant opposition. A staunch opponent of paper money and central banking, Jackson is ironically featured on the $20 bill. He favored hard currency, like gold and silver, and his "war on the bank" is well-documented.

After Jackson won a plurality of popular and electoral votes in the 1824 presidential election but lost in the House of Representatives, his supporters claimed that John Quincy Adams and Henry Clay had made a "corrupt bargain." Jackson continued to nurse this grudge and attacked his opponents for years, even after winning the presidency in 1828.

President Jackson was known for his strong will and fiery temper. Despite his early exposure to education and the potential for a ministerial career, he was deemed too "hot-tempered." This passionate and often aggressive nature was a defining characteristic throughout his life. Jackson's aggressive nature often influenced his political decisions and interactions with others.

Jackson's personality was marked by fiery patriotism, strong partisanship, and a tendency to personalize disputes. He was known to demonize his opponents and hold grudges. In the infamous *"Petticoat Affair,"* he even rearranged his cabinet due to societal treatment of his Secretary of War's wife, according to the White House Historical Association. This incident further highlighted his willingness to defy social conventions and act on personal convictions.

Andrew Jackson's disregard for criticism offers insight into leadership and governance. There are several principles this covers: the dangers of unchecked executive power, the importance of diverse viewpoints, potential for detrimental outcomes and the influence of personal animosity on policy. While some praise Jackson for his strength, his resistance to criticism serves as a cautionary tale about unchecked authority, considering diverse perspectives, and the potentially destructive consequences of decisions made without regard for opposing viewpoints or established legal processes.

HOW DO YOU DO THIS?

Leaders can cultivate openness to criticism by fostering a culture of psychological safety; actively listening to feedback; and reframing criticism as an opportunity for growth. This involves recognizing that criticism is a natural part of leadership, learning to detach personal feelings from feedback, and seeking to understand the perspective of the critic.

Here's a more detailed look at how leaders can be open to criticism:

1. Cultivate Psychological Safety:
- Leaders should create an environment where team members feel comfortable sharing feedback without fear of reprisal.
- This involves actively demonstrating that feedback is valued and that diverse perspectives are welcome.

2. Embrace Criticism as a Tool for Growth:

- Leaders should view criticism as an opportunity to learn and improve, rather than a personal attack.
- Recognize that criticism, even if uncomfortable, can highlight areas for development and strategic adjustments.

3. Listen Actively and Without Defensiveness:

- When receiving feedback, leaders should listen attentively, ask clarifying questions, and strive to understand the critic's perspective.
- Avoid interrupting, arguing, or becoming defensive, as this can shut down communication and discourage future feedback.

4. Disengage from Personal Feelings:

- Leaders should aim to separate feedback from their own ego or sense of self-worth.
- Remember that criticism is often about the situation or the action, not the person.

5. Reflect and Learn:

- After receiving feedback, take time to reflect on its validity and potential implications.
- Consider how the feedback can be used to improve future decisions and actions.

LEADERSHIP CHALLENGE

Here is my challenge to you:

This week we learned about President Andrew Jackson, a leader who was not open to criticism.

Are you open to criticism? Are you cultivating a work center that allows criticism?

"Be open to criticism, but don't be affected by it. Criticism is meant to help you be a better person. Learn from it."

- Yankee Doodle Dave

Being open to criticism in the workplace is crucial for professional growth and a healthy work environment. It involves actively listening to feedback, understanding its potential benefits, and responding constructively rather than defensively. This fosters a culture of learning, improvement, and stronger relationships.

Here are a few techniques on how to cultivate a culture that allows criticism:

Cultivate a Positive Mindset:
- View Criticism as an Opportunity
- Separate Feedback from Your Identity
- Avoid Being Defensive
- Focus on Understanding Their Perspective
- Acknowledge the Feedback
- Thank the Person for Their Input
- Develop an Action Plan

This week different concepts were discussed that can help leaders further be open to criticism and develop an environment that welcomes criticism.

What concepts do you plan to put in place to be more open to criticism and develop a work center that welcomes criticism?

---

*"People are remarkably open to criticism
when they believe it's intended to help them."*
- Adam Grant

Know Your Limits, Aim to Push Beyond Them!

"Since his days are determined and the number of his months is with you, and since you have set limits that he cannot exceed."

- Job 14: 5

HISTORICAL FIGURE:
Jimmy Carter, 39th President of the United States

This week's lesson deals with the concept of knowing your limits. Knowing your limits is crucial for personal growth, well-being, and success. Once you know what those limits are strive to push beyond them!

Knowing your limits means understanding your physical, mental, and emotional capabilities and boundaries, and acting accordingly. It's about recognizing what you can and cannot do; what you're good at and not good at; using that knowledge to make informed decisions; and set appropriate boundaries. It's not about limiting yourself, but rather about being self-aware and making wise choices to avoid overexertion, stress, or potential harm.

To explain this concept allow me to share a few stories about our 39th President of the United States. That is of course President Jimmy Carter, who served in office from 1977-1981.

Jimmy Carter was born in rural Georgia in 1924. Carter's childhood was shaped by hard work on a farm and the Baptist faith.

He was raised in a time and place marked by segregation, but his mother, Lillian Carter, instilled in him a more progressive view on race. This early experience of racial division and a developing sense of moral duty would later form his political actions. His military career in the Navy's nuclear submarine program, under the demanding leadership of Admiral Hyman Rickover, reinforced his discipline and attention to detail.

On December 12, 1952, a series of mechanical failures and human errors caused a partial meltdown of the NRX reactor at the Chalk River Laboratories in Ontario. This led to overheating fuel rods, a hydrogen gas explosion, and the flooding of the reactor's basement with over a million gallons of highly radioactive water.

The U.S. Navy was asked to assist Canada's clean-up efforts. Lieutenant Jimmy Carter, then a 28-year-old nuclear engineering officer working under Admiral Hyman Rickover, was chosen to lead a 12-man team. Their task was to help disassemble the damaged reactor core.

To prepare for the dangerous work, Carter's team built an exact replica of the reactor on a nearby tennis court to practice their dismantling procedures. This allowed them to meticulously rehearse each move before entering the contaminated area.

The radiation levels inside the reactor were so high that workers could only enter for 90 seconds at a time. Carter himself took multiple shifts, recalling in his book, *Why Not the Best?*, that he would dash in to loosen as many bolts as possible before being withdrawn. For months afterward, his urine tested radioactive.

Carter's political career began in the Georgia State Senate. This is where he earned a reputation for tackling difficult issues like racial discrimination and government waste. He successfully ran for governor and then the presidency, campaigning on a platform of honesty and competency in the post-Watergate era. He faced significant challenges, including a challenging economy and foreign policy crises. He worked to address the energy crisis, combat inflation, and promote human rights as a cornerstone of U.S. foreign policy. He achieved significant successes in foreign policy, including mediating the historic *Camp David Accords between Egypt and Israel.*

Jimmy Carter understood the importance of honesty and integrity. Carter emphasized their importance in public service. In his inaugural address, he vowed to never lie to the American people. This conviction, while lauded, also sometimes made it difficult for him to navigate the political landscape and build relationships with those who did not share his uncompromising approach.

President Carter's post-presidency was marked by decades of tireless humanitarian work, focusing on diplomacy, human rights, and the fight against disease through the *Carter Center,* which he co-founded with his wife, Rosalynn Carter. He also gained recognition for his long-standing commitment to *Habitat for Humanity.* His dedication earned him the *Nobel Peace Prize* in 2002. This phase of his life arguably reshaped public perception, highlighting his unwavering commitment to service and making a positive impact on the world.

Jimmy Carter openly discussed the concept of limits, acknowledging past shortcomings and recognizing the ongoing need for growth and learning. He believed in continuous improvement, pushing beyond perceived limitations and striving for excellence in all areas of his life. In a poignant letter to his 12-year-old self, he advised against limiting ambitions, to recognize and address discrimination, to prioritize learning and service, and to always do one's best. He also stressed the importance of re-examining causes of failure, reassessing talents, and setting higher goals after every setback.

In essence, Jimmy Carter's life story is a testament to the idea that "*knowing your limits*" isn't about accepting limitations, but rather about understanding them as opportunities for growth, learning, and striving for continuous improvement. His post-presidency demonstrated a powerful and impactful dedication to service that transcended the boundaries of traditional political roles.

HOW DO YOU DO THIS?

Leaders can identify their limitations through self-reflection, seeking feedback, and understanding their "circle of competence." This involves recognizing areas where they need improvement, acknowledging when they lack expertise, and actively seeking input from others.

Here's a more detailed breakdown:

1. Self-Reflection and Assessment:

- **Evaluate Strengths and Weaknesses:** Regularly assess both personal and professional strengths and weaknesses to understand areas of competence and areas needing development.
- **Identify Areas of Expertise:** Understand your *"circle of competence"*—the areas where you have genuine expertise and can make informed decisions.

2. Seeking Feedback:

- **Ask for Constructive Criticism:** Actively solicit feedback from team members, mentors, and peers on your performance and leadership style.
- **Don't Be Afraid to Ask for Help:** Recognize when you need support or guidance from others and don't hesitate to ask for it.

3. Understanding Limitations in Context:

- **Recognize Situational Limitations:** Understand that what works in one situation or with one team may not work in another.
- **Delegate Effectively:** Identify tasks that can be delegated to others who possess the necessary skills and expertise.

4. Importance of Knowing Limitations:

- **Decision-Making:** By acknowledging their limitations, leaders can make more informed decisions by seeking input from experts.

"*Know your limits but never stop trying to exceed them.*"

- Yankee Doodle Dave

LEADERSHIP CHALLENGE

Here is my challenge to you:

Do you know your own limitations? Are you cultivating a work center that allows your staff to express their own personal limitations?

In this week's lesson there was a story involving President Jimmy Carter and his knowing his own limits. He did not necessarily accept those limits but continued to grow beyond them.

Knowing your limitations is particularly crucial when building teams. Good leaders who understand their limitations use that knowledge to ensure they have balance in their teams. Having people around you who complement you with strengths that are your weakness, is key.

This week different concepts were discussed that can help leaders know their limits and develop an environment that allows your staff to recognize their limits as well.

What concepts do you plan to put in place to understand your own limits and develop a work center that allows staff members to understand their limits?

____

____

____

____

____

____

____

____

____

____

____

____

"Believe in your infinite potential.
Your only limitations are those you set upon yourself."
- Roy T. Bennett

Mastering Soft Data

"Do you know that your bodies are temples of the Holy Spirit, who is in you, who you have received from God? You are not your own; you were bought at a price. Therefore, honor God with your bodies."
- 1 Corinthians 6: 19-20

HISTORICAL FIGURE:
President Ronald Reagan - "The Great Communicator"

Effective leaders are adept at interpreting qualitative information, such as body language, tone of voice, and subtle cues, to understand their team's needs and concerns.

Soft data, also known as qualitative data, refers to information that is subjective, descriptive and often based on opinions, feelings, and experiences. Unlike hard data, which is numerical and measurable, soft data focuses on understanding the *"why"* behind the numbers. It's often gathered through methods like interviews, surveys, and open-ended questionnaires.

This week's lesson deals with the concept of mastering soft data.

One of the best examples I can think of would be our 40th President of the United States—President Ronald Reagan.

Before Ronald Reagan became President, he mastered the art of soft data in film and television. He appeared in 53 movies and numerous television shows. His first starring role was in the 1937 movie *"Love Is on the Air."* He was also a prolific radio performer and television host before entering politics. During his time in the military, he also produced over 400 training films.

President Ronald Reagan, often dubbed "*the Great Communicator*," masterfully integrated body language with his verbal communication to connect with audiences on a deeper level. His acting background played a significant role in his ability to use non-verbal cues effectively.

Reagan's facial expressions, gestures, posture, and eye contact reinforced his messages and engaged his listeners, creating a more impactful delivery. He understood the importance of aligning his body language with the emotions he was trying to convey. For example, in a somber speech, his posture and facial expressions reflect grief, but also strength and resolve.

Reagan used his body language to establish a connection with his audience, making them feel like he was speaking directly to them and sharing their feelings.

President Reagan commanded the stage, using eye contact, facial expressiveness, and a varied vocal tone to keep his audience engaged and interested. He could shift his demeanor to convey different messages. When delivering an important point about American determination, for example, his features would take on a steely resolve.

Following the *Challenger* space shuttle disaster in 1986, Reagan delivered a powerful speech that exemplified his use of body language to connect with a grieving nation. He started by sharing the nation's pain, bearing his emotions and empathizing with the audience. His facial expressions conveyed grief, with a slightly downturned mouth and forehead muscles contracted as if struggling with his thoughts. However, throughout the speech, he maintained straight shoulders and a head held high, demonstrating strength in the face of tragedy. When speaking about America's commitment to space exploration, his features became resolved, conveying determination and hope.

Reagan deliberately avoided political jargon, choosing instead to communicate in a simple, conversational style that resonated with everyday Americans. He explained complex problems using everyday language that people could easily grasp, making his policies feel like common sense.

President Reagan was a master of using anecdotes about individual Americans to humanize his policies and illustrate his points. He would often end a speech by telling a touching story about a family or a hero, giving his audience a powerful emotional takeaway.

At his best, Reagan presented a larger narrative about America as a "*shining city on a hill*," where hardworking, common people were the heroes. This framing gave his followers a sense of shared purpose and destiny.

Reagan's use of body language in this speech allowed him to grieve alongside the nation while also displaying leadership and resilience. His gestures and demeanor were in harmony with his words, creating an authentic and impactful delivery that resonated with the American people.

President Reagan's "*Great Communicator*" persona came from a strategic and authentic deployment of body language that resonated with his audience and enhanced his message. Mastering body language is an essential component of effective communication and leadership.

HOW DO YOU DO THIS?

Leaders can significantly enhance their communication and influence by improving their body language and facial expressions. This involves projecting confidence through posture; maintaining eye contact; using open and purposeful gestures, and ensuring facial expressions align with their message. By consciously controlling and utilizing these nonverbal cues, leaders can build trust, foster connection, and effectively convey their message.

Here is a more detailed look:

Body Language:

- **Posture:** A confident posture, like standing tall with shoulders back, conveys authority and self-assurance. Avoid slouching, which can signal disinterest or low energy.
- **Contact:** Maintaining consistent eye contact demonstrates attentiveness and sincerity, fostering trust. Aim for around 50% eye contact when speaking and 70% when listening, briefly breaking contact every few seconds to avoid staring.
- **Gestures:** Open and purposeful gestures, such as using hands to emphasize points, can enhance communication making the message more engaging. Avoid fidgeting, which can appear nervous or anxious.
- **Space:** Respecting personal space is crucial. While maintaining an appropriate distance, avoid crowding others, which can make them uncomfortable.
- **Mirroring:** Slightly mirroring the body language of the person you are communicating with can help build rapport and connection.
- **Facial Expressions:** Smiling a genuine smile makes a leader appear approachable, friendly, and confident. However, excessively smiling can be perceived as insincere.
- **Emotions:** Ensure facial expressions align with the message being delivered. For example, if discussing a serious issue, a serious expression is appropriate. Avoid expressions that contradict the verbal message.
- **Reading Others:** Develop the ability to recognize and interpret the emotions expressed through facial expressions in others. This helps you better understand their reactions and adjust your communication accordingly.

Additional Tips:

- **Be Mindful:** Pay attention to your body language and facial expressions in various situations.

- **Practice:** Regularly practice your body language and facial expressions in front of a mirror or with a trusted friend to identify areas for improvement.
- **Seek Feedback:** Ask for feedback from colleagues, mentors, or friends on your nonverbal communication skills.
- **Align Verbal and Nonverbal:** Ensure your verbal and nonverbal communication are consistent. A lack of alignment can lead to confusion and distrust.

By focusing on these aspects of body language and facial expressions, leaders significantly enhance their communication effectiveness. This builds stronger relationships and inspires greater confidence in their teams.

"Body language refers to nonverbal communication expressed through physical behaviors like facial expressions, posture, gestures, and eye contact. It can reveal a person's true feelings and add impact to their message. Understanding body language allows for deeper emotional awareness and more effective communication."

- Yankee Doodle Dave

LEADERSHIP CHALLENGE

Here is my challenge to you:

This week we learned about President Ronald Reagan and his understanding of *"soft data."* His background in film and television was instrumental in understanding concepts like body language and tone of voice.

Does the idea of understanding "Mastering Soft Data" stress you out? When you are in conversations are you attentive to subtle cues, such as body language and tone of voice?

Subtle cues and body language play a crucial role in workplace communication, influencing how colleagues perceive and interact with each other. Understanding these cues improves communication, builds rapport, and projects a professional image. Conversely, negative body language can create mixed messages and undermine verbal communication.

Positive Body Language Cues:

- **Eye Contact:** Maintaining appropriate eye contact shows engagement and sincerity.
- **Posture:** Standing tall and maintaining a good posture conveys confidence and authority.
- **Facial Expressions:** Smiling and maintaining a neutral expression enhances communication.
- **Gestures:** Using open and inviting gestures help emphasize points and create a welcoming atmosphere.
- **Tone of Voice:** A clear and confident tone can reinforce your message.
- **Open Posture:** Avoiding crossed arms and leaning in can signal engagement and interest.

Negative Body Language Cues:

- **Lack of Eye Contact:** Looking away or down can suggest disinterest or discomfort.

- **Slouching:** A slumped posture can indicate a lack of confidence or disinterest.
- **Fidgeting:** Nervous movements can be distracting and create a negative impression.
- **Crossed Arms:** This posture can be interpreted as defensive or unapproachable.
- **Avoiding Touch:** A weak handshake can convey a lack of confidence.
- **Staring:** Prolonged, intense staring can make others uncomfortable.

Other Important Cues:
- **Mimicry:** Subtle mirroring of another person's body language can build rapport.
- **Hand Gestures:** Animated gestures can emphasize points, but excessive gestures can be distracting.
- **Legs and Feet:** Tapping the feet can indicate impatience, while feet pointing away might signal a desire to leave
- **Voice Tone:** A flat or monotone voice can convey disinterest or lack of engagement.

This week we discussed different concepts to help leaders "master soft data" (attentive to subtle cues, such as body language and tone of voice). What concepts do you plan to put in place to help master soft data and be attentive to subtle cues, body language, and tone of voice?

____

____

____

____

"The most important thing in communication is hearing what isn't said."
- Peter Drucker

God Does Not Make Mistakes. There Is Only One of You. Be Authentic.

"Therefore, putting away falsehood, let each one of you speak the truth with his neighbor, for we are members of one another."

- Ephesians 4:25

HISTORICAL FIGURE: Martin Luther King Jr., American Minister and Civil Rights Leader

Being authentic means being true to oneself, one's own personality, values, and spirit, regardless of external pressures. It involves acting in alignment with one's inner self and being honest with oneself and others. Authenticity is about expressing one's true thoughts, feelings, and beliefs, rather than presenting a false or idealized version.

This week's topic is one that some people may not discuss. This is the concept of being authentic and true to oneself.

Dr. Martin Luther King Jr. was a leader of the American Civil Rights Movement who championed equality and justice through nonviolent resistance.

Here is a rather lesser-known story about Martin Luther King Jr. Believe it or not, he was a passionate *Star Trek* fan. He considered himself the *"biggest Trekkie"* on the planet. He and his wife, Coretta

Scott King, allowed their children to stay up late to watch *"Star Trek,"* calling it the only show they approved for their children.

Martin Luther King Jr. was a passionate *Star Trek* fan and a strong supporter of Nichelle Nichols, the actress who played Lt. Uhura. He convinced Nichols not to leave the show, emphasizing the importance of her role as a strong, intelligent Black woman in a diverse, optimistic vision of the future—a message that resonated with his civil rights goals

Martin Luther King said her presence demonstrated that a Black woman could be intelligent, beautiful, and hold a position of authority in a hopeful, egalitarian future—a stark contrast to the realities of the 1960s. Nichols was deeply affected by King's words and the realization of the role's profound impact. She returned to *Star Trek*, and King's encouragement helped her stay with the show, which went on to have a lasting cultural and social impact.

His authenticity stemmed from his deep-seated commitment to his principles, even in the face of great personal risk. He believed in the power of nonviolence, drawing inspiration from his Christian faith and the teachings of Mahatma Gandhi. King's authenticity was also evident in his willingness to sacrifice for his beliefs, including being arrested and jailed for his activism.

Dr. Martin Luther King Jr. consistently advocated peaceful methods of protest and civil disobedience, even when faced with violence and opposition. He remained steadfast in his principles of justice, equality, and nonviolence, even when it meant personal sacrifice and danger. King inspired millions through his powerful speeches and his unwavering dedication to the cause of racial equality, earning him the respect of people across the nation. King's journey involved questioning religious dogma and embracing a more progressive vision of Christianity, which ultimately fueled his activism. His example inspired countless individuals to participate in the *Civil Rights Movement* and to fight for a more just and equitable society.

Dr. King's leadership in the *Montgomery Bus Boycott* demonstrated his commitment to nonviolent resistance and his ability to mobilize a community. His leadership in Birmingham, Alabama, involved acts of civil disobedience that drew national attention to the injustices of segregation.

Dr. King's iconic *"I Have a Dream"* speech at the March on Washington for *Jobs and Freedom* encapsulated his vision of a racially integrated society. His later work focused on addressing economic inequality and poverty, demonstrating his commitment to a broader vision of social justice.

Dr. Martin Luther King Jr.'s authenticity was not just a personal attribute, but a driving force behind the *Civil Rights Movement*. His unwavering commitment to his principles, his willingness to sacrifice, and his ability to inspire others made him a truly authentic leader.

Dr. Martin Luther King Jr. embraced being authentic in all aspects of his life. Everything from being the "biggest Trekkie" to standing up for what he believes in as a Civil Rights Leader, he was authentic. He is widely regarded as an authentic leader due to his unwavering commitment to his principles and his ability to inspire others to action. A leadership rooted in his deep-seated belief in nonviolence and equality was demonstrated through his words and actions throughout the *Civil Rights Movement*.

HOW DO YOU DO THIS?

Leaders can foster an authentic work center by encouraging open communication, demonstrating vulnerability, and actively listening to their team members. This includes creating a safe space for employees to share ideas and concerns without fear of judgment. Furthermore, leaders should be self-aware, practice ethical decision-making, and prioritize the development of their team members.

Here's a more detailed look at how leaders can foster authenticity:

1. Encourage Open Communication:

- **Example:** Authentic leaders are transparent about their own thoughts and feelings, which encourages others to do the same.
- **Various Channels:** Provide various ways for team members to communicate, like face-to-face meetings, emails, and instant messaging, catering to different preferences.
- **Practice Active Listening:** Pay attention, show empathy, and respond thoughtfully to show team members that they are heard and valued.

2. Foster a Culture of Trust and Safety:

- **Be Vulnerable:** Share your own experiences, including mistakes, to show that it's okay to be imperfect and human.
- **Promote Healthy Debate:** Encourage diverse perspectives and respectful disagreement, recognizing that no one has all the answers.

3. Focus on Individual Development:

- **Invest in Training and Development:** Provide opportunities for employees to learn new skills and grow professionally.
- **Offer Coaching and Mentorship:** Support individual growth through coaching and mentorship programs, helping employees develop self-awareness and improve their communication skills.
- **Recognize and Appreciate Strengths:** Acknowledge and celebrate the unique talents and contributions of each team member.

4. Lead with Integrity and Empathy:

- **Align Actions with Values:** Make decisions that are consistent with the organization's values and ethical principles.
- **Demonstrate Empathy:** Show genuine care and concern for your team members' well-being.

- **Be Consistent:** Maintain a consistent approach in your leadership style and interactions with your team.

By implementing these strategies, leaders can create a work environment where employees feel safe, valued, and empowered to be their authentic selves, leading to increased job satisfaction, productivity, and innovation.

"Authenticity is the daily practice of letting go of who we think we are supposed to be and embracing who you are."

- Yankee Doodle Dave

LEADERSHIP CHALLENGE

Here is my challenge to you:

Would someone describe you as a person that they believe is an honest person?

Are you a person that is genuine and true to yourself?

In this week's lesson there was a story involving Dr. Martin Luther King Jr. Through all the trials and tribulations he endured, his leadership remained true and "authentic."

Being authentic in the workplace means being genuine and true to yourself while navigating professional expectations. It involves being honest, being transparent, and showing vulnerability, which fosters stronger relationships and a more positive work environment. Authenticity can lead to increased job satisfaction, creativity, and overall better job performance.

This week different concepts were discussed to help leaders be more authentic and help foster an environment that allows your staff to be more authentic as well.

What concepts do you plan to put in place to help your team members be more authentic?

*"Always be a first-rate version of yourself
and not a second-rate version of someone else."
— Judy Garland*

Embracing Discomfort

"I have said these things to you, that in me you may have peace. In the world you will have tribulation. But be of good cheer; I have overcome the world."
> *- John 16: 33*

HISTORICAL FIGURE: Grover Cleveland, 22nd and 24th President of the United States

This week's topic may resonate with my fellow brothers and sisters in the military. There is a slang term utilized in the military to discuss this concept: It is simply *"Embrace the Suck!"*

Grover Cleveland's life story is a powerful illustration of embracing discomfort and overcoming adversity. What is truly fascinating is that many of his medical conditions were not provided to the public.

Grover Cleveland was the 22nd and 24th President of the United States. He suffered from several medical conditions that he simply dealt with and the public was not aware of.

President Cleveland was not exactly the healthiest of individuals working in the White House. He stood at 5 feet 11 inches tall and weighed around 260 pounds. His family gave him the nickname *"Uncle Jumbo"* since his weight was a common topic of conversation. Not only did he have a strong distaste for exercise he had a fondness for rich foods, beer and cigars. There are some people that state he could have even suffered from sleep apnea as well.

During his second term in 1893, President Cleveland noticed an unusual spot on the roof of his mouth. An examination by Robert O'Reilly, the presidential doctor, revealed a lesion about the size of a quarter, which later proved to be cancerous.

The lesion had to be surgically removed, but Cleveland feared that news of the cancer could have catastrophic political consequences for him. As a result, it was decided that the president would have surgery in secret aboard a yacht belonging to Cleveland's friend Elias Benedict. O'Reilly led a surgical team that also included dentist Ferdinand Hasbrouk. He acted as an anesthesiologist and removed two of the president's teeth.

Later, when addressing rumors of the surgery, White House aides used Ferdinand Hasbrouk as a convenient cover, reporting only that the president had a bad tooth removed. Cleveland was fitted with a prosthesis, which allowed him to regain his normal speaking voice and facial appearance. The truth about Cleveland's surgery was not revealed to the public until 1917, almost a decade after his death.

Although the surgery was a success, the removal of some tissue in Cleveland's palate affected his speech. A specialist was brought in to create a special implant, which worked well. However, Cleveland was never the same after the surgery. He grew increasingly depressed and irritable and never held public office again.

Cleveland suffered from gout throughout his life, which likely caused him pain and limited his mobility at times. During his 1892 presidential campaign, for example, gout restricted his public appearances.

Beyond the specific incidents, the combination of his health problems and the economic crisis during his second term reportedly left him "thinner, hearing-impaired, and even more irritable and stubborn."

Cleveland chose to keep his health issues, especially the cancer surgery, private to avoid causing public panic during a time of financial instability. This desire for secrecy surrounding his health was not unique among presidents of that era.

It is fascinating to think of what Grover Cleveland accomplished while experiencing so many medical issues. Grover Cleveland's two non-consecutive presidential terms were marked by several notable actions. He is known for his strong stance against corruption and his efforts to reform the civil service. In his first term, he signed the *Interstate Commerce Act,* regulating the railroad industry, and the *Dawes Act,* which impacted Native American lands. In his second term, he faced the *Panic of 1893,* a major economic depression, and controversially used federal troops to suppress the *Pullman Strike.* He also resisted expansionist policies, notably opposing the annexation of Hawaii. President Cleveland accomplished all those things, and the public had no idea what he was dealing with medically.

Despite these challenges, Cleveland was able to fulfill his presidential duties and maintained a degree of normalcy in his public life thanks to the secrecy surrounding the surgery and the successful prosthetic device. Cleveland continued his duties, though his health remained a concern. He died in 1908, several years after leaving office. In summary, Grover Cleveland confronted his discomfort by taking decisive and sometimes unpopular actions. This often meant risking his political standing or defying prevailing norms.

HOW DO YOU DO THIS?

Leaders embrace discomfort by actively seeking out challenging situations, fostering open communication, and promoting a culture of continuous learning. This involves stepping outside of their comfort zones, encouraging feedback, and creating a psychologically safe environment where team members feel comfortable expressing concerns and taking risks.

Here's a more detailed look:

1. Seeking Out Discomfort as a Deliberate Practice:

- **Challenge Assumptions:** Leaders can push themselves to explore new perspectives by intentionally engaging in activities that make them uncomfortable, like learning a new skill, taking on a difficult project, or seeking feedback from those with different viewpoints.
- **Normalize Discomfort:** By sharing their own experiences of discomfort, leaders can create a culture where it's seen as a normal part of learning and development, rather than something to be avoided.

2. Fostering Open Communication and Psychological Safety:

- **Active Listening:** Leaders should actively listen to their team members' concerns and perspectives, even when those perspectives are challenging or uncomfortable to hear. Feel comfortable sharing their ideas and concerns without fear of judgment or punishment.

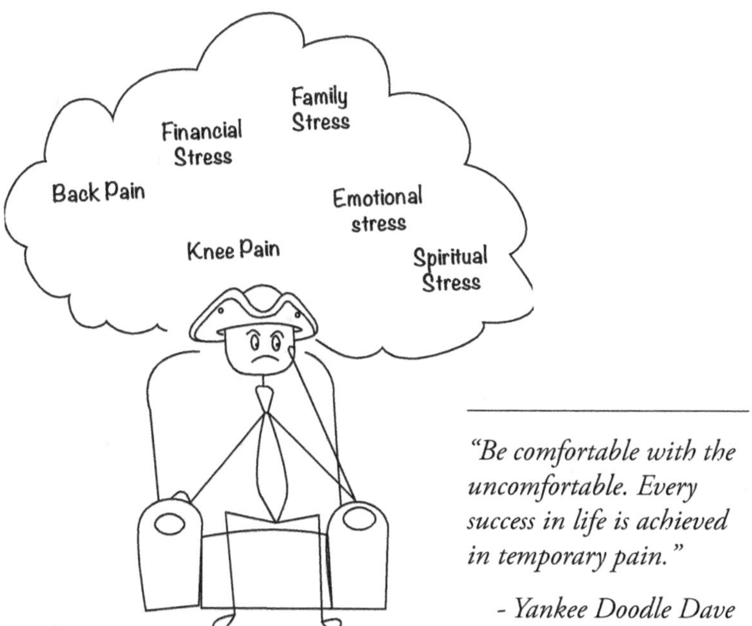

"Be comfortable with the uncomfortable. Every success in life is achieved in temporary pain."

- Yankee Doodle Dave

LEADERSHIP CHALLENGE

Here is my challenge to you:

What happens in your life when things get a little difficult? What happens when things begin to suck?

In this week's lesson we learned a little about the life story of President Grover Cleveland and how he lived a life of embracing discomfort. President Cleveland was diagnosed with cancer and had a massive surgery that effected his speech and the appearance of his face. He did not let that slow him down one bit. In fact, he went on to successfully complete two (2) terms in the White House.

Embracing discomfort in the workplace involves actively seeking out challenging situations and new experiences to foster personal and professional growth. It is about recognizing that discomfort as a natural part of learning and development, and using it as a catalyst for innovation, resilience, and stronger relationships.

Here are a few techniques on how to be authentic in a workplace:

- Recognize that discomfort is a natural part of growth and learning.
- Understand that everyone experiences discomfort at times, and it does not mean you are failing.
- Develop the ability to bounce back from setbacks and challenges.
- Engage in activities that push you out of your comfort zone, such as public speaking or taking on a new project.

This week different concepts were discussed that can help leaders be more comfortable in uncomfortable situations.

What concepts do you plan to put in place to help you embrace uncomfortable situations and develop a work center that allows staff members to embrace uncomfortable situations?

"The only way to become successful is to embrace the discomfort of hard work."
- David Goggins

Do Your Homework! Be Prepared!

*"Put on the full armor of God, so that you can take
your stand against the devil's schemes."*
                                        - Ephesians 6:11

HISTORICAL FIGURE: Theodore Roosevelt, 26th President of the United States

To "do your homework" and "be prepared" means to diligently study, research, and practice beforehand to gain a comprehensive understanding of a subject or situation, ensuring you are equipped to handle it successfully.

This week's topic is based on the concept of being prepared. This week I want to share a story about being prepared. This is the story of President Theodore "Teddy" Roosevelt.

As a young boy, Theodore Roosevelt suffered from severe asthma and was often sickly. Due to his health, he was homeschooled by private tutors and his family. Despite the challenges, he developed a love for learning and reading widely. He was particularly interested in natural history and even founded the *"Roosevelt Museum of Natural History"* in his family's home, collecting and studying various specimens.

Concerned about his son's health, Theodore Roosevelt Sr. took young "Teddy" aside and delivered a life-altering ultimatum: *"Theo-*

dore, you have the mind, but you have not the body, and without the help of the body, the mind cannot go as far as it should. You must make your body."

According to family accounts, the determined boy immediately replied, *"I will make my body."* His father then installed a gymnasium in their home, and the young Roosevelt began a regimen of weightlifting, swimming, and boxing.

This discipline was tested shortly after. After a confrontation with two bullies on a stagecoach, Roosevelt found his physical conditioning was not enough. He was unable to defend himself, and when he told his father, the elder Roosevelt encouraged him to take up boxing. The discipline and skill he gained helped him learn to defend himself and deepened his commitment to physical fitness to build character and mental toughness.

President Theodore Roosevelt established the first formal U.S. military physical fitness standards in the early 1900s, requiring officers to pass endurance tests like a 50-mile walk within three days. Driven by a concern that officers were becoming physically unfit, Roosevelt issued orders for the Marine Corps and Navy in late 1908 and early 1909, mandating that passing these tests be a condition for promotion. While initially met with complaints, his initiatives championed a "Strenuous Life" and set a benchmark for military physical readiness that influenced subsequent fitness programs.

Marine Corps Field Officers were required to take a 90-mile riding test over three days, while Line Officers (captains and lieutenants) had to complete a 50-mile walk in three days, with 20 hours of actual marching time.

A Navy General Order included an annual test of a 50-mile walk in three days (within 20 hours), a 90-mile horseback ride, or a 100-mile bicycle ride, all over three consecutive days.

Roosevelt also implemented standards for the Army and even led the General Staff on an expedition that included hiking through dense forests and climbing inclines. Roosevelt, an avid athlete himself, was concerned that urbanization and office work were making soldiers weaker.

He believed that officers needed to possess the "average physical strength of their companies" to prevent men from being held back in battle, leading to defeat.

For the first time, passing these endurance tests became a requirement for officer promotion.

The standards initially faced resistance from some within the Navy, who found them too demanding. However, Roosevelt's push for physical fitness set a precedent for military physical training and remains a historical touchstone for military fitness, with Army Reserve Officers today still marching 50 miles to honor his initiatives.

For Roosevelt, a physically prepared body was not just about strength but about cultivating courage, determination, and a readiness to face life's challenges. From overcoming his childhood asthma to charging up San Juan Hill with the Rough Riders, his life was a testament to his belief that a strong body was the vessel for a strong, prepared mind.

One of the key takeaways from Theodore Roosevelt's life is the importance of preparedness. He believed that while one might not be able to create opportunities, one could be ready to seize them when they arrived. Roosevelt's life is a reminder that preparedness involves a holistic approach. This includes acquiring knowledge and skills, cultivating physical and mental resilience, embracing challenges, and constantly striving for self-improvement. Theodore Roosevelt believed that exercising his body was crucial for preparedness, not only for himself, but for the nation.

HOW DO YOU DO THIS?

Effective leaders *"do their homework"* in the workplace by thoroughly preparing and immersing themselves in the details to gain a deep understanding of their responsibilities, their team, and the broader organizational context. This preparation goes beyond surface-level understanding and involves several key actions:

1. Dedicating Time for People and Team:

- **Invest in the Team:** Good leaders understand that their success is tied to the collective intelligence, performance, and output of their team, organization, and surrounding ecosystem.
- **Focus on the Collective:** Being mindful of the team's importance and investing in developing a sense of purpose and mission helps to engage and motivate team members.

2. Embracing a Commitment to Continuous Learning:

- **Adapting to Change:** Leaders must stay informed about evolving industry trends, technologies, and market dynamics to anticipate disruptions and seize opportunities.
- **Expanding Knowledge:** Continuous learning, through various methods like reading, attending conferences, and seeking mentorship, enhances decision-making and problem-solving skills by providing a broader perspective.
- **Inspiring Others:** By prioritizing their own learning, leaders set a powerful example, fostering a culture of innovation and continuous improvement within their teams.
- **Addressing Skill Gaps:** Leaders need to be aware of their strengths and weaknesses and proactively seek learning opportunities to fill any skill gaps as their roles evolve.

3. Actively Engaging in Business Research:

- **Understanding the Market and Customers:** Researching market trends and customer needs is essential for effective strategic planning and adapting to changes.
- **Analyzing Competition:** Understanding competitors' strengths and weaknesses allows leaders to identify areas for improvement and develop competitive strategies.
- **Informing Decision-Making:** Business research provides valuable, data-driven insights that help leaders make well-informed decisions regarding operations and financial planning.

4. Ensuring Effective Communication:
- **Clear Expectations:** Leaders must clearly define goals, deadlines, and responsibilities for their team members.
- **Open and Honest Dialogue:** Creating an environment where employees feel safe to share feedback and raise concerns is crucial for gathering important information.
- **Utilizing Various Channels:** Effective leaders use a mix of communication tools like emails, instant messaging, team meetings, and project management systems to ensure information is conveyed effectively.

In summary, leaders who *"do their homework"* in the workplace are committed to continuous learning, engage in thorough business research, and prioritize effective communication to stay informed and guide their teams toward success.

LEADERSHIP CHALLENGE

Here is my challenge to you:

Would someone describe you as a preparer? Do you like to make lists and check things off when you have completed them? Do you have a "To Do List?"

In this week's lesson we learned about President Theodore "Teddy" Roosevelt and his life of wanting to be prepared and continuously do "his homework." Despite a sickly childhood, he maintained a strenuous physical regimen, becoming physically robust. Proactively working on physical and mental well-being allows one to face challenges with resilience and energy.

Being prepared in the workplace involves proactive planning, anticipating potential challenges, and having the necessary resources and knowledge to respond effectively. This can lead to increased productivity, reduced stress, and a more productive work environment.

Here are a few techniques on how to be authentic in a workplace:

- Organize your workplace
- Ensure you prepare your materials ahead of time
- Set a positive mindset
- Get enough sleep

This week different concepts were discussed that can help leaders be more prepared and ensure that their department is prepared.

What concepts do you plan to put in place to be prepared?

____

____

____

____

____

____

____

"Before anything else, preparation is the key to success."
- Alexander Graham Bell

____

"By failing to prepare, you are preparing to fail."

- Yankee Doodle Dave

Willing to Learn New Things
(The Power of a Curious Mind)

"Teach me to do your will, for you are my God!
Let your good Spirit lead me on level ground."
- Psalm 143:10

HISTORICAL FIGURE:
Benjamin Franklin, Founding Father of the United States

This week's topic of being open to learning new things should identify with many people. Surveys indicate a strong willingness among adults to learn new things, both for personal and professional reasons.

This week I want to share a few stories about the importance of being open to learning new things. This is the story of one of our founding fathers, Benjamin Franklin.

Even as a young man, Franklin's formal education was limited, ending at age ten. However, he understood the value of self-education.

"I was fond of reading, and all the little money that came into my hands was ever laid out in books," he said.

He read books extensively, often late into the night, in search of knowledge and insight.

He was a man that had a truly curious mind. Benjamin Franklin, a true Renaissance man, embodied a remarkable willingness to learn throughout his life, driven by an insatiable curiosity and a belief in the power of knowledge.

The first takes place in 1717. At the age of 11, Benjamin Franklin, an avid swimmer, invented a pair of wooden swim fins for his hands, inspired by his desire to swim more efficiently and "like a fish." These first fins were hand-held paddles with a hole for his thumb, which helped him propel himself faster but tired his wrists. He also tried fitting fins to his feet, but found them clunky and less effective, eventually deciding he swam better without the paddles altogether.

Benjamin wanted to swim better and make the swimming strokes more efficient and allow him to swim faster. This is where the power of his curious mind took over. He began thinking and came up with a design using wood, like modern paddles. His design was two oval-shaped pieces of wood, each about 10 inches long and 6 inches broad, with a hole in the center for the thumb. The idea would be he would grasp the planks with his hands, pushing the edges forward and striking the water with their flat surfaces. The hand fins increased his speed but also fatigued his wrists. His attempt to make fins for his feet was less successful.

His childhood invention influenced the development of modern flexible swim fins, based on the same fundamental principle of increased surface area for propulsion.

The second story takes place during Franklin's adult years. His dedication to learning led him to implement a structured approach to self-improvement. He set aside an hour each weekday for deliberate learning, including reading, writing, contemplation, and experiments. This *"five-hour rule"* highlights his commitment to continuous growth, reflecting his belief that *"An investment in knowledge pays the best interest."* He also used a system of daily self-assessment, creating lists of virtues he aimed to cultivate and noting his progress.

Benjamin's fascination with electricity fueled ground-breaking experiments and ultimately led to the invention of the lightning rod, protecting buildings and people from storms. He meticulously researched and documented findings, sharing discoveries and becoming part of an international network of scientists. He also charted the Gulf Stream, studied the causes of storms and aurora borealis, and investigated lead poisoning, demonstrating diverse interests and contributions to various fields.

Franklin's willingness to learn went beyond simply acquiring knowledge; he was also open to changing his mind based on new information. In a letter regarding the *U.S. Constitution*, he acknowledged that, having lived a long time, he had experienced many instances where better information led him to alter his opinions, even on important subjects. This humility and adaptability were key to his success as a thinker and leader.

Benjamin Franklin's story demonstrates the power of a curious mind and a willingness to learn. His life serves as an inspiration, demonstrating that, through dedication, exploration, and openness to new ideas, individuals can transform their own lives and contribute to the betterment of society.

HOW DO YOU DO THIS?

Leaders can foster a culture of learning by actively seeking knowledge, staying curious, and being open to new ideas. This involves embracing a *"learning mindset,"* where they view every experience, even setbacks, as an opportunity for growth and improvement. Leaders should also encourage experimentation, cultivate respectful conflict, and lead by example, demonstrating a commitment to their own development.

Here's a more detailed breakdown:

1. Cultivate Curiosity and Seek Knowledge:

- **Be a Lifelong Learner:** Leaders should prioritize continuous learning by engaging in activities like reading, attending workshops, and networking with other leaders.

- **Ask Questions and Listen Actively:** Leaders should be genuinely interested in understanding different perspectives and actively listen to their team members and colleagues.
- **Embrace Discomfort:** Learning often involves stepping outside of one's comfort zone. Leaders should be willing to challenge the status quo and try new things, even if they are initially unsure of the outcome.

2. Foster a Learning Environment:

- **Lead by Example:** Leaders who demonstrate a commitment to learning inspire their teams to do the same.
- **Provide Resources and Support:** Ensure that your team has access to the resources and support they need to learn and grow, including time, funding, and mentorship.

*"If you are not willing to learn, no one can help you.
If you are determined to learn, no one can stop you."*

- Yankee Doodle Dave

LEADERSHIP CHALLENGE

Here is my challenge to you:

Do you feel like you know everything you need to complete your job? Have you ever said something like "If it is not broken why should we change?" Simply changing because of change does not make sense.

In this week's lesson we learned about the story of Benjamin Franklin and his lifelong pursuit of knowledge. He lived a life where he constantly pursued learning new things. Franklin was a champion of education for all. He played a key role in founding the first public library and the establishment of the University of Pennsylvania. He also used his knowledge in inventing practical items such as the lightning rod and bifocals. Benjamin's diplomatic skills helped secure crucial alliances during the American Revolution.

Being open to learning new things in the workplace is highly valued by employees and can lead to greater career opportunities and job satisfaction. It demonstrates a growth mindset, adaptability, and a proactive approach to professional development, which are all beneficial for both the individual and the organization.

Here are a few techniques how leaders can learn new things in the workplace:

- Believe in your ability to learn
- Learn from colleagues and mentors
- Explore learning methods (online courses, workshops, on-the-job training, audiobooks, etc.)
- Make time in your schedule for learning

This week different concepts were discussed that can help leaders be able to foster an environment that enables a willingness to learn.

What concepts do you plan to put in place to ensure your work center has an environment of willingness to learn?

"Wisdom is not a product of schooling but of the lifelong attempt to acquire it."
- Albert Einstein

Take Work Seriously, Not Yourself

"Do not be overly righteous, not be overly wise, why should you destroy yourself? Do not be overwicked, and do not be a fool—why die before your time? It is good to grasp the one and not let go of the other. Whoever fears God will avoid all extremes."

- Ecclesiastes 7:16-18

HISTORICAL FIGURES:
MGEN Fox Conner & Maj. Dwight Eisenhower

This week's topic is something that I personally need to work on. This is the concept of taking work seriously, but not yourself. For those that know me on a personal level, I have a habit of taking myself way too seriously. Taking oneself seriously can be a defensive mechanism to avoid showing vulnerability. People may feel that being serious protects them from being perceived as weak or unprofessional.

This week I want to share a historical story about the concept of taking work seriously, not yourself. This is the story of a General in the United States Army and a Field Grade Officer.

The year was 1922. Major General (MGEN) Fox Conner commanded the 20th Infantry Brigade in the *Panama Canal Zone*. It is not an exact amount, however there are estimations that state there were roughly between 3,000 and 5,000 soldiers under MGEN Conner's command.

Major Dwight Eisenhower reported to the 20th Infantry Brigade to be on MGEN Conner's staff.

Before we get much further it is important that you understand how significant Major General Conner was. MGEN Fox Conner was perhaps the most influential officer in the United States Army between *World War I* and *World War II*. He was General John J. Pershing's right-hand man in building the *American Expeditionary Force (AEF)* in *World War I*. Conner was also a military historian and thinker of great reputation inside the Army. Significantly, he numbered among his protégés two of the greatest American leaders in *World War II*: George C. Marshall, Army Chief of Staff, and Dwight D. Eisenhower, Supreme Commander of American and British forces in the European Theater of Operations.

Conner served as a mentor to Eisenhower and imparted valuable leadership lessons, including the maxim: *"Always take your job seriously, never yourself."*

This advice deeply influenced Eisenhower's leadership style throughout his career.

MGEN Conner was an outstanding commander and mentor for Eisenhower. Through persistent instruction he taught Eisenhower the love of the military. He ordered Eisenhower to read Count Yorck von Wartenburg's biography of Napoleon, *Clauewitz's On War* (actually three times), Steele's *Campaigns* and many other historical classics. Conner tested Eisenhower daily on his reading, re-fought the great battles with his protégé, and scrutinized the errors made in wars in the past.

Conner especially emphasized instruction in working with allies in war, which Conner thought would prove crucial in the next world war. Conner knew that the Allies would have to be more coordinated than they were in *World War I*. They needed a single chain of command, and such a task would require considerable diplomatic skills in addition to military acumen.

Eisenhower, who would go on to command vast armies and

later serve as President of the United States, viewed the responsibilities bestowed upon him with immense gravity. However, he maintained a humble perspective on his own importance, seeing himself simply as "*Ike,*" a human being doing his best. He believed that the power, wealth, or fame that could come from such roles were secondary to the duty and responsibility itself.

Eisenhower's focus remained on achieving the mission at hand, understanding that a sense of humor and approachability helped with building morale and getting things done.

He recognized the value of building coalitions and using political influence to accomplish goals, rather than relying solely on issuing orders.

Eisenhower wasn't afraid to admit when he didn't know everything, recognizing that others possessed valuable expertise. He also kept his ego in check, managing the egos of others for the greater good.

This approach, fostered by General Conner's advice, allowed Eisenhower to effectively lead diverse groups, manage complex operations, and ultimately achieve incredible successes, all while remaining grounded and focused on the work itself.

HOW DO YOU DO THIS?

Leaders can effectively balance the seriousness of their work with a healthy dose of self-awareness by focusing on results, demonstrating humility, and fostering a positive work environment. This approach involves taking responsibility for outcomes while avoiding the pitfalls of ego and self-importance.

Here's a breakdown of how leaders can achieve this balance:

Taking Work Seriously, Not Yourself:

- **Focus on Results:** Leaders should be dedicated to achieving goals and producing high-quality work. This involves attention to detail, effort, and a commitment to excellence.

- **Humor and Lightheartedness:** Using humor appropriately can create a more relaxed and positive atmosphere, showing that while work is important, the leader doesn't take themselves too seriously.
- **Recognize Your Imperfections:** Acknowledging that no one is perfect and that mistakes are part of the learning process can reduce pressure and encourage open communication.
- **Don't Sweat the Small Stuff:** Leaders who can let go of minor setbacks and maintain a sense of perspective are better equipped to handle challenges and maintain a positive attitude.
- **Find Humor in Setbacks:** Being able to laugh at yourself and learn from failures can make you more resilient and approachable.
- **Focus on the Bigger Picture:** Leaders should remember that the work is about achieving goals and serving others, not about personal glory or validation.

LEADERSHIP CHALLENGE

"Don't take yourself so seriously, but take your work very seriously."

- Yankee Doodle Dave

Here is my challenge to you:

Have you ever been told you are too serious or maybe you sweat the small stuff?

In this week's lesson we learned about the story of MGEN Fox Conner, and how his mentorship helped a young Major Eisenhower not take himself too seriously.

The key to a healthy work-life balance is to take your work seriously, but not yourself. This means focusing on the quality and effort you put into tasks, while also maintaining a sense of perspective and not letting your job define your entire identity.

Here are a few techniques on how to be authentic in a workplace:

- Find humor, or empathy when others act out.
- Build immunity to your fears.
- Be compassionate and kind to yourself.
- Focus on the work itself, not your ego.

This week different concepts were discussed that can help leaders maintain a healthy work-life balance.

What concepts do you plan to put in place to ensure your work center has an environment that respects and promotes a healthy work-life balance? By prioritizing the work, but not letting it define their self-worth, leaders can create a more positive, productive, and fulfilling work environment. They can also build stronger relationships with their teams and inspire others to do their best work.

Empower Your People

"Therefore encourage one another and build each other up, just as in fact you are doing."
                                        - 1 Thessalonians 5:11

HISTORICAL FIGURE:
Harriet Tubman, American Abolitionist and Social Activist

Autonomous leadership focuses on empowering individuals and teams by granting them the freedom to make decisions and manage their work independently. It emphasizes trust, adaptability, and providing necessary resources and tools for success, rather than constant supervision.

This week's topic deals with the concept of empowering your people. Here is a historical story that helps illustrate how a leader empowered their people. The story I want to share with you deals with Harriet Tubman.

She was born in March 1822 and had the birthname of Araminita "Minty" Ross. Born into slavery in Dorchester County, Maryland, she was beaten and whipped by enslavers as a child. Early in life she suffered a traumatic head wound when an irate overseer threw a heavy metal weight, intended to hit another slave. Instead, the metal weight hit her instead. The injury caused dizziness, pain, and episodes of hypersomnia. This affected her throughout her life. After her injury, Tubman began experiencing strange visions and vivid dreams, which she ascribed to premonitions from God. These experiences, combined with her Methodist upbringing, led her to become devoutly religious.

Harriet Tubman changed her name from Araminta "Minty" Ross to Harriet Tubman after her marriage to John Tubman around 1844.

In 1849, she escaped and found refuge in Philadelphia. However, she couldn't stand the thought of her family and friends remaining enslaved. This is where her empowering journey truly began.

Tubman became a conductor on the *Underground Railroad,* a secret network helping enslaved people escape to freedom. She made about 13 dangerous missions back to Maryland, risking her life to guide around 70 individuals, primarily family and friends, to the North. She was known for her courageous leadership and success in navigating the routes.

Tubman demonstrated incredible bravery by repeatedly venturing into slave states despite the risks and bounties on her head. She used various strategies to evade capture and guide people to safety, including disguises, knowledge of the land, and secret codes through songs. Tubman prioritized the freedom of others over her own safety, showcasing a profound sense of responsibility and dedication. Her actions inspired not only those she helped but also others in the abolitionist movement and beyond.

Tubman's fight for justice didn't end with her work on the *Underground Railroad.* During the *Civil War,* she served as a spy, nurse, and cook for the Union Army. After the war, she continued to advocate for women's suffrage and civil rights, demonstrating her belief in equality for all.

There is another rather unknown story I would like to share that illustrates Harriet Tubman's leadership and ability to empower people. In June 1863, she guided Colonel James Montgomery and the 2nd South Carolina Black regiment around Confederate torpedoes in the Combahee River. The successful raid liberated over 750 enslaved people. This was a significant blow to the Confederacy and a historic achievement for the Union Army. The event solidified Tubman's reputation as the *"Black she-Moses"* and was recognized by a military honor in 2021 when the U.S. Army Military Intelligence Corps Hall of Fame inducted her as a full member.

Harriet Tubman's life story is a powerful example of self-empowerment leading to the empowerment of others. Her unwavering determination, courage, and dedication to freedom continue to inspire people today.

HOW DO YOU DO THIS?

Empowering a team involves giving team members autonomy, resources, and support to make decisions and take ownership of their work, fostering a sense of trust and value. Effective leaders create an environment where individuals feel confident, capable, and motivated to contribute their best, ultimately driving team success.

Leaders can empower their followers in practical ways by:

1. Providing Clear Direction and Expectations:

- **Communicate the Vision and Goals:** Ensure team members understand the overall company mission and how their work contributes to it.
- **Define Roles and Responsibilities:** Clearly outline what each person is responsible for to avoid confusion and empower them to take ownership.
- **Set Measurable Objectives:** Help employees establish clear, attainable goals aligned with the broader strategy.

2. Offering Continuous Support and Resources:

- **Provide Training and Development:** Offer opportunities for employees to learn new skills, expand their knowledge base, and advance their careers.

- **Make Resources Accessible**: Ensure team members have the tools, technology, and information they need to succeed.
- **Offer Ongoing Guidance:** Be available to support your team, helping them set goals and overcome challenges.

3. Cultivating Trust:

- **Be Transparent and Honest:** Share relevant information openly, even during challenging times, to build credibility.
- **Show Empathy and Respect:** Build genuine relationships by actively listening to concerns and valuing diverse perspectives.
- **Follow Through on Commitments:** Demonstrate reliability and dependability by being consistent in your words and actions.

4. Encouraging Autonomy and Decision-Making:

- **Delegate Tasks and Responsibilities:** Give employees ownership of projects and the authority to make decisions related to their work.
- **Allow Calculated Risks and Experimentation:** Create a safe space for employees to try new approaches and learn from potential setbacks.
- **Involve Employees in Decision-Making:** Solicit feedback and incorporate employee suggestions where possible, showing you value their input.

5. Providing Feedback and Recognition:

- **Offer Constructive Feedback:** Provide regular, specific feedback that helps employees understand their strengths and areas for improvement.

"Leadership is about empowering others to achieve things they had no idea that they thought they could achieve."

- Yankee Doodle Dave

LEADERSHIP CHALLENGE

Here is my challenge to you:

When in your work center do you have a lack of confidence in your team's abilities to complete a task? Or do you feel that your position is so critical that no one can complete what you do?

In this week's lesson we learned about the story of Harriet Tubman and her ability to empower countless people.

Empowering a team in the workplace means providing team members with authority, autonomy, and resources to make decisions and take ownership of their work. This fosters a sense of responsibility, increases engagement, and ultimately leads to improved performance and a more positive work environment.

This week different concepts were discussed that can help leaders empower their team.

What concepts do you plan to put in place to trust your team and build a culture of empowerment?

Create More Leaders

"To equip the saints for the work of ministry, for building up the body of Christ."
                              - Ephesians 4:12

HISTORICAL FIGURE: Baron Friedrich von Steuben - Training Continental Army Soldiers

Creating more leaders in the workplace is crucial for enhancing employee engagement, boosting productivity, and improving retention. A strong leadership pipeline ensures a more agile and resilient organization, better equipped to navigate challenges and capitalize on opportunities.

This week's story is based on the concept of creating more leaders. To illustrate this concept, I would like to share a small historical story. This is a story that takes place during the *Revolutionary War* and the leaders in the *Continental Army* realized their troops needed more training.

In 1777, Benjamin Franklin and Silas Deane, American ambassadors to France, who initially met with and were impressed enough by Baron Friedrich Wilhelm von Steuben to recommend him to help the *Continental Army*.

The reason they contacted him was because the *Continental Army* at Valley Forge was in desperate need of organization and training. Franklin and Deane recognized Steuben's military experience, having served as an aide-de-camp to Frederick the Great of Prussia. They hoped Steuben could bring order and professional military discipline to the *Continental Army*.

They essentially recruited him with the hope that he would be appointed by Congress to help General Washington. Following Washington's recommendation, Congress did appoint Steuben as Major General and Inspector General of the Continental Army

Baron von Steuben, a Prussian military officer, played a crucial role transforming the *Continental Army* into a disciplined, effective fighting force during the *American Revolution*.

Baron Friedrich von Steuben thought the American soldiers had a lacking in formal training and organization. However, he believed they possessed a remarkable fighting spirit that could be cultivated into a professional army through discipline, standardized drills, and clear explanations for orders. He was initially dismayed by the poor conditions and unprofessionalism of the *Continental Army* but grew to respect the soldiers' tenacity, which he believed could be transformed into a formidable fighting force.

He had a key part of what was his systematic approach to developing leadership within the ranks, particularly among Noncommissioned Officers (NCOs). Von Steuben identified the Noncommissioned Officer (NCO) as the most important soldier in the army. He understood their potential to influence and train the soldiers under their command.

To implement his training, he selected a group of 150 to 200 soldiers, including officers and NCOs, to form a *"model company."* This company underwent rigorous training in Prussian drill techniques.

Von Steuben's direct and *hands-on approach* to training, along with his emphasis on standards and precision, helped instill a sense of pride and professionalism in these chosen individuals.

Once the model company was proficient, these trained officers and NCOs then spread out to their respective units to replicate the training they had received. This created a cascading effect, effectively developing leadership at various levels of the army. Von Steuben's drill manual, the *Blue Book,* codified his instructions and provided a consistent framework for training across the entire army. This ensured that training methods were uniform and that essential military knowledge, including the duties and responsibilities of NCOs, was readily available.

In essence, von Steuben's model company approach, coupled with his understanding of the importance of empowered NCOs and his standardized training methods, created a system for developing leaders throughout the *Continental Army,* a system that helped lay the foundation for the American military's training structure that endures to this day.

HOW DO YOU DO THIS?

Leaders cultivate more leaders by actively developing the leadership potential in others through mentorship, providing opportunities, and fostering a culture of growth and learning. This involves identifying individuals with potential, offering them training and coaching, and providing practical experience in leadership roles.

Here's a more detailed look:

1. Identifying and Nurturing Potential:

- **Find Promising Individuals:** Leaders should actively look for team members who demonstrate leadership qualities like initiative, communication skills, and problem-solving abilities.
- **Provide Mentorship and Coaching:** Offering guidance, support, and constructive feedback to help individuals develop their leadership skills is crucial.
- **Create Development Opportunities:** Assigning challenging tasks, delegating responsibilities, and providing opportunities for individuals to lead projects or initiatives can accelerate their growth.

2. Fostering a Leadership Culture:

- **Promote a Growth Mindset:** Encourage a culture where learning from mistakes is seen as a valuable part of the development process.
- **Offer Leadership Training:** Provide formal training programs or workshops to equip individuals with the knowledge and skills needed for leadership roles.
- **Lead by Example:** Leaders should demonstrate the very qualities they want to see in their future leaders, such as integrity, vision, and commitment to growth.

3. Empowering and Delegating:

- **Delegate Challenging Tasks:** Empowering team members with increased responsibilities and autonomy allows them to develop their decision-making and problem-solving skills.
- **Give Them Space to Lead:** Allow individuals to take ownership of their work and make their own decisions, even if it means making mistakes.

"Leadership is about building people up, not tearing them down, and helping them become the best versions of themselves."

- Yankee Doodle Dave

LEADERSHIP CHALLENGE

Here is my challenge to you:

Do you have decreased morale at your workplace? Is turnover surprisingly high within your company? Do you have a lack of innovation?

In this week's lesson we learned about the story of Baron Friedrich Wilhelm von Steuben and his ability to train the *Continental Army* in the *Revolutionary War*.

Effective leaders foster leadership qualities in others, building a pipeline of future leaders through mentorship, coaching, and providing opportunities for growth. This involves identifying potential, offering support, and allowing individuals to learn through experience.

Here are a few techniques on how to be authentic in a workplace:

- Mentorship and Coaching
- Leadership Training Programs
- Enhance Communication Skills
- Creating a Supportive Environment
- Providing Opportunities for Mentees to Shadow Mentors

This week different concepts were discussed to help leaders train and make new leaders.

What concepts do you plan to put in place to create an environment where you make more leaders?

____

____

____

____

A Note from the Editor

What an honor to help bring this book to the American public.

David Ocheltree, a Navy man, served his country for 26 years. As a corpsman on the battlefield, he makes split-section decisions. Can he be both warrior and healer? When the injured is calling out for Doc…can he risk his own life to reach the wounded? Can he comfort a dying man in his arms, "You're going to make it"…as eternity is claiming his soul.

He will carry these scars for life—the wounds of the American horror story of war in Iraq.

This book could be called "Holy Ground" when you read the stories of these American leaders. Brilliance, fate, and common sense came together in these men and women.

Military leadership is at the essence of this book…that and God!

Chapter to chapter you will cherish the wisdom of a Bible verse woven into the attributes of 250 years of American leaders from presidents to scientists. Each lesson teaches what shapes a leader, maybe even a hero.

Yankee Doodle Dave, a character from the American Revolution leads the way through the book.

He is special to me. My grandfather, George Washington Kreisher, who I loved dearly, was born on July 4, 1890. What a fun person. I can still see him dancing and playing his fiddle singing, "I'm a Yankee Doodle Dandy, A Yankee Doodle do or die…a real live nephew of my Uncle Sam, born on the 4th of July!"

Flags, red, white, and blue, fireworks—it was always a birthday celebration! I do this work as a member of The Daughters of the

American Revolution. I honor my ancestors and my patriots who fought to birth a new nation under God. God Bless them—Simon Seyfert and Jonas Knerr—and all who have served this great nation.

As you are reading this book may your heart and soul be touched as you march into leadership with Yankee Doodle Dave. God Bless America!

Love what you see?
Share the story!

Find more great books or
grab another copy for a friend.

———————————————

**Enjoy FREE shipping
on your first order!**

———————————————

Use promo code: SHIP4FREE

www.masthof.com